RELIGION AND HUMAN RIGHTS

COLUMBIA UNIVERSITY SEMINAR SERIES

The University Seminars at Columbia University welcomes this study, *Religion and Human Rights: Competing Claims?* edited by Carrie Gustafson and Peter Juviler, to the Columbia University Seminars Series. The study has benefited from Seminar discussions and reflects the advantages of scholarly exchange provided by the Seminar Movement.

Aaron W. Warner
Director, University Seminars
Columbia University

THE FUTURE OF AMERICAN BANKING
James R. Barth, R. Dan Brumbaugh, Jr., and Robert E. Litan

THE EVOLUTION OF U.S. FINANCE, VOLUME I
FEDERAL RESERVE MONETARY POLICY: 1915–1935
Jane W. D'Arista

THE EVOLUTION OF U.S. FINANCE, VOLUME II
RESTRUCTURING INSTITUTIONS AND MARKETS
Jane W. D'Arista

HOW CREDIT-MONEY SHAPES THE ECONOMY
THE UNITED STATES IN A GLOBAL SYSTEM
Robert Guttmann

THE ANTITRUST IMPULSE, VOLUMES I AND II
AN ECONOMIC, HISTORICAL, AND LEGAL ANALYSIS
Theodore P. Kovaleff, editor

FROM MALTHUS TO THE CLUB OF ROME AND BACK
PROBLEMS OF LIMITS TO GROWTH, POPULATION CONTROL, AND MIGRATIONS
Paul Neurath

TOWARD SUSTAINABLE DEVELOPMENT?
STRUGGLING OVER INDIA'S NARMADA RIVER
William F. Fisher, editor

DEBT, CRISIS, AND RECOVERY
THE 1930S AND THE 1990S
Albert G. Hart and Perry Mehrling

CHANGING STRUCTURE OF MEXICO
POLITICAL, SOCIAL, AND ECONOMIC PROSPECTS
Laura Randall, editor

REFORMING MEXICO'S AGRARIAN REFORM
Laura Randall, editor

RELIGION AND HUMAN RIGHTS
COMPETING CLAIMS?
Carrie Gustafson and Peter Juviler, editors

RELIGION AND HUMAN RIGHTS
Competing Claims?

**CARRIE GUSTAFSON
PETER JUVILER**
Editors

M.E. Sharpe
Armonk, New York
London, England

1999

Copyright © 1999 by M. E. Sharpe, Inc.

All rights reserved. No part of this book may be reproduced in any form without written permission from the publisher, M. E. Sharpe, Inc., 80 Business Park Drive, Armonk, New York 10504.

Library of Congress Cataloging-in-Publication Data

Religion and human rights : competing claims? Carrie Gustafson and Peter Juviler, editors.
  p. cm. — (Columbia University seminar series)
Includes bibliographical references and index.
ISBN 0–7656–0261–X (alk. paper). — ISBN 0–7656– 0262–8 (pbk. : alk. paper)
  1. Human rights—Religious aspects. I. Gustafson, Carrie, 1966–.
    II. Juviler, Peter H. III. Series.
      BL65.H78R44 1998
      291.1′77—dc21   98–21719
                CIP

Printed in the United States of America

The paper used in this publication meets the minimum requirements of
American National Standard for Information Sciences—
Permanence of Paper for Printed Library Materials,
ANSI Z 39.48-1984.

BM (c)	10	9	8	7	6	5	4	3	2	1
BM (p)	10	9	8	7	6	5	4	3	2	1

To Professor Louis Henkin, who inspires so many.

Contents

Foreword
    Donald W. Shriver Jr.   ix

Acknowledgments   xiii

1. Introduction: Ambiguities of the Divine
   Peter Juviler   3

2. Human Rights and Public Theology: The Basic Validation of Human Rights
   Max L. Stackhouse   12

3. **Reply:** Human Rights: Religious or Enlightened?
   Louis Henkin   31

4. Human Environmental Rights and/or Biotic Rights
   Larry Rasmussen   36

5. **Reply:** Rights of Creation to Rites of Revolution
   Patricia A. Daly   53

6. Religion and Societal Change: The Struggle for Human Rights in Latin America
   Margaret E. Crahan   57

7. **Reply:** Religion and Societal Change: The Struggle for Human Rights in Latin America
   James F. Joyce   81

8. Gandhi's Philosophy of *Satyagraha*: Cautionary Notes for the International Penal Lobby
   Carrie Gustafson   88

9. **Reply:** Secular Eschatologies and Class Interests of the Internationalized New Class
   Kenneth Anderson   107

10. Speaking/Seeking a Common Language: Women, the Hindu
    Right, and Human Rights in India
    Arati Rao   117
11. **Reply:** Reconceptualizing the Relationships Between Religion,
    Women, Culture, and Human Rights
    Julie Stone Peters   140

12. Feminism, Jewish Orthodoxy, and Human Rights:
    Strange Bedfellows?
    Blu Greenberg   145
13. **Reply:** Jewish Orthodoxy, Modernity, and Women's Rights
    Alan F. Segal   174

14. Islamic Law and Human Rights: Conundrums and
    Equivocations
    Ann Elizabeth Mayer   177

About the Editors and Contributors   199

Index   203

Foreword

Two hundred years ago, Immanuel Kant testified to the two realities that held him in awe: "the starry heavens above and the moral law within" each human being. Like other philosophers of the European Enlightenment, Kant was not astronomically intimidatable. Whatever the size of the galaxies, humans had a special relation to it all: a rationality that relates them to something ultimately precious in the universe.

These two centuries later many of us would like to emulate this Kantian confidence, but we are burdened with two difficulties: We are less sure of our unique status in that very large universe, and we are even less sure that as members of the same species we all have access to that "moral law within."

To be sure, in this fiftieth anniversary year of the adoption by the United Nations of its Universal Declaration of Human Rights, we hope for an earth-wide consensus that we humans owe profound, non-negotiable mutual respect to each other. But we have little consensus as to whether Thomas Jefferson was on firm ground when he claimed that we humans have "certain inalienable rights" because our divine Creator has "endowed" us with them. Was this Jeffersonian rhetoric decorative only? Do we have to bring God into any claim that we are to respect ourselves and each other always as "ends" and never as "means"—the Kantian ethical maxim?

The authors of the essays in this collection are fully aware that our experience of our neighbors in this twentieth century, especially in our politics, has left us anything but confident in the moral status of human being. Where was the "moral law within" when the trench warfare of 1914 began? When the university-trained Nazis devised the concentration camps? When the annihilation of whole cities became standard strategy for victory in war from 1939 to 1945? When at the end of this century, as a world "community," we had compiled a record for organized killing in the range of 150 million? The pre-Enlightenment French philosopher Blaise Pascal spoke of the "grandeur and misery" of human nature. We know about the grandeur in our moon walks, our computers, and our Declarations of Human Rights. But on some deep levels, we are haunted by the misery.

Were I to propose a test question for all the authors here, I would ask:

Does your vision of human rights concepts, justifications, and enforcement do justice to both the dignity and the corruptibility of us humans? It is quite possible that religious systems have accented the corruption to the neglect of the dignity, while secular human rights thinking has accented the reverse. The latter may not agree that the democratic system of government requires advocates who take good and evil with equal seriousness, but it is hard to avoid the balance of wisdom in Reinhold Niebuhr's famous aphorism: "The human capacity for justice makes democracy possible; the human inclination to injustice makes democracy necessary."

Do both religion and secularism have contributions to make to this possibility and this necessity? Most writers in this collection are cautious but hopeful on both scores. They seem to agree that the frequent antagonism between the claims of religious institutions and the claims of human rights advocates is not necessarily good for either. Like everything else in history, religion certainly has a checkered record for defining, legitimating, and implementing the rights of even its own adherents, not to speak of those who, on occasion, are considered its enemies. "Error has no rights" has been the maxim of many an inquisition in alliance with governmental killing of both kinds of heretics: religious and political.

In general the record of governments has been equally problematic for the cause of human rights. In the twentieth century governments have violated the human right to *life* on a scale beyond the technical ability of the inquisitions and witch hunts of long ago. Human rights require protection from both politics and religion, it seems. One of the occasional exceptions in the institutions of both, however, is their provision for criticism and rebuke of themselves—by their own constituents, their own law, or the divine law. As the Hebrew author of Psalm 15:4 put it, the righteous are those "who swear to their own hurt." Religion, at least at its most authentic, has a built-in ability to challenge autocratic power. In this respect it can offer some solution to the problem that Madison identified in the *Federalist Papers:* "You must first enable the government to control the governed, and in the next place oblige it to control itself."

Instead of swearing at each other, advocates of religious faith and advocates of human rights may need to offer to each other their grounds for acknowledging both the grandeur and the misery of humanity. On its side, religion needs to show why it helps salvage human self-respect if one insists that we are precious to God even when we display little care for each other. In more wonderment than doubt the Hebrew psalmist lifted the prayer: "What are human beings that you are mindful of them?" Then the prayer praises the Creator for "crowning us with glory and honor." Abraham Joshua Heschel defined a human person as "a being whose anguish may reach the heart of God." On that ground, the prophets of Israel stood up to kings on behalf of the poor, believing that God was on their side. Moral revolutions, as well as immoral ones, have been effected by leaders who were convinced that the "Judge of all the earth" demands a justice that kings defy.

Modern secular democratic advocates of the rights of all people have also on occasion reminded leaders of both government and religion that neither has the right to lord it over the minds, hearts, and freedoms of their constituents. Even if citizens sometime use their freedom for corrupt ends, freedom—that is, response-ability—remains as one salvageable part of their dignity. Even criminals and heretics have rights.

Both sides seem to clasp hands here in an agreement that is momentous for democracy: Government is not God, neither is religion. There is a separation of powers necessary for the social and personal lives of humans. No power, no matter how old or authoritative in its own "right," can usurp the right-full power reserved for oneself, one's neighbors, and neighboring institutions. Rights (and their embodiment in diverse institutions) nudge each other. They do not fit together neatly in logic or in practice. They guarantee abrasions as well as peace between citizens. They call for debates between interests, claims, and centers of power. For their exercise they require social pluralism, diverse power centers, and possible appeals to diverging ultimate authorities.

By whatever other name, a conflict of ultimates is itself religious. Not always noticed by either the religious and the secular, however, is the crucial difference between ultimate *views* and views *of* the ultimate. The famous confession of Martin Luther in 1521—"Here I stand. I can do no other," sometimes suffers in quotations that omit the final recorded words: "God help me." In that qualification there opens the parallel passion of Oliver Cromwell, who exclaimed to a certain quarreling Scottish regiment, "By the mercies of Christ, think that you may be wrong!" Here gleams the one protection that the genuinely religious spirit has against its own temptation to fall into autocratic tyranny. It is bound to an appeal to an Authority above its own authority. By this theological standard, not even religious freedom is absolute. It may be conditioned by other freedoms and other rights. Supremely it is conditioned by Another whose freedom transcends that of any human.

Such a principle parallels the famous words of Judge Learned Hand: "The spirit of liberty is the spirit that is not too sure it is right." Many will blame Cromwell for not following his own advice, and fear of another Cromwell was rightly in the minds of the 1787 American Constitution-makers. They separated governmental powers. They both restricted and legitimated the power of religious bodies, the press, and individual citizens to challenge government. They even allowed for challenges to its very Constitution. They made it *amendable*. They left to future citizens the right and responsibility of discerning how it might need to be amended under criteria yet to be discerned. Nothing human is beyond amendment, and this reminder, this humility, is essential democratic wisdom. It may be equally essential to both religious and secular accounts of what keeps human life human.

Donald W. Shriver Jr.

Acknowledgments

The editors express their thanks to Dr. Aaron Warner, director of Columbia University Seminars, for his encouragement; also to Jessie Strader, assistant to the director, and Anissa M. Bouziane, administrative assistant. We are grateful for support from the Leonard Hastings Schoff Publications Fund. The Columbia University Center for the Study of Human Rights and its executive director, Dr. J. Paul Martin, and the Pew Fellows Program in Religion and Human Rights inspired the theme for the University Seminar meetings that led to this book. We have enjoyed and gained from working with our contributors and appreciate the input of all participants in the seminar discussions. We have benefited from the encouragement, patience, and guidance of editors at M.E. Sharpe, Peter Coveney, Stephen Dalphin, Esther L. Clark, and Eileen Maass.

RELIGION AND HUMAN RIGHTS

1

PETER JUVILER

Introduction: Ambiguities of the Divine

Introduction

The Universal Declaration of Human Rights and derivative global and regional covenants, as well as numerous national constitutions, proclaim the basic human right to freedom of thought, conscience, and religion.[1] Some countries' path to religious freedom lies, as in Germany, through state support to religions. The path of others lies in the establishment of one religion, such as the Church of England, or the de facto establishment of one religion, as in Russia. Still other countries adhere to the principle of the separation of church and state as the preferred path to religious freedom. In defiance of international law, governments persecute or harass religious persons and institutions in many lands, ranging from Eastern Europe and the former Soviet Union, to Sudan, Iran, India (by condonation), and China.[2] The sequence is familiar and relatively clear cut. Governments single out one or more religions for suppression or discrimination, in violation of their members' human rights—the rights that they have as human beings.[3]

This symposium depicts religion not as victim, however, but as an ambiguous force for both progress and reaction. Religion can provide "an arena of innovation and ever-new gifts for the human family," says the World Future Society. But it may also "tend to promote fixity of ideas so that concepts of breakthrough and religion are often seen as mutually exclusive."[4] Religion can be a formidable force for and against human rights, John Witte points out, because of its resonance in the "human heart, soul, and mind" through its teachings and liturgy that embrace questions of "the ultimate origin, meaning and purpose of life, of existence."[5] Irene Bloom's analysis captures the situation quite well: Religions can present in their traditions both challenges to human rights, and challenges to those who

3

would violate those rights, depending on the particular context of religion's encounter with issues of human rights.[6]

Validating and Promoting Human Rights

Professor Robert Thurman, a leading authority on Tibetan Buddhism, has suggested that world religions "have demonstrated over centuries that they are capable of providing a source of common identity that can occasionally and at least partially transcend differences of clan, tribe, nation, and even race."[7] Professor Thurman foresees the possibility of a "new global civility," the key to which is "a sense of *spiritual* membership, transcendental identity with an infinite life force, conceived of as either a Creator God or a Truth Presence Enlightened Being." His religion, Buddhism, can inspire such universalist support for ideas of human rights.

In the same spirit of religious universalism, Max Stackhouse opens our symposium with a critique of today's secular validation of human rights, and its association of them with particular centuries and social changes. He depicts human rights theory in justification of global norms as ephemeral and culture-bound, despite its universalist intent. Only a religious morality expressed in a new public theology, Max Stackhouse avers, can realize that universalist intent. Public theology can transcend particular religions, cultures, special interests, and time itself. He calls for inter-religious and cross-cultural dialogue to develop such a theology that views human beings as divinely endowed holders of their rights and that will foster "righteous ways of human dealing." Louis Henkin questions the possibility of a universal religious validation in this culturally diverse world. "For our time," he writes, "one ... has to justify human rights by some contemporary universal version of natural law, *whether religious or secular,* by appeal to a common moral intuition of human dignity." Despite disagreement, these and other writers welcome the idea of alliances between religious and secular advocates of human rights.[8]

Religious vision has opened up new perspectives on human rights. "Ecotheology" is one such trailblazer. It propounds a theological vision of humans as part of nature's realm, and as obligated to preserve the global biosphere that nature forms.[9]

In this vein, the theologian and environmentalist Larry Rasmussen brings to this symposium his critique of human rights theory as a source of insight on human relations with our planet's biosphere. Notions of rights are morally incomplete, he says, and potentially harmful without religion's sense of life's sacredness and human beings' membership in the "earth community" of all living things. Professor Rasmussen points to the anthropocentrism of human rights and, indeed, of some religious outlooks. He suggests a divine basis for the conception of non-human life as possessing "biotic rights" not to be harmed by humans. Humans' recognition of their obligations of environmental preservation are in their own self-interest. "Ecocide is homicide." The ardor and vision of religions can add a crucial dimension to campaigns for the rights of humans and of all life forms to be spared the ravages of human pollution.

Religion inspires not only the validation of human rights, but also the advocacy of human rights.[10] As testimony, religious inspiration, religious leaders, and congregations in hundreds of U.S. inner cities spark neighborhood and human renewal, and serve the cause of human rights (to life, health, education, and work) without necessarily ever invoking them specifically. "Overwhelming evidence," writes David Kuo, "suggests that faith is not only important, it may be the factor in determining whether an at-risk child, a welfare mother, or a convicted criminal is able to turn his or her life around."[11] Theology and the institutional and pastoral issues of activism come together in Margaret Crahan's account of the efforts of the Catholic Church in Latin America to carry out a rights-oriented social mission of "a preferential option for the poor." Professor Crahan traces how the church attempts to harmonize its established confessional mission with its new social mission. As an institution the church has faced the challenge of maintaining internal unity and retaining its multi-class constituency while paying special heed to the unmet needs of the vast Latin American underclasses.

The ending of civil conflicts and blatant authoritarianism in most of Latin America posed new challenges to unity within the institutional church and its societal constituencies. With some pressures off human rights, the church drew back partly from its politicized and activist mission, for the sake of internal and pastoral unity. The concern for social justice and basic rights continues within the ideologically diverse Catholic Church in Latin America. One might add that the old social conflict and liberationist struggle carries over and draws some churches and church leaders, at considerable risk once again, over to the side of the armed Zapatista movement in the Mexican state of Chiapas, which seeks social justice and democracy.[12]

Father Jim Joyce puts Margaret Crahan's chapter in the context of Catholic social doctrine and its espousal of a social theology of which the moral basis is concern for the impact of global and local economies on the poor and on labor rights. Margaret Crahan's account of such concerns expressed by high Latin American prelates to heads of the IMF, World Bank, and Inter-American Development Bank prompts Father Joyce's critique of such organizations and the systems of trade and finance they foster, and his call for ongoing solidarity among rights advocates and church supporters of the human rights of labor and the poor.

Religion, Punishment, and Reconciliation

Religion has inspired approaches of truth and reconciliation in societies recovering from grave abuses of human rights as an alternative or complement to criminal punishment of the perpetrators of such crimes. The upsurge of brutal internal wars, genocide, and ethnic cleansing has prompted the formation of interim tribunals such as the War Crimes Tribunal in The Hague and Arusha, following the precedent of the Nuremburg war crimes trials of 1945–46. "A strong and independent court," according to Human Rights Watch, "could be a powerful supplement to the Security Council, since it promises to deter the gross abusers of human rights who lie behind most of today's threats to international peace."[13]

Massive human rights abuses have sped along the planning of an International Criminal Court. In the search for responses to crimes against humanity, an argument for the ICC rather than for truth commissions (such as those in Chile and El Salvador, or the South African Truth and Reconciliation Commission with its powers of amnesty for confessed criminals) is that international prosecution for such crimes appears to be the only option in places such as former Yugoslavia. There, in Theodore Meron's view, "the prospects for truth and reconciliation were poor from the beginning," and indicted war criminals remain at large, "thriving on extreme nationalism and violence." For supporters of criminal punishment for war criminals, the principle is not in doubt. The difficulties are practical ones of enforcement and independence. Enforcement could be jeopardized by inadequate international support, and lack of funds, staff, and an independent court, which the United States would like to put under the UN Security Council.[14]

Religious traditions of non-violence find support in a diverse range of Western and Eastern religions and exponents. Principles of non-violence and reconciliation have inspired measures of truth and reconciliation through the exposure of the truth about past human rights violations, in preference to criminal punishment.[15]

Carrie Gustafson evokes principles of non-violence in her case against international criminal prosecutions. She questions both the morality and the efficacy of war crimes tribunals, observing that to inflict suffering through penal institutions runs counter to religiously inspired principles of non-violence, such as imbue Gandhi's doctrine of *satyagraha,* meaning truth-force or holding to the truth, and *ahimsa* or non-violence. Punishment creates the illusion that we are eliminating causes, when we are dealing only with symptoms. Ms. Gustafson suggests that we weigh the benefits of punitive justice against the divisiveness involved. Kenneth Anderson links support of the ICC with a "top-down internationalism" originating in religious visions and the postulates and class interests of economic globalists.

Religion, Politics, and Human Rights

When, on the contrary, visions of religion and human rights clash and advance competing claims, they do so to the detriment of religious freedom and of human rights. Human rights issues often involve conflicts of rights. The exercise of religious freedom, or measures in the name of that freedom, may conflict with other human rights.

In the most complete report to date on religious freedom, co-editors Kevin Boyle and Juliet Sheen conclude that the inclinations of religions to view themselves as the sole guardians of truth can tempt them to intolerance and "to fight against whatever [each] defines as deviant, either within [their] own faith or at [the] boundaries." Moreover, the mix of the religious and the political fuels and entrenches conflicts.[16] Barnett Rubin notes the lethal melding of religion and politics when religious organizations "sacrelize" conflicts over issues of identity, power, territory, and assets.[17]

The sharing of traditional rituals and creeds provides members of religions with moral guidance and a sense of belonging. Sociologist Rhoda Howard cites examples of Jewish and Roman Catholic feminists for whom the importance of their religious communities and associated traditions causes them to pursue equality with men within the group rather than abandon the group.[18] The ranks of Jewish feminists have grown to include Orthodox Jewish women, working within their own community, and their Orthodox male supporters.

Blu Greenberg combines devotion to her Orthodox community and its traditions with a championing of women's rights within that community in divorce, liturgy, learning, leadership, ritual, and other matters. Blu Greenberg regards her movement within Orthodoxy for women's equal rights as something that should be promoted mainly from within her community, as a change that invigorates and preserves, rather than subverts. The movement's success, writes Alan Segal, will determine whether Orthodoxy remains open to change or ossifies into a "fundamentalism" of the Jewish variety.

India remains a more religiously diverse society than does Iran. Unlike Iran, India is formally a secular state. But communal violence has plagued the country ever since the bloodbath of 1946–1948 that accompanied partition.

The main source of violence lies in its incitement by politicians, especially the Hindu Right. The government's condonation has contributed to anti-Muslim violence, as with its inaction during the 1992 destruction by Hindu extremists of the Ayohdya Mosque in the state of Uttar Pradesh.[19]

Arati Rao makes clear that religious infringements on women's human rights originate in sources outside of as well as within religion. Witness the colonial legacy of discriminatory laws, the diversity of Hindu traditions and teachings, and concessions of the supposedly secular Indian government to Muslims on family law. Out of that poison brew, politicians of the Hindu Right, in their quest for popular support, can concoct caricatures of Muslims as barbarian threats to Hindu women. The hundreds of militant groups among Hindus, Sikhs, and Muslims all feature ideals of the "good woman" and the espousal of severe penalties against women who transgress the boundaries of subordination and the militant ideals of familyhood. The extremists have succeeded in drawing women into leadership and grass-roots participation, at a cost to unity among women and to their influence as advocates for women's human rights.

Julie Stone Peters finds in the Indian experience another instance of religion's part in both the violation and the enhancement of human rights. Central to that experience is the complex diversity of religious teachings and traditions that lends itself to selective, politicized, and often divisive interpretations. Women are at once continuers of the subordinating traditions upheld by fundamentalists, and the potential force for their own liberation. Indian justice provides no meaningful example of an as yet rare case where a court recognizes the precedence of international human rights laws and obligations over local law as regards women's rights.[20]

Religious scriptures and commentaries can allow for contradictory interpretations of human rights, such as the rights of women, depending on how one chooses to interpret these texts. Islam, Ann Elizabeth Mayer conveys in her wide-ranging contribution, presents no exception to the ambiguity of religion as upholder of human rights. This holds especially where Islamic law collides with civil and political human rights in matters ranging from punishment to women's rights. Islam and interpretations of its laws can become prisoners of its politics, Professor Mayer reveals. In Iran, the interpretation of Islamic law is subject to the balance of power between reformers and traditionalists who put the *shari'a* law above international law—not the least as regards women's inequality imposed by the Islamic revolution of 1979. Iranian Islamic feminists and liberal male Islamic scholars accept the need for the law to change along with society; they return to the Qu'ran for more egalitarian and humane principles than emerge in (male-created) commentaries and laws expanding on those texts.

The ultimate authority over religion and politics in Iran remains in the hands of the *velayat i faqih* (guardian of Islamic jurisprudence), at this writing Ayatollah Ali Khamenei. Mohammed Khatami's surprise election to the lesser post of presidency came amid a vigorous debate that saw theocracy under attack "not just from fringe elements and exiles," according to Tarek E. Masoud, "but from university professors, moderate critics, and younger members of society."[21] The emergence of freer-thinking generations linked by the Internet, satellites, and other means of formal and informal networking could pose new challenges to traditional limitations of human rights. In Iran as in other Muslim countries, paths to human rights lie within Islam, to the extent that dialogue can grow between traditionalists and innovators.[22]

Dr. Jeanette Wakin was, unfortunately, prevented by illness from completing her written commentary on Ann Mayer's contribution. In her presentation, Dr. Wakin agreed that a fuller delineation of Islamic law is essential to refute purported Islamic alternatives to secular law. Focusing on Egypt, Dr. Wakin discussed the obstacles faced by President Mubarek in his defense of secular family legislation. She spoke of conservatives' ongoing campaign in Parliament to impose inegalitarian principles of the *shari'a*.

Conclusion

Religion is a powerful force for good, and for evil. It draws on wellsprings of mystery, fear (of the unknown and death), hope, morality, exaltation. It can help validate or repudiate human rights for all. It can unite and divide societies. Whether on secular or religious grounds, the ongoing struggle for human rights calls not for the rejection or suppression of religion but for dialogue within each country and internationally between the upholders and questioners of traditions that run counter to human rights. Advocacy builds within conflicted groups and societies, as an essential part of resolving the conflicts of rights engendered by religion. One of the tasks remaining is to promote efforts within religions to transcend boundaries of gender, and to eliminate exclusive identities that foreclose inter-religious dialogue and cooperation. Meanwhile, religious champions of human rights press on toward a balance between religious freedom and other human rights; between advocacy from outside countries, cultures, and religions and advocacy from within them; between the harm of intervention and the costs of indifference to violations of human rights committed in the name of religion. We hope that this symposium will contribute to furthering that progress.

Notes

1. Article 18, Universal Declaration of Human Rights and International Covenant on Civil and Political Rights; article 9, European Convention for the Protection of Human Rights and Fundamental Freedoms, *Twenty-Five Human Rights Documents* (New York: Center for the Study of Human Rights, Columbia University, 1994).

2. John Witte Jr., and John D. Van der Vyver eds., *Religious Human Rights in Global Perspective: Legal Perspectives* (The Hague/Boston/London: Martinus Nijhoff, 1996); Geoffrey Goldberg, "Washington Discovers Persecution," *New York Times Magazine,* December 21, 1997, passim; "Statement of the Advisory Committee on Religious Freedom Abroad," Washington, U.S. Department of State, February 13, 1997.

3. On human rights, see Jack Donnelly, *International Human Rights* (Boulder, CO: Westview Press, 1997); Louis Henkin, *The Age of Rights* (New York: Columbia University Press, 1990).

4. *Preliminary Program: Trend Watch: Technology, Society, and Values,* July 17–19, 1997, 2. For an overview on religion and its relation to human rights, see Martin E. Marty, "Religious Dimensions of Human Rights," in Witte and Van der Vyver, eds., *Religious Human Rights in Global Perspective: Religious Perspectives,* 1–16.

5. John Witte Jr., "Law, Religion, and Human Rights," *Columbia Human Rights Law Review* vol. 28, no. 1 (1996), 1–31, at 4; see also Arlene Swidler, ed., *Human Rights in Religious Traditions* (New York: Pilgrim Press, 1982).

6. Irene Bloom, "Introduction," in Irene Bloom, J. Paul Martin, and Wayne L. Proudfoot, eds., *Religious Diversity and Human Rights* (New York: Columbia University Press, 1996), 1–11.

7. Robert Thurman, "Foreword," *The United Nations and the World's Religions: Prospects for a Global Ethic* (Cambridge: Boston Research Center for the 21st Century, 1995), viii. See also the Dalai Lama, *A Policy of Kindness* (Ithaca, NY: Snow Lion Publications, 1990).

8. Witte, "Law, Religion, and Human Rights," 31.

9. Seyyed Hossein Nasr, *Religion and the Order of Nature* (New York: Oxford University Press, 1996).

10. Lowell W. Livezy, "U.S. Religious Organizations and the International Human Rights Movement," *Human Rights Quarterly* vol. 11, no. 1 (1989), 14–81.

11. David Kuo, "Poverty 101: Liberals and Conservatives Can Learn from One Another," 36–38: 37; William A. Schambra, "Local Groups Are the Key to America's Civic Renewal," 16–22; William A. Galston and Peter Levine, "America's Condition: A Glance at the Evidence," 23–26: 25, all in *Brookings Review* (Fall 1997).

12. "Urgent Action Alert of SIPAZ, November 7th, 1997, Armed Attack on Bishops Samuel Ruiz Garcia and Raul Vera Lopez," http://www.nonviolence.org/sipaz.

13. *Human Rights Watch World Report 1998* (New York: Human Rights Watch, December 1997), xv.

14. Theodore Meron, "Answering for War Crimes: Lessons from the Balkans," *Foreign Affairs* vol. 76, no. 1 (January–February 1997), 2–8: 3.

15. Desmond M. Tutu, "Preface," ix–xvi; and J. Bryan Hehir, "Religious Activism for Human Rights: A Christian Case Study," 97–120, both in Witte and Van der Vyver, eds. *Religious Human Rights in Global Perspective: Religious Perspectives.*

16. Kevin Boyle and Juliet Sheen, eds., *Freedom of Religion and Belief: A World Report* (New York: Routledge, 1997), xv.

17. Barnett Rubin, Presentation for the Program of Pew Fellows in Religion, Columbia University Center for the Study of Human Rights, October 15, 1997. Chester Crocker refers to religious ideas and values that legitimate the struggle for resources and

political power, as in Sudan. "Religion, Nationalism and Peace in Sudan," *Peace Watch* vol. 3, no. 6 (Washington, DC: U.S. Institute for Peace, 1997), 1.

18. Rhoda E. Howard, *Human Rights and the Search for Community* (Boulder, CO: Westview Press, 1995), 9.

19. *Slaughter Among Neighbors: The Political Origins of Communal Violence* (New York, NY: Human Rights Watch, 1995), 33–44; Ian Buruma, "India: The Perils of Democracy," *The New York Review of Books,* December 4, 1997, 14–18.

20. India is a party to the UN Covenants on Civil and Political Rights, Economic, Social, and Cultural Rights, and the Elimination of Discrimination Against Women. *Country Reports on Human Rights Practices for 1997* (Washington, DC: U.S. Government Printing Office, 1998).

21. Tarek E. Masoud, "Misreading Iran," *Current History* vol. 97, no. 615 (January 1998), 38–43: 40.

22. Abdullah Ahmed An-Na'im, "Human Rights in the Moslem World," in Henry J. Steiner and Philip Alston, *International Human Rights in Context: Law, Politics, and Morals* (Oxford: Clarendon Press, 1996), 210–18.

2

MAX L. STACKHOUSE

Human Rights and Public Theology: The Basic Validation of Human Rights

The Triumph of and Threat to Human Rights

As we approach the fiftieth anniversary of the United Nations Declaration on Human Rights, the prospects for actualizing a modicum of human rights around the globe have never been brighter. While many people continue to suffer horrendously, more societies are democratic than ever in human history, more nations in more parts of the world have the idea of rights built into their constitutions, and more attention is focused on the violations of human rights by international agencies and media than ever before. Those who violate human rights by the use of forced labor, unjust imprisonment, torture, or the denial of basic civil and political access have to hide their actions ever more carefully, or claim that such violations are only temporary policies made necessary by emergency conditions. It has become more difficult to justify the denial, abuse, or violation of rights before the court of world opinion.[1]

But for all the support for human rights around the world and in American lore, they are not universally acknowledged, and they are under attack from several quarters. For one thing, the idea of human rights is often confused with inchoate appeals to entitlements and freedoms that are not clearly rights, although it is a testimony to the power of the idea of human rights that every cause, right and left, high and low, attempts to use the language of rights to claim legitimacy. The constant multiplication of claimed rights, and the fact that many of these claims conflict with other claims, blurs the concept.[2] Nevertheless, Americans seem especially eager to defend the idea of rights, in part because they are deeply planted in a tradition that can be found in various colonial bills of rights and in the first paragraph of the Declaration of Independence, the first official text of the new nation. Its opening paragraph proclaims: "We hold these truths to be self-evident: that all men are created equal; that they are endowed by their Creator with certain unalienable rights; that among these are life, liberty and the pursuit of happiness."

To be sure, some of the purported defenders of human rights leave themselves open to critique and the unwitting discrediting of the human rights ideas they wish to defend. For instance, Rhoda E. Howard and Jack Donnely argue that the idea of human rights "is rooted in structural changes that began to emerge in the late medieval and early modern Europe."[3] However, if it is so that such ideas are little more than a by-product of a particular historical and social context, it becomes very difficult to argue that they ought to be taken as governing principles when the context has changed substantially, or is not contiguous with other areas of the world. Of course, we may believe that some inexorable logic of universal history moves toward ever fuller and fuller actualization of rights and autonomy everywhere, along with social, political, and economic change. But such a quasi-religious conviction is beyond the evidence and beyond most people's confidence in history's logic. History does not seem to warrant a rollicking confidence in an innate drive to do good once life is liberated from all religious and social constraint, as some thinkers of the Enlightenment wanted so much to be the case. Nor is it obvious that autonomy should be the highest moral purpose.[4]

We might better believe, given the evidence of the twentieth century, that domination and ideology are the natural tendency of human experience, unless they are constrained by decisive insights about transcendent moral laws that demand regard for the rights of all. Such moral laws inform us that we are less autonomous beings than creatures under universal principles, not of our own making, and that the arrogant notion that these are nothing more than human products of will and wisdom leads to the worst forms of tyranny and exploitation by those who have the will and think themselves wise, not subject to any pre-given law.[5] Some traditions honor moral principles beyond human artifice, and they offer a stronger account of why human rights, in every context, should be advocated, sustained, and encouraged even where they are not present in the social history of this or that group. In short, the presumptions of Howard and Donnelly leave the door open to a reductionist faith that invites the easy dismissal of what they want to advocate.

If no other possible source for normative principles is imagined than the changing socio-historical conditions that emerge in a particular cultural context, and if each ethical or juristic principle is simply a cultural adaptation to those changing conditions, then the "values" of the Declaration of

Independence are ripe for challenge. To insist on them in another time or place or cultural history is simply an exercise in anachronistic cultural imperialism. For instance, some may denigrate these values of the Declaration by pointing out that rights of the founding fathers were, in fact, for "men"—that they were designed only to protect the interests of white, propertied males. This is a species of the belief that moral and legal principles are attempts by the temporary victors of history to legitimate their dominance over their victims. Such arguments disallow the possibility that the "fathers" rightly, but only partially, discerned a universal moral principle when they said "*all* men."[6]

When confronted with such claims, we are forced to grapple with some very basic questions. How are we to think about the sources and character of normative ideas? What role do they play in history and society? How are scholars and theorists to assess such ideas in an age when a host of theorists, from Feuerbach to Freud, from Nietzsche to Foucault, and their devotees over several generations, have regarded moral, theological, and jurisprudential first principles as mere artifacts, constructed to meet irrational needs? Are they, or we, to become high journalists of our time, scribbling down the prevailing sentiments of the day? Are they, or we, to become today's sophists who construct meaning, building the images and myths, the models and paradigms that project a semblance of order on a chaotic world, for a price, of course? Are they, or we, intellectual pioneers who find our way through thickets and deserts, making paths for the next generation to follow? Or pilots at the intellectual guidance center of the ships of states who, by careful discernments and prudent instructions, help captains and crews bring society through the ever-perilous tides of history—or, if mistaken, send it to shipwreck? Or is it possible that they, or we, should seek to be closer to prophets and sages of the common life, seeking to identify the permanently valid principles to be actualized always and everywhere, even if generations and cultures and social developments betray or ignore them in particular times or places?[7]

If human rights are the product of scribblers and sophists only, or even of pioneers and pilots, they will not long endure. Sentiments will change, and other construals will be imagined, other paths found, other channels dug. Human rights will be like civil rights—what is promulgated by one ruler or passed by one legislature can be rescinded by the next. The erosion of the gains for human rights could easily occur, at tremendous human cost, if the idea of human rights is based on nothing more than the changing course of historical experience and discourse about it. They, or we, would then neglect or deny the possibility that, in the final analysis, the idea of human rights depends on the sort of thing to which the phrase "endowed by their

Creator" points. They, or we, presume to be wiser than sages and prophets if it is held that without theological roots all rights, if they can be conceived to exist, can be made inalienable.

The Indispensability of Theology

The purpose of this essay is to argue that certain theological principles are indispensable to the sustaining of the idea of human rights. I should make clear that I am not disputing the question of whether people should be able to base their public ethics on religious convictions, or whether the freedom of religion should be acknowledged as a human right, or whether one nation may act internationally to prevent the violation of religious oppressions in other cultures.[8] I think the answer to all these questions is a decided "yes," if, but only if, it is true that there is a firm and comprehending basis for holding to human rights as a universal guide in ethical and juridical argument. It should also be made clear from the outset that I do not claim that all religions necessarily support human rights, for many do so only irregularly and indirectly. Nor do I claim that every religion has elements that could be theologically developed to support human rights, although this claim is closer to my views and does demand a distinction between *religion* as a mythic account of meaning or belief with a ritual practice that reinforces a group's sacred identity, and *theology* as a discipline by which we analyze the comparative worth of various religious claims according to their capacity to offer a viable comprehending view of life and meaning for all.

Of course, some who study and advocate human rights view the very idea of rights itself as a virtually all-encompassing ethical worldview, and work eagerly to see that it is applied to political orders, to criminal justice systems, to economic life, to educational opportunity, to health care, to family life, and equally to all religions, cultures, ethnic groups, and genders—eagerly drawing support from as many groups as possible.[9] Such understandings are laudable in their intent, and can be in alliance with what I here argue. Surely, people ought not harm or dehumanize others, and every institution of life ought to be so structured as to support and sustain the flourishing of humane existence. Yet, this view is often intellectually thin in that it does not supply the moral grounds for saying that we ought to help and not harm our neighbor, that everyone is a neighbor, and that even if much in every religion is identity-based and culturally particular, some theological—that is, some God-given and reasonable—normative insights bind all humanity together.[10]

The point of this argument, however, is that although the idea of human rights involves a quite profound and potentially universal set of implications about human nature, it is not ultimately a fully comprehending idea. It lacks the rationally defensible understanding that we all stand under a universal moral law, and that each person is constituted by a divinely endowed core that is the ultimate basis for the "right to have rights" before this law. Such ideas are more comprehending than the idea of human rights itself, and certainly more than any code, covenant, or declaration about them. Such ideas are theological in nature, not merely religious in the sense that there are many religions, and that each one will have its own dogmas and cultic practices that are not shared by outsiders.[11] Theological ideas may be fed and supported, or resisted and contradicted in various degrees by particular religious traditions. But the "logos" of "theos" may well be the most rational ground for holding to human rights in the first place. Indeed, theological ideas are often the unacknowledged and indispensable root of those non-religious universalist philosophies that also support human rights.[12]

Some contemporary thinkers may regard ideas about the "soul" or the "image of God" or "spark of the divine" as quaint or unconvincing. But what such ideas point toward is quite permanent and persuasive: each person by virtue of being human must be accorded a dignity and a respect that precludes violation of his or her person, relationships, and convictions. Still further, because all peoples and cultures stand under a universal "higher authority" that humans did not construct and cannot deconstruct, people may seek to change the unjust laws of various nations, the unjust conventions of any cultures, or the unjust practices of any religion that permits or advocates violation of that core. Of course, they must be persuaded to make these alterations, for respect for their convictions demands recognition that the soul ought not, and probably cannot, be coerced. Persons or societies or religious movements may, of course, ignore the reality of a universal law or the dignity of the soul or the necessity of persuasion for a time; but the results lead to disaster.[13]

This theological perspective suggests that the powers of government should be limited because some things are so sacred that no regime is competent to control their existence. Every society requires a political order to organize the common life, and that entails some regulative authority over aspects of every other area of life—family life, law, education, economy, medicine, and so forth—where violence or the violation of rights occurs. But government must also be subject to and supportive of those bondings of affection, principles of justice, processes of learning, laws of economics, arts of healing that make these other areas possible. This regulative authority within respectful limits applies, above all, to those institutions where the "metaphysical-moral" presumptions by which people wrestle with ultimate issues, those which no regime can generate or control, are cultivated, celebrated, and propagated.[14]

If such theological principles are recognized, then certain arenas of human activity must have a zone of relative freedom, a "social space" to carry out their proper functions. Many today discuss vital arenas such as (1) the family in sustaining intimate relationships and forming new generations, (2) the importance of governance under law, (3) the role of media, school, and university to seek truth and inform people, (4) various associations to assist quests for material betterment (whether unions, corporations, or advocacy groups) or cultural identity (ethnic, musical, artistic, or cultural-linguistic groups), and (5) most important: the church, synagogue, mosque, and temple, because these are the historical root of the other social spaces that seek to clarify the ultimate, spiritual ground for humans to deal with the mysteries of sexuality, justice, wisdom, beauty, health, and plenty. No regime must be allowed free rein to dictate or coercively control the internal content of these.[15] Thus, not only a universal moral law, and not only a sense of a metaphysically and morally grounded understanding of personhood, but also a structural pluralism in society, all theologically grounded, are required for an enduring theory of human rights.

Doubt About the Universality of Human Rights

Such ideas are clearly not universal in one sense. They have not been present historically at all times; they are not recognized in many places. When Ira Glasser of the American Civil Liberties Union went to Russia for a human rights conference three years ago, for example, he discovered that neither the concept of rights prior to those granted by the state nor the idea "of an organization outside of government to restrain government" existed in the common vocabulary.[16] Yet, in another sense, such ideas are universal. The Russians quickly recognized the importance of such concepts and of such organizations, once they had a chance to explore them. A major project is now under way to translate and publish books on these matters for use in Russia.[17]

Elsewhere, resistance to such ideas and organizations persists, even in international forums. The idea that human rights imply a potentially shared universal morality has been challenged by some delegates to the 1993 United Nations Conference on Human Rights in Vienna, the 1995 meeting in Beijing on women, and the 1996 meeting in Helsinki on poverty. These delegates have argued that the citizens of their respective states have no obligation to obey "Western" ideas of human rights, for these could destroy their social, cultural, and sometimes religious distinctiveness.[18] The arguments have been particularly intense in regard to East and Southeast Asia.[19]

Recently, Xiaorong Li offered a summary and critique of what are today called "Asian Values" by those who resist the developing international standards of human rights. The "Asian" (the term itself obscures the variety in Asia) claims are these: "Rights are culturally specific," "the community takes precedence over individuals," "social and economic rights take precedence over civil and political rights," and "rights are a matter of national sovereignty." Xiaorong argues that not only does the first of these claims commit the "genetic fallacy"—the view that a norm can only be suitable to its place of origin—she goes on to suggest that the cultures they defend have not only drawn on norms that derive from "foreign" roots, but could benefit by adopting these norms too.

Xiaorong also argues that proponents of so-called Asian values confuse "community" with state or regime. They use the obfuscation to dissolve any non-governmental organization that the state does not create or control, to the detriment of community, and without letting the people participate in the definition of the communities to which they would give loyalty. Moreover, she argues that leaders who limit civil and political rights in the name of social and economic ones are nearly always in political positions that guarantee them social and economic privileges, while they silence advocates of poor and illiterate peoples from speaking of their needs and discontents, and prevent the middle classes from gaining in political influence.

Finally, she points to the fact of the changing definitions of community in an emerging global society, and the debate about patterns of justice in civil, political, social, and economic life that all reflect transnational realities, where political sovereignty is inevitably compromised by intercultural exchange. Life is in fact shaped by realms of meaning that are not rooted in any one society or history or cultural heritage, and to deny this is morally dishonest. In brief, Xiaorong argues that those who oppose human rights by invoking sovereign cultural values do so on very suspect intellectual and moral grounds.[20]

However, it must be said that while some non-Western voices challenge universalist ideas in international law and public policy, we face the odd and awkward situation that many Western defenders of human rights do so on grounds that are held by many contemporary thinkers to be no less suspect intellectually and morally. They doubt that ethics or jurisprudence has a serious metaphysical or epistemic ground, for they doubt that anything can be grounded *onto-theo*-logically—the classic basis for universalistic ethics and jurisprudence. But if it is the case that human rights are based essentially in what the powerful members of the international community of nations impose on the rest of the world, even with the best of intentions, it is difficult to escape anything but a Hobbesian society and a Nietzschean philosophy.[21]

Ironically, one of the leading international advocacy organizations for human rights, Amnesty International, has sponsored lectures by outstanding political philosophers that reveal the fragility of contemporary secular thinking about universalistic principles. In their defenses of human rights, they provide thin, mutually contradictory, and often precisely Hobbesian or Nietzschean, grounds for doing so.[22] For the most part, they say, human rights emerge under sociological conditions of modernity as an assertion of the will of sovereigns. They offer no explanation as to when, where, or why these social conditions arose, or when, where, or why this will was exercised. Some, to be sure, turn to the nature of human imagination, with its presumptions of linguistic construction, to see what the character of language and discourse itself tells us. And while they note that it has a grammar, it is not clear that one can get from grammar to human rights, for the opponents of human rights also have a grammar. Their arguments read thin precisely because they share a disregard of, sometimes a contempt for, theology as a possible resource in the interpretation of, or the guidance of, the common life. The dependence on sociological or linguistic analysis alone (although sometimes a blend of the two) as the bases for ethical and jurisprudential values suggests that, in substantial measure, political philosophy as practiced today is groundless and more culturally and contextually variable than theology. These philosophers tend to share the Enlightenment view that theology is the more or less rationalized articulation of otherwise quite irrational religious dogmas. This questionable view is suspect on empirical and rational grounds, and remains quite unaware of the traditions of "public theology" in relation to human rights.[23]

Public Theology and the Genealogy of Modernity

The term "public theology" first appeared in 1974, although it appeared as a summary of a long tradition. It has been developed systematically by several authors in recent years.[24] The term, although still disputed, has been increasingly used by those concerned about the ethical fabric of contemporary life.[25] The term "public" is used to stress the point that "theology," while possibly related to intensely personal commitments or to particular communities of worship, is at its most profound levels neither merely private nor a matter of distinctive communal identity. Rather, it is an ongoing discipline that seeks to discern the way things are and ought to be, one that is decisive for public discourse and necessary to the guidance of individual souls, societies, and indeed the community of nations. It responds to the problems that human experiences do not interpret themselves, but require various modes of public discourse to discern their meanings. Therefore we turn to several "publics" to establish the relative validity of any serious claim about meaning.

First, we may speak of the *religious* public, which can be identified by asking: What can and should be preached and taught among those who seek faithful living and thinking according to the most holy, the most comprehensive, most righteous, and most enduring reality to which humans can point? Second, we may refer to the *political* public by asking: What can provide those in authority with a vision of and motivation to establish just institutions in society so that the common life can flourish? In this connection, it is a mistake to identify "public" only with government, for other spheres of human activity form, or reform, construct or overthrow governments. Third is the *academic* public, identified by asking: What can offer reasons and withstand critical analysis, offering convincing arguments and evidence for the positions it advances in the context of serious dialogue between informed scholars? To these three publics must be added at least the *economic* public and the *legal* public. All these "publics," which together constitute much of civil society, are decisive for human rights, and are shaped by theological influences.

The rejection of theology as a decisive influence in civil society and in the development of constitutional democracy and human rights, or the use of theology as an ideological weapon, has led to great difficulties. For example, when contending rulers combined particular traditions with this or that militant national or class loyalty and posed them against all outside institutions or dissenting people or alternative faiths, Europe was plunged into a time of war, with each side claiming that God was on its side. No small number of scholars and jurists, statesmen and artists began to wonder whether theology could be public. Was it not so that "wars of religion" de-civilized what theology had once civilized? And was theology not laden with a history of crusades, inquisitions, witch burnings, and pogroms?

These are the questions that "modernity," as many today call the Enlightenment period of Western intellectual history, puts to theology. The Enlightenment did not entirely deny the fact that "religion," and even "dogmatics" or "polemics," were powerful forces in people's lives; it simply relegated these to the "private" sphere of subjective, irrational preferences. On the one hand, this evoked an intense examination of the subjective and irrational forces within the human personality. On the other hand, it denied theology a public role. Insofar as a case for theology could be made, it would have to be made on the grounds of secular philosophy or social utility. This raised a pressing question: Why is "theology" necessary to intellectual and social life at all, for are not philosophy and social analysis sufficient to the task?

Those of us who claim the legacy of public theology hold that philosophical thought, social analysis, and moral judgment are unstable by themselves. They bend easily to the unscrupulous interests that lurk in the very heart of the best of us if they are not rooted in a holy, true, just creativity that is greater than we humans can achieve in our rationalizations—if they are not ultimately grounded in that reality which we call God. For the human wisdom of philosophy, the ordering systems of societies, and the ethical judgments of individuals express the irrational elements of human fantasy no less than much religion does. And all of them need to be seen as subject to standards, purposes, and an unconditioned reality greater than our wisdoms, systems, judgments, and religions can generate or discover alone. "Logos" requires "Theos." Theology is required.

In this view, the greatest horrors derive not from religion and theology, but from all sorts of forces—philosophical, scientific, legal, political, economic, sexual, and artistic—when they become disconnected from their reasonable ground. Indeed, it is those movements that have repudiated theology that have been the source of the greatest destruction of our times, the greatest violators of human rights. One might speak of Papa Doc's Haiti, of Pol Pot's Cambodia, of Marcos's Philippines, of Mao's China, of Stalin's Soviet Union, and of dozens of petty tyrants in Latin America and Africa—all of whom rejected theology in favor of "modern scientific" approaches to social reality. Of course, South Africa and Iran would also have to be mentioned, but a thorough analysis is unlikely to find developments there to be genuinely theological, even if they were religious. It was precisely in reaction to the barbarism of the Nazi movement that the UN Declaration of Human Rights was written.

From the recent explosion of literature on this topic, I would like to draw attention to the current "Special Communications" of the *Journal of the American Medical Association.* In a series of articles it shows that the most advanced centers of medical and legal research (all working on post- or anti-theological bases) were among the most energetic legitimators of the most grotesque travesties.[26] They drew from Hume, Rousseau, Darwin, and Ploetz, all of whom developed the idea of "racial hygiene" and fostered the notion of "eugenics."[27] The lead article also points to a Dr. Leo Alexander, who offered in the Nuremberg Doctors Trial the testimony that a combination of Hegelian theories of historicist development and notions of "rational utility" were the guiding principles of the recent dictatorships, and that these had displaced "moral, ethical, and religious" values.[28] All the decisive theorists thought that one or another form of post-theological theory could supply the foundations for modern thought, politics, law, and morality without the need for anything beyond "nature" and "history," "culture" and "human creativity," anything such as "God."[29]

Challenges to Modernity

One of the several challenges to modernity may be called "premodernism" or "traditionalism." It sees modernity's repudiation of the synthesis of religion, philosophy, and social wisdom cultivated over centuries as a pretentious denial that human thought and civility is cumulative, a pompous presumption that we can dispense with all that went before us, an arrogant conceit that the past is but prologue. What some call Enlightenment, they call ruin.[30]

A second attack on modernity in its progressive, liberal form is the "hypermodernism" of revolutionary humanism. This is the view that evolutionary progress was a bourgeois dream, and that change must be aided by the seizing of power and the mobilization of the forces that actually transform life—economic, political, and ideological power. The enemy of modernization, in this view, is not only inherited ideas, and trust in natural development, but popular religion, conventional morality, and accepted patterns of leadership. To the hypermodernist, these are all pillars and symptoms of false consciousness. But a consciousness that discovers the logic of historical life by the analysis of human material interests can become the guiding power of nature and society.

Hypermodernism has taken one of two forms—libertarian individualism (centered on individualist, rational-choice economic theories) and liberationist collectivism (centered on bureaucratic theories of state planning). What we know as democratic capitalism or as democratic socialism are of course the moderate forms of these extremes that have preserved some sense of human rights. Doubts about the more radical forms of hypermodernism have increased in recent years, especially since the "Fall of the Wall" in 1989. While they are sometimes credited with helping to dismantle colonial and imperialist power, they have been unable to build a viable civilization, develop a compelling philosophy of life, or generate a profound culture. Where they have been most successful, various forms of hypermodernism have tended to become a "secular religion," demanding a degree of faith in their analysis of human interests and material forces that the evidence does not seem to warrant. They do not seem to evoke enduring loyalty or provide the moral or spiritual foundations to guide souls or civilizations, particularly in regard to human rights.

"Postmodernism," a third critique of modernism, rejects premodern traditionalism, much of hypermodernist revolutionism, and modernism itself. Its chief claim is that none of these is reliable; they are all nothing more than mental constructs imposed on a chaotic and fluctuating world in which all reality is interpretation, all morality is preference, and all truth is opinion.

Some religious writers love this view, believing that it supports their claim that everything must be based on blind faith alone. Thus, they feel free to believe anything they wish to believe, and feel no obligation to defend their views. If every view is equally arbitrary, one can be a Fundamentalist of any kind, purely on the basis of an act of will. Seldom do those who embrace this view recognize that they have acceded to a Hobbesian/Nietzschean world in which nihilism, not a just divine reality, has the final word as it deconstructs, decodes, and delegitimates all normative belief—including faith, morality, theology, and human rights.

It may be wise to suggest that all the struggle over modernity, by such premodernists, hypermodernists, and postmodernists as are sketched here, is not only a manifestation of contemporary Western thought but another version of a longer and deeper and wider set of debates that have gone on in many contexts over many centuries. Certainly, comparable debates may be found in some measure in those settings where theistic faiths—such as Judaism, Christianity, Islam, and major parts of Hinduism—have influenced or substantially formed complex, inclusive, ethically guided civilizations. These movements nearly always have their traditionalist reactionary, their militant revolutionary, and their fideist voluntarist wings, although they seldom carry the day. The current resurgence of religious movements in Israel and in Islamic and Hindu regions,[31] and the rapid growth of Evangelical and Catholic communities in both formerly pagan areas and in recently secularized areas of the world, can be seen as a reactionary resistance to modernization, or a frightening revolutionary drive to a new theocracy, or as a fundamentalist fideism; but they might better be seen as an alternative postmodern attempt to recover and recast more stable and reliable ways of thinking about how things are and ought to be.[32]

All of these current trends tend to believe that the modern thinkers understood their own foundations. But the premodern traditionalists think they are false and that we need to repudiate them and return to sounder, ancient ones. The hypermodernist enthusiasts think they are absolutely valid and thus turn modernization into a secular religion. And the postmodern nihilists think that they, and every other claim about foundations, are simply the imposition of conscious constructions on a chaotic context. All of these take their clues from what modernity says about itself.

Reflections on the bases for human rights, however, suggest that modernity does not understand itself.[33] Growing evidence suggests that the Enlightenment is more deeply rooted in theological presuppositions than it acknowledges. If that is so, both the modernist and the traditionalist, who see the Enlightenment as the repudiation of the syntheses of previous epochs, are mistaken. The continuity may be greater than the discontinuity, and the difference may be that of profound foundation and superficial appearance. If so, the hypermodernist who worships the presumptions of the Enlightenment is worshiping superficial images, and the postmodernists are correct in saying that what they say is groundless, without foundations.

A deeper, more persuasive view is provided, I think, by the resurgent development of public theology, as suggested earlier. From this perspective, we may look again at what are purported to be the turning points in modernity, and note that they rest on a more enduring basis than usually recognized. The French philosopher Descartes, for example, was able to discover a real self at the root of consciousness when he tried to doubt all, because the microscope of perception through which he examined consciousness was formed by a refined theological engagement with the soul. He did not discover what the Buddha discovered when he plumbed his own consciousness, namely the bliss of no-thing-ness; nor did he discover what Marx talked about when he spoke of these matters, namely that self was merely an "ensemble of social relations." Similarly, the British philosopher of religion and constitutional law, John Locke, could speak of "self-evident truths and natural rights" of justice, because he believed that all humans were endowed by their Creator with the image of God (and thus had the capacity to recognize what was reasonable and fair), and that these truths and rights ought not be violated by political or religious authority. So also the German philosopher of science and morality, Immanuel Kant, could speak of *a priori* truths in "the starry heavens above and the moral law within," because he thought within a framework of discourse that viewed these spheres as established by a divine will, both capable of reasonable argument.

Religion, Theology, and the Bases for Human Rights

In the final analysis, these theistic understandings of reality may well provide more promising bases for universal definitions of human rights than any social, historical, cultural, or legal view, because they focus on the only truly universal moral reference for understanding our common humanity, despite differences among and within the various groups in their interpretations of the reality to which they all point. They may differ because they interpret the reality of God in ways that link their views to particular aspects of society or experience, but they tend to hold, in common, a sense of the human person as a moral entity with a soul and a relationship to a universal, just God who is the source and guarantor of moral law. To be sure, the differences shape the ways in which civil society is generated and organized under their influence, so that only some enhance human rights in all areas of life, but the potential for universality is scripted into the ultimate convictions of them all.[34]

Indeed, every culture in every age seems to have faced issues roughly comparable to what is here outlined. If so, we must all, once and again, ask what, finally, is holy, true, just, and creative. What shall we give our minds, our time, our energies to as we try to assess who stands under the same standards that pertain to us? And that is likely to drive us to theology. Decisive in this regard is that there be a dialogue of the world religions, joined specifically in a quest for a common social ethic. This would of course require both the further development of a reasonable public theology, and the kind of open social context in which people could be persuaded that they ought to reaffirm or reform their inherited religion, convert from one religion to another, or from no religion to a religion, or from a religion to suspicion of the kind of religion they previously knew.[35] We dare not fail to note how decisive this is. The right to convert, to become persuaded that one relationship to God (and thus to humanity) is better than another, and the right to attempt to persuade others individually and to reorganize society as a whole on that basis, are the core indicators of the flourishing of human rights. Once people have the right to have rights—that is, have "souls"—they then have the basis of the right to free speech and press, of academic freedom, of the right to organize religious and advocacy groups of all sorts, of the right to transcend ascribed identities (race, sex, class, nation), and of the right to dissent from the dictates of any temporal political regime.

It is most remarkable that when a new barbarism broke out in the West, at the hands of Hitler, it was not only to the legacies of such Enlightenment thinkers, but even more to the wider, deeper framework on which they are dependent, to which the world turned. Indeed, the United Nations can enshrine such ideas as these in "covenants" because the social and intellectual heritage that has generated contemporary public theology possessed a way of thinking about these matters that can be, and has been, recognized by many peoples who are not historically party to this mode of discourse as containing something universally valid. Indeed, the contemporary development of global interactions of people beyond world wars is possible because of the increasingly widespread actualization and acceptance of certain universal principles—ones that were first stated in biblical terms and refined through long, complex encounters with philosophy, jurisprudence, and complex cultures by theology. We cannot, then, simply dismiss modernity's claims about human rights, any more than we can take them as the basis of a new secular faith, or claim that they are without grounding.

However, it is important to acknowledge that the public to which Western theology has spoken is still much too narrow and shallow. Today, if anything like a public theology is to be developed further, it must include a much enlarged conversation. For the philosophy, law, and culture it must engage are no longer confined to the Mediterranean, European, or American (North and South) life. The modernity that theology generated in these areas has expanded and been adopted, and modified, all over the world. True, the West's contribution to it has sometimes been in ways that we now know to have been imperialistic, colonialist, and exploitative. But we judge these as false, unjust, and unethical because the same theology that prompted expansion in these ways also bears within it universal principles that demand both a self-critical judgment when its best contributions are distorted, and a wider willingness to learn from other publics than those of the West. This theology holds that it is not true that there is nothing like a universal humanity. It rejects the cynical belief that there are no moral laws under which the whole of humanity stands. Some things simply ought not to be done to people, and people ought not to do some things. If this became most clear in the context of a very particular biblical insight at a particular time or space, it is nonetheless valid for all and defensible on grounds recognizable in other contexts.

Public theology also implies, in our world, that we take seriously the humanism of Confucius and Mencius, the religious philosophies of Ramanuja and Ankara, the wisdom of Saicho (who bridged Chinese and Japanese cultures and also became known as Dengyo Daishi) and Ibn-Rushd (who bridged Islamic and Western culture and also became known as Averroës), and of those leaders in many fields who, because of their considered convictions, work out righteous ways of human dealing. They must all be taken as theological dialogue partners in the redefinition of a broader public. The great philosophies and world religions that have demonstrated that they can shape great and complex civilizations over centuries must be given a place in this redefinition.

Similarly, public theologians will applaud when politicians, lawyers, social historians, and activist advocates defend human rights in public discourse. And they will acknowledge that many will do so on grounds that are not, overtly or consciously, theological. Some will oppose any introduction of theology into the discourse at all, due to the irrational presuppositions they have about theology. Nevertheless, they are allies, and not the enemies of public theology, unless they deny the possibility of allowing theology to offer its resources as the deepest and most enduring basis for human rights that can be identified. At that point, their objection becomes not only a violation of the human rights of those who hold these views, but ultimately an undercutting of what is likely the only secure basis for defending universal human rights in all societies and cultures. Public theology discerns in the claims of human rights publicly recognizable and universal truths. These are: (1) that each person has a dignity conferred by God, (2) that all live under a divine, universal moral law, (3) that no state, even an international federation of states, is competent to control all matters since some aspects of human activity are sacred beyond political agreement or social expediency, and that therefore a social pluralism is required, (4) that persons have to come to non-coerced conviction about matters at this level, so that freedom of religion is demanded, and (5) that there are valid continuities between the great and classical insights of sacred history and the present, and between present understandings and those emerging from new encounters and conversations with the world's great religions and philosophies. All these are theological points that sooner or later are best acknowledged as such, and as the grounds for human rights.

Notes

1. This is the central finding of John Witte Jr., and Johan D. Van der Vyver, eds., *Religious Human Rights in Global Perspective,* 2 vols. (The Hague/Boston/London: Martinus Nijhof, 1996).
2. Darryl M. Trimiew, *God Bless the Child That's Got Its Own: The Economic Rights Debate* (Atlanta: Scholars Press, 1997).
3. See "Human Dignity, Human Rights and Political Regimes," *American Political Science Review* vol. 80, no. 3 (September 1986): 801.
4. I take seriously, on this point, the arguments of Nicholas Wolterstorff against Robert Audi in their debate, *Religion in the Public Square* (Lanham, MD: Rowman and Littlefield, 1996). Kent Greenawalt presents an extremely helpful overview of the major current arguments about the role of religion in public discourse in *Private Consciences and Public Reasons* (New York: Oxford University Press, 1995), although some of his arguments seem to be effectively refuted by Michael J. Perry, *Religion in Politics* (New York: Oxford University Press, 1997).
5. It is the greatest insight of the Mosaic tradition, which makes Judaism a perpetual light to the nations, that a moral law is recognized as given to humanity even where there is no settled society and no organized state. The fact that every other religion and culture can recognize the truth of these principles and that no just society or government can be formed without comparable provisions confirms the universality of them.
6. I have elsewhere argued that however ambiguous the views of the "fathers" when they approved the phrase "all men," the Jacksonian and Emancipation movements of the nineteenth century and the Civil Rights and Feminist movements of the twentieth century have properly recognized that the "all" is more definitive for the meaning of the word "men" than the biases of the authors. See R.C. White Jr., et al., eds., *An Unsettled Arena: Religion and the Bill of Rights* (Grand Rapids: Eerdmans, 1990), 92–114. When these principles become the basis for a foreign policy, the "all" is considerably broadened again. The question is the legitimacy of this expansion.
7. The debate over these matters is quite old and rather well defined. From the late medieval scholastics to the modern defenders of "natural rights," as found in Thomas Reid, John Locke, and the U.S. founding fathers, we find the argument that law that was based only in "sociality" (not in God) was mistaken, for the knowledge of just law implied also obligation to follow it, and that sense of obligation cannot be derived from

sociality. "A de facto feature of human nature, such as sociality, could not impose obligation, for a self-imposed obligation arising from such a drive towards social living could be dissolved as easily as it could be assumed and was therefore no obligation at all." Knud Haakonssen, *Natural Law and Moral Philosophy: From Grotius to the Scottish Enlightenment* (New York: Cambridge University Press, 1996), 141.

8. These issues are widely and profoundly debated in Greenawalt, *Private Consciences;* Perry, *Religion in Politics;* and with a longer historical perspective in N.B. Reynolds and W.C. Durham Jr., eds, *Religious Liberty in Western Thought* (Atlanta: Scholars Press, 1966).

9. See, for example, Robert Traer, *Faith in Human Rights* (Washington, DC: Georgetown University Press, 1991).

10. John Kelsay and Sumner Twiss, eds., *Religion and Human Rights* (New York: Project on Human Rights, 1994), approximate this view, but tend to avoid theology in favor of a purely sociological view of religion.

11. See Mark Heim, *Salvations* (Maryknoll, NY: Orbis Press, 1995). Even if there are quite competing senses of what the ultimate ends of life are in various religions—of what humanity is to be saved from and saved for, so that Moksha or Nirvana seems ultimately irrational to those who believe in Paradise or heaven or a New Jerusalem—the debate about these ultimate ends can only take place if and when a recognition of universal moral law and a respect for the other is accepted as theologically valid.

12. The evidence stands against the common reading of history found, for example, in Charles P. Henry's "Introduction: On Building a Human Rights Culture," in *International Rights and Responsibilities for the Future,* K.W. Hunter and T.C. Mack, eds. (Westport, CT: Praeger, 1996), xviii, where he asserts that "the first generation of human rights—personal, civil, and political—may be ascribed to the French philosophy of the Enlightenment and the French and American human-rights declarations from the late 1700s." This ignores the tradition of rights established in ecclesiastical and civil law under theological influence long before the French Revolution, as well established by Georg Jellinek, *The Declaration of the Rights of Man and of Citizens: A Contribution to Modern Constitution History* (Westport, CT: Hyperion Press, 1982) reprint; A.S.P. Woodhouse, *Puritanism and Liberty* (Chicago: University of Chicago Press, 1932); and Reynolds and Durham, eds., *Religious Liberty in Western Thought.* Henry also conveniently ignores the "Terror" of the French Revolution against human rights.

13. The threat may even lurk in some ways of advocating human rights, as suggested by David M. Smolin, "Will International Human Rights Be Used as a Tool of Cultural Genocide?" *Journal of Law and Religion* vol. 12, no. 1 (1995–96): 143–71. The peril is particularly acute if the only two centers of reference in human rights analysis are the self and the state—especially if the state is global in scope.

14. I use the term "metaphysical-moral" to indicate those philosophical-theological attempts to articulate a trans-physicalist or spiritual (sometimes also called transcendental) reality that is constitutive of ethically normative characteristics. This reality is conceived in ontological or theistic terms and is held capable of being discussed in reasonable discourse. It is both "metaphysics" and any "onto-theo-logical" reality that is today doubted by many.

15. I have elsewhere argued the larger historical case (and shall return to the argument below) that the roots of human rights ideas derive from no other source than the biblical heritage, in conversation with philosophical and social thought, although it is very clear that some parts of this tradition too have been hostile to human rights. However, a strand reaching from the ancient prophets through early church, the Catholic conciliar, and Reformation developments, gradually persuaded the West that certain of its presuppositions were valid. On this basis modernity affirmed human rights. See my

Creeds, Society, and Human Rights: A Study in Three Cultures (Grand Rapids: Eerdmans, 1985; republished, Nashville: Parthenon Press, 1996).

16. "Translating Civil Liberties into Russian," *New York Times*, August 26, 1996, B-4.

17. The American Civil Liberties Union vigorously defends the freedom of religion, but it does not acknowledge that the civil liberties it advocates may be substantially rooted in a theological heritage, one only marginally developed in the Russian Orthodox wing of Christianity. See Tamás Földesi, "The Main Problems of Religious Freedom in Eastern Europe"; and Harold Berman, "Religious Rights in Russia at a Time of Tumultuous Transition," in Witte and Van der Vyver, *Religious Human Rights in Global Perspective*, 243–62, 285–304. My own experience in Eastern Europe and current debates about freedom of religion in Russia suggest that the non-Orthodox religious groups are the most effective groups in bringing new concepts of human rights to that region.

18. The latter view is held especially by Islamic representatives. See Abdullahi Ahmed An-Na'im, ed., *Human Rights in Cross-Cultural Perspectives* (Philadelphia: University of Pennsylvania Press, 1992).

19. Christina Cerna, "Universality of Human Rights and Cultural Diversity," *Human Rights Quarterly* vol. 16, no. 4 (1994): 740–52.

20. " 'Asian Values' and the Universality of Human Rights," *Philosophy and Public Policy* vol. 16, no. 2 (Spring 1996): 18–23. See also my "The Future of Human Rights: Multiculturalism in Vienna," *Christian Century*, June 30/July 7, 1993, 660–62. The main arguments employed in regard to Asia were also used by a number of Latin American countries, sometimes under the influence of Marxist-dominated "liberation thought" and sometimes that of right-wing nationalism—until the recent, if still fragile, turn to democracy in that region.

21. This, of course, is what the noted Jewish philosopher Leo Strauss says is the foundation of human rights. See his *Natural Right and History* (Chicago: University of Chicago Press, 1950). The view is also held by a number of Roman Catholic thinkers, for example, Ernest Fortin, *Collected Essays*, vol. 2, J.B. Benestad, ed. (Lanham, MD: Rowman and Littlefield, 1996).

22. See note 3 above. The lecturers are Steven Lukes, John Rawls, Catharine MacKinnon, Richard Rorty, Jean-François Lyotard, Agnes Heller, and Jon Elster. For a critique of several of these contributions, see my essay, with Stephen Healey, "Religion and Human Rights: A Theological Apologetic," in Witte and Van der Vyver, eds., *Religious Human Rights in Global Perspective*, 485–516.

23. The following discussion is, in part, drawn from my "Public Theology and Moral Judgment," prepared for an October 1996, Consultation at the University of Beijing in honor of the opening of a new Religion Department. It is being translated for publication in China, but has also appeared in *Theology Today* vol. 54, no. 2 (July 1997): 165–80.

24. Martin E. Marty, "Reinhold Niebuhr: Public Theology and the American Experience," *Journal of Religion* 54 (October 1974): 332–59. See also David Tracy, *The Analogical Imagination: Christian Theology and the Culture of Pluralism* (New York: Crossroad Books, 1981).

25. The most recent overview of the development of this idea is in Robert Benne, *The Paradoxical Vision: A Public Theology for the Twenty-First Century* (Minneapolis: Fortress Press, 1995).

26. Jeremia A. Barondness, "Medicine Against Society," 1657–61; Jay Katz, "The Nuremberg Code and the Nuremberg Trial," 1662–66; Ruth Faden, et al., "U.S. Medical Researchers, the Nuremberg Doctors Trial, and the Nuremberg Code," 1667–71; all in *JAMA* vol. 276, no. 20 (November 27, 1996).

27. Barondness, "Medicine Against Society," 1657–58.

28. Ibid., 1658, drawing from R.N. Procter, *Racial Hygiene: Medicine Under the Nazis* (Cambridge: Harvard University Press, 1988); and S. Kuehl, *The Nazi Connection* (New York: Oxford University Press, 1994).

29. This is also the obvious presumption of Ronald Dworkin, *Taking Rights Seriously* (Cambridge: Harvard University Press, 1977), and Jack Donnelly, *Universal Human Rights in Theory and Practice* (Ithaca: Cornell University Press, 1989). But they are challenged by Mary Ann Glendon, *Rights Talk: The Impoverishment of Political Discourse* (New York: Free Press, 1991); and Arthur Dyck, *Rights and Responsibilities: The Moral Bonds of Community* (Cleveland: Pilgrim Press, 1994).

30. All these views can be found in what may well be the most profound text for the "neoconservative" revival in America today, Leo Strauss and Joseph Cropsey, eds., *History of Political Philosophy*, 2nd ed. (Chicago: Rand McNally, 1972). Other influential works that press comparable issues into contemporary discussions include Alasdair MacIntyre, *After Virtue* (Notre Dame: Notre Dame University Press, 1981); Richard John Neuhaus, *The Naked Public Square* (Grand Rapids: Eerdmans, 1984); and Allan Bloom, *The Closing of the American Mind* (New York: Simon and Schuster, 1987).

31. See, for example, Peter van der Veer, *Religious Nationalism: Hindus and Muslims in India* (Berkeley: University of California Press, 1994); Mark Juergensmeyer, *The New Cold War?: Religious Nationalism Confronts the Secular State* (Berkeley: University of California Press, 1993); and Abdullahi Ahmed An-Na'im, *Toward an Islamic Reformation: Civil Liberties, Human Rights, and International Law* (Syracuse: Syracuse University Press, 1990). My own views are found in my *Creeds, Society, and Human Rights,* Chapters 8–10, and "Public Theology and the Future of Democratic Societies," in *The Church's Public Role,* ed. D. Hessel (Grand Rapids: Eerdmans, 1993), 63–83.

32. See David Martin, *Tongues of Fire: The Explosion of Protestantism in Latin America* (London: Basil Blackwell, 1990); Lawrence E. Harrison, *Underdevelopment Is a State of Mind: The Latin American Case* (Cambridge, MA: University Press of America, 1985); and my *Christian Social Ethics in a Global Era,* with Peter Berger, Dennis McCann, et al. (Nashville: Abingdon Press, 1995).

33. See, for example, Roy A. Clauser, *The Myth of Religious Neutrality: An Essay on the Hidden Role of Religious Belief in Theories* (Notre Dame: Indiana University Press, 1991).

34. This is a major conclusion of my *Creeds, Society, and Human Rights,* where I argue that humanism without theology crushes human rights, and that religious conviction opposed to the reasonable defense of its convictions in public discourse limits moral engagement with other traditions and with the multiple sectors of civil society in complex societies, and thus constricts the development of human rights, even if the theistic, metaphysical-moral basis is present.

35. Efforts to conduct serious dialogue are already under way. See, for example, Hans Küng, et al., *Christianity and the World Religions* (New York: Doubleday, 1986); Hans Küng, *Christianity and Chinese Religions* (New York: Doubleday, 1988); and Hans Küng, *Global Responsibility* (New York: Crossroad, 1991). See also, Witte and Van der Vyver, *Religious Human Rights in Global Perspective.* Fascinating alternative views can be found in Mark Heim, *Salvations* (Maryknoll, NY: Orbis Press, 1995); and David Krieger, *The New Universalism: Foundations for a Global Theology* (Maryknoll, NY: Orbis Press, 1991).

3

REPLY   LOUIS HENKIN

Human Rights: Religious or Enlightened?

Professor Stackhouse brings, from the world of religion, support for the idea of human rights, for the universality of human rights, for human dignity as the foundation of human rights, and for the largely agreed upon content of human rights. One may cavil at some of Professor Stackhouse's "asides." One may wonder which "inchoate appeals to entitlements and freedoms" are not clearly rights. Is there a moral distinction between "rights" and "entitlements"? Which freedoms are rights and which are not "clearly rights"? Might Professor Stackhouse be rejecting economic and social rights? Group rights?

Nor is it necessary to take sharp issue with Professor Stackhouse's deprecation of those who identify the human rights idea with the seventeenth and eighteenth centuries, with the Enlightenment, with "structural changes in Europe."[1] Professor Stackhouse does not deny that historic forces and non-religious ideas may have contributed, indeed may have been necessary, to realize and give expression to the religious values he sees as basic to human rights. For their part, those who locate a birth date for human rights in the seventeenth and eighteenth centuries need not insist that the human rights idea is *only* "a product of history." They need not deny that religion may also have presided at that birth, in the person of John Locke, or of Immanuel Kant, even of Thomas Jefferson. In the eighteenth century, as today, whether as "scribblers" or "sophists," or as "high journalists," supporters of the human rights idea should welcome support for it from religious ideas and ideology.

Professor Stackhouse's thesis is that the human rights idea depends on certain "theological points," and that these "are best acknowledged as such, and as the grounds for human rights." It is important to note what Professor Stackhouse does not claim for these "theological points." He does not claim

31

that "religion," and religions, have always supported human rights either in principle or in practice. Religion, religions, he would probably admit, have not been prominent in promoting human rights as a moral idea, as a political ideology. Some religions have had difficulty rooting human rights in their "theology" or in finding support for it in their hagiography. Religion, religions (some of them surely, at times) have found the idea of human rights anthropocentric, egoistic, even narcissistic; and they have resisted the human rights commitment to individual autonomy, and its implicit challenge to authority, including religious authority, as anarchic—"every man whatsoever is right in his own eyes."[2]

Furthermore, religion—virtually every religion—has, at some time, included some dogma that the human rights idea and its devotees decry. I single out several: Denial of religious freedom to others, including the freedom to abandon one's religion or to convert to another religion (and—in the past—the freedom to worship idols). Religions have not been notable for commitment to gender equality. Some religions have not escaped the brush of slavery. Some religions have been charged with propagating, or tolerating, hatred of some group or another (e.g., antisemitism). At various times, in various places, religion—some religion—has not avoided practices that are horrendous, or surely highly questionable from the human rights perspective.

Professor Stackhouse avoids such strictures by distinguishing between religion (or religions) and theology. He posits a "public theology," which he defines as "a discipline by which we analyze the comparative worth of various religious claims according to their capacity to offer a viable comprehending view of life and meaning for all." His theology is not bound to, or represented by, or responsible for, any particular religion; public theology seems to be a distillation of what—for him—all religions, at bottom, represent or have in common.

Professor Stackhouse identifies certain "publicly recognizable and universal truths" in "the claims of human rights":

> (1) that each person has a dignity conferred by God, (2) that all live under a divine, universal moral law, (3) that no state, even an international federation of states, is competent to control all matters since some aspects of human activity are sacred beyond political agreement or social expediency, and that therefore a social pluralism is required, (4) that persons have to come to non-coerced conviction about matters at this level, so that freedom of religion is demanded, and (5) that there are valid continuities between the great and classical insights of sacred history and the present, and between present understandings and those emerging from new encounters and conversations with the world's great religions and philosophies. All these are theological

points that sooner or later are best acknowledged as such, and as the grounds for human rights.

If Professor Stackhouse's public theology—the "viable comprehending view of life and meaning for all"—is, or comprehends, acceptance, respect for, and commitment to the full panoply of human rights, the human rights movement and all persons of good will should rally to that "theology." But would all religions, and all who represent them today, embrace it? Should we not examine whether every religion now offers a "viable comprehending view of life and meaning for all?" (Including women? Including those committed to other religions, including various infidels, and other "others"?)

In any event, the world is not yet educated to Professor Stackhouse's distinction between religion and theology, and it is likely to continue to judge "theology" by what religion, or particular religions, profess and practice and preach. His articulation invites religion, all religions, to "clean up" their *particular* theologies so as to eliminate elements that are inconsistent with his "public theology," with his "theological points." If there is to be understanding and dialogue, theologians have to assume the task of educating the world, including the religious world, to the essentials of their own religion, and to the central place of human rights in their theology. That should help bridge, if not blend, the representatives of the human rights movement and the representatives of theology into a common bond in support of human rights, in support of its universality, in dismissing "cultural relativism" and "Asian values."

The heart of Professor Stackhouse's essay, its purpose, "is to argue that, over time, certain theological principles are indispensable to the long-term sustaining of the idea of human rights"; that "without theological rootage, all rights, if they can be conceived to exist, are alienable." For him, the idea of human rights is, and can only survive as, a religious idea. There can be no firm, lasting, legitimate, logical basis for human rights, except religion.

Professor Stackhouse seems to revisit here an old controversy between deists and *a-deists:* Can there be morality outside religion? Without religion, is morality rooted? Can it stand? Can it last? I do not deem it necessary to reopen and enter that fray. Since I—and no doubt he—have known highly moral persons who are atheists, agnostics, humanists, *Enlightened,* Professor Stackhouse must be saying, "yes, but their morality is not firm, lasting." Since I—and no doubt he—have known religious persons, institutions, creeds that he and I would agree are immoral, at least in respect of some principle or some practice, he must be saying, again, "yes, but those are aberrational."

My principal point of resistance to Professor Stackhouse's thesis is of another kind, at another level. As a philosophical, ideological, political idea, as the idea of our times as it is epitomized in the Universal Declaration, the human rights idea aspires to universalism. Therefore, it needs a base that has universal appeal, or at least general acceptance. Surely, that is not supplied by a theology, "public" or otherwise, that has religion as its basis. (More than half the world was, until recently, officially committed to atheism.) Any person, of any religion or of no religion, committed to human rights, should welcome Professor Stackhouse's expression of the principles implicit in human rights. But—for some—the references to God and divinity are unnecessary, exclusionary, and divisive. Whatever one's view of the history and the development of the human rights idea, whether in the seventeenth century, the eighteenth century, or the twentieth century, why should we deny the plausible claims, and forfeit the support, of the Enlightened world?

One should be pleased to see religion, religions, religious institutions, religious leaders, religious individuals embrace and support the idea of human rights. One should be pleased to see them join in the human rights movement, work in it, even lead it. One should be pleased to honor their claims to *parentage* of the idea of human rights, or of cognate ideas. But one might hope that those who fly the banners of religion would not exclude or discourage the large world of non-religious, or differently religious, from working to realize human rights for all, everywhere.

Accepting human rights as they have been defined here, I conclude that religion has made an important contribution to the definition—the idea of justice, for instance. (A major, perhaps *the* major, contribution to understanding justice was provided by Aristotle, whom we do not think of as a spokesman for religion, although some religions later adopted and adapted him.) Religion contributed also the idea of the brotherhood of man. But Professor Stackhouse's claims for religion are wider and deeper. He asserts that religion is essential to human rights; that we must base human rights on a firm intellectual foundation; that no "rational" foundation is possible, and that religion—and only religion—provides such a foundation.

If there were a religion that made human rights central, if that religion commanded universal, or nearly universal, adherence, such a religion might indeed provide a strong foundation for human rights. But I know of no such religion, and no religion would serve for those who do not believe in it. Indeed, for the present—alas—religion, the religions we know, have sometimes been more of a danger to, than a foundation for, human rights.

We do need an intellectual foundation for human rights; but, for very many, religion, even "public theology," cannot provide it. The religious commitment to human rights, the identification of a common public theology, provides a welcome support for human rights, but it is only recent, is not yet universal, and may not last.

For our time, one can—one has to—justify human rights by some contemporary universal version of natural law, *whether religious or secular,* by appeal to a common moral intuition of *human dignity.* If that is not good enough, it will have to do. May it last! If it does not last, all will be to do again, in another century, another age.

Notes

1. See Louis Henkin, *The Rights of Man Today* (New York: Center for the Study of Human Rights, Columbia University, 1988), 1–15; Louis Henkin, *The Age of Rights* (New York: Columbia University Press, 1990), 1–10.
2. Deuteronomy 12:8.

4

LARRY RASMUSSEN

Human Environmental Rights and/or Biotic Rights

Introduction

Several matters set this discussion. First, the Universal Declaration on Human Rights, together with most interpretations of rights, says nothing about environmental bases or dimensions of human rights. Common rights discourse ventures even fewer claims for the rights of non-human life, often referred to as biotic rights.*

The reason has oft been cited: "Rights" are socially constructed. Their form and content are embedded in cultural narratives. In the modern era, when current rights discourse came on the scene, a specific narrative about human nature prevailed. Kant's rendition is perhaps the most influential: humans, as autonomous beings possessing reason's self-given law, are not means but ends in themselves.

This assertion of individual human dignity issues in a refusal to make humans instruments only. When this refusal is guaranteed with a legal structure, it takes on the status of an entitlement deemed a "right." A moral claim about human dignity grounds a legal one, and both reside in a certain account of human nature as rational and sovereign.

That account goes well beyond Kant, of course. It is more broadly the culture of the European Enlightenment, even when it builds upon sources

---

*For the discussion of this chapter, to have "rights" or a "right" means simply to hold a legitimate claim or entitlement to something, the recognition of which is required of others. Within this broad definition I distinguish between "human environmental rights" and "biotic rights." Human environmental rights are an extension of the moral framework and discourse that has grounded human rights; biotic rights reside in a different framework with a different rationale.

such as the Reformation's distinction between the person and the person's works, a distinction that asserted individual dignity as given by God. This Enlightenment narrative understood humanity as a species apart, just as it conceived the rest of nature in Cartesian and Kantian terms. Kant himself was utterly clear: "Animals are not self-conscious and are there merely as a means to an end. That end is man."[1]

"Nature," "natural rights," and "natural law" are, to be sure, serious moral, religious, and metaphysical subjects and key terms in Enlightenment rights discourse. The appeals of Locke, Rousseau, Jefferson, Paine, and other such champions of this good cause rest here. But the attention is anthropocentric without qualification.

Descartes is prototypical. In his famed quest for a practical philosophy based in certain knowledge, he cites two possibilities—then essentially chooses the first—it will be knowledge "I . . . find within myself, or perhaps in the great book of nature."[2] He then, like Kant and the Enlightenment generally, gives centrality to the nature and resources of the autonomous, rational self, with reliable knowledge rooted in human subjectivity. "Natural law" and "natural rights" refer to the laws and rights of human nature only. When "the great book of nature" is in view, "nature" there other than human is essentially without consciousness and is apprehended in mechanistic terms. Nature is an array of objects serving the ways of active, purposive human subjects. For "rights," then, the reference is to human subjects alone and apart. This holds even when the claims go theological. ("We hold these truths to be self-evident, that all men are created equal, that they are endowed by their Creator with certain unalienable rights, that among these are Life, Liberty and the pursuit of Happiness.")

A chapter such as this, periodically engaging religious perspectives, cannot forgo a development parallel to the intensified anthropocentricity* of the "turn to the subject" in Enlightenment epistemology and ethics. In tandem with the assertion of human moral autonomy—namely, freedom consists in giving ourselves the laws by which we will live—is the move away from theocentrism in ethics. Kant himself is still quite serious about God, as a transcendental idea. But his innumerable prodigy lack any God-requisite, or even God-reference, in their grounding of ethics and rights. The scope of rights changes over time, to be sure. Rights come to claim a wider range of

---

*"Androcentricity" is more accurate. Women and children, indigenous peoples and peoples of colors, Jews, Muslims, and slaves did not share equal rights even when Enlightenment rights language was "universal" in voice and even when that universalism offered a moral trajectory that opposed these inequalities.

human subjects as deep-seated prejudices against slaves, women, and non-Western peoples and religions are combated in the name of a more genuine and hard-won universalism. Yet the essential moral grounding does not change, and rights debates proceed *etsi Deus non daretur*, as if God did not exist. The theocentric universe of medieval cosmology, with all nature alive as an ocean of symbols linking earth to heaven, is thoroughly secularized in the same broad movement that set the thinking, judging human self at the center of rights discourse and ethical theory. God, and nature as a fecund expression of divine emanations, are discarded in favor of morally self-sufficient humans set over against mechanistic and passive nature.[3] For better or worse, then, rights language arises within and inhabits a moral world that is neither theocentric nor biocentric, but anthropocentric.

Moreover, it is anthropocentric in a certain way. As noted, the legitimacy of rights is not grounded in an objective order (the city of God, or the polis, or nature beyond human nature). Rights are grounded in the subjectivity of sovereign individuals who voluntarily enter the contractual relationships that compose society. These are essentially non-relational, freely consenting individuals who possess certain qualities, such as rationality, that comprise "nature" and warrant "natural rights." In this rendition of human nature, tradition, culture, religion, family, and the world of non-human nature do not belong in any essential way to rights and their legitimation.[4]

In short, the moral and legal provenance of the Universal Declaration of Human Rights, like the rights formulations of the English Bill of Rights (1689), the American Declaration of Independence (1776), the French Declaration of the Rights of Man and the Citizen (1789), and the first ten amendments to the Constitution of the United States known as the Bill of Rights (1791), is empty of any significant notions of human environmental rights or biotic rights. Human rights are not integrally related to the moral standing of other species. Non-human life has little or no moral standing at all, except as human property and means. I call this style of moral thought "apartheid" thinking.[5] It assumes segregated worlds and separate development. Thomas Berry calls it "moral autism" because, while it speaks in universal terms about human beings, it considers humans a species essentially non-relational and self-encased.[6]

Conclusion: If we are to speak of human environmental rights and/or of biotic rights, the standard rights framework will need to be changed rather drastically, or another framework substituted.

The second matter framing the discussion is a planet in jeopardy. Virtually all the natural systems of the planet are experiencing deterioration, some of them at historically unparalleled rates. While there are very significant regional differences, on the planet as a whole soil erosion is exceeding soil formation, carbon emissions are exceeding carbon fixation, forest destruction is exceeding forest regeneration, fresh water use is exceeding aquifer replenishment, species extinction is exceeding species evolution, while half the world's coastlines—the most densely populated human areas—are imperiled as life systems. The ominous, if bland, word for all this together, stamped like a big stencil on a large crate, is "UNSUSTAINABILITY."

The Ecological Society of America, having documented the range of threats to basic life systems, says straightforwardly: "Achieving a sustainable biosphere is the single most important task facing humankind today."[7] Achieving a global ethos focused on sustainability is the chief task of ethics itself now, and a part of the larger human endeavor. Environmental rights are, in turn, a part of the necessary global ethos. "We ought to maintain a sustainable biosphere"[8] should be among the truths held to be self-evident.

The reason is as firm as any can be: Ecocide is homicide. Human rights and social justice, much less minimal survival requirements, cannot be realized in an environment unfit for human habitation. Differently said, realizing any human right depends on realizing human environmental rights or biotic rights—or at least "environmental well-being," should rights language itself be rejected.[9]

Perilous social and environmental degradation, together with the revelation of our dull sense of obligation to the Community of Life as a whole, has turned human environmental rights and/or biotic rights into pressing international subjects. The report of the World Commission on Environment and Development, titled "Our Common Future" and popularly known as the Brundtland Report, pushed the environmental responsibilities of nation-states to the fore in its preparation for the UN Conference on Environment and Development (the Rio Earth Summit). NGOs (non-governmental organizations) were perhaps even more active than nation-states in pressing environmental rights as a subject of law, morality, and policy.[10] One key effort, the attempt to write and sign onto an "Earth Charter" as a parallel-of-sorts to the Universal Declaration of Human Rights, failed in Rio. However, it is still being actively pursued under UN and NGO auspices and features prominently in the "Rio Review + 5" process (a monitoring of progress since the Earth Summit). The efforts of theologian Hans Küng and friends to develop the principles of a "Global Ethic" and to garner international support is another development, this one an initiative of the Parliament of World Religions. In the conciliar movement for "Justice, Peace and the Integrity of Creation," the World Council of Churches has also sought to link the realization of human rights with efforts to sustain and restore people's comprehensive environments.

It should be added that there is growing pan-religious support for what is now dubbed an "eco-justice" ethic. Human rights and rights protective of the rest of nature are considered indivisible in this perspective, in the firm conviction that environmental devastation and social injustice go hand-in-hand.[11] Tenets such as the following are supported by religious convictions that cross virtually all the world's religions—tenets basic enough to support an eco-justice framework: the ancient and continuing claim of a global human unity, and an ethic of care for the earth, of generosity toward all creatures, of compassion for all that suffers, of seeing all things together in or before the divine, and of seeing all things as precious, indeed holy.

So a second matter: The compellingness of environmental rights, for the sake of surviving and thriving, sits side-by-side with the first—the absence of a voice, substance, and framework for environmental rights in canonical rights discourse.

To move the discussion (or non-discussion!) off dead center, any number of things are necessary. One is to visit the cases made for human environmental and biotic rights. This entails moral, metaphysical, and empirical arguments as these center on the understanding and status of nature vis-à-vis the human. Another is to ask whether the current framework for rights can be bent around to include human environmental rights, assuming a case for such inclusion is made. Yet another is to ask whether something in the way of religious and moral sensibilities and commitments is necessary and/or helpful to the realization of environmental rights. In the pages remaining, these three questions will be addressed in interlocking ways.

Nature and the Human

The realization of human environmental rights and/or biotic rights will not happen apart from a cosmology (an overarching understanding of reality) or a narrative different from the one that gave us modernity. Modernity has construed humans as a species apart and as the sovereign subject, with the rest of nature as subordinate object and infinite resource for a world of our own making that is, to use Francis Bacon's image, "hammered out" by us on the "anvil of nature."[12] Surmising that the significant problems we face cannot be addressed with the same broad thought patterns that created them, an alternative cosmology with a basis for rights is necessary. It might be something like the following, in bare-bones version, drawing on the work of environmental philosopher and theologian Holmes Rolston III, and on philosopher Paul Taylor and theologians Sallie McFague and James Nash.

Holmes Rolston, unlike some deep ecologists, argues that nature does not provide the norms for morality (and, derivatively, for rights). Nature is always a teacher, to be sure, but not always a teacher of morality. "Compassion and charity, justice and honesty, are not virtues found in wild nature. There is no democracy there, nor any laws recognizing any creature's rights."[13] Categorical moral imperatives we might subscribe to—"One ought to keep promises," "Tell the truth," "Do unto others as you would have them do unto you"—are not imperatives of the rest of nature. No natural decalogue parallels the Ten Commandments or other classic religious and legal formulations for the baselines of life together.[14]

This does not end the matter, however. Nor does it lead to the conclusion that moral standing and the content of morality and rights pertain only to that peculiar species distinguished by reasoned choice and moral agency. There may be goods (values) in nature to which humans ought to conform, for their own sake and the sake of other citizens in the Commonwealth of Life. Animals, plants, and ecosystems, though not moral agents themselves, may carry a kind of value that, though non-moral, nonetheless counts morally when moral agents encounter it and relate to it in a common and interdependent world. Natural entities may be value(d) objects even when they are not moral agents and tutors.[15]

Value found in nature beyond human beings can be conceptualized in at least two different ways. One yields grounds for biotic rights, the other for human environmental rights. Grounds for such rights may themselves be religious or non-religious. One designation of value is commonly termed "inherent value" or worth, or sometimes "intrinsic value." It offers a parallel for non-human life to Kant's strictly anthropocentric "ends-in-themselves." It is value presumed to be there before, and independently of, humans; value not first fabricated when humans arrive late in the evolutionary drama to join other life.

The grounds for inherent value are often expressed religiously. "As independently good expressions of divine activity, all creation has moral standing before God" is a plausible and commonplace formulation, though it is usually more briefly put: "And God saw that it was good," from the Genesis creation account, is one example. Against the broad stream of the Enlightenment, this view rejects the dominant modern notion that the sovereign human self is the sole determiner of moral significance and the sole subject of moral value. Instead, creation is a community populated by literally innumerable subjects whose value to God and for life establishes them as morally significant in their own right. Regarding human environmental rights, such a religiously based case might, for example, argue for the right of creatures to realize their evolutionary potential free from human-induced extinction, or from human cruelty and abuse, or, more broadly, argue for the right to a healthy habitat.[16]

Non-religious grounds can be offered as well. Paul Taylor argues that non-human creatures have "a good of their own" independent from humans by virtue of their being members of the biotic community. For moral agents (i.e., human beings) this translates as a prima facie duty to promote or preserve these creatures' good. Minimally it means that non-human lives are worthy of (moral) respect and consideration. Legal respect and consideration follow, and take the form of rights.

In short, whether on religious or secular grounds, non-human entities have moral standing such that "rights," including biotic rights, is an appropriate agenda for what is necessarily universal (global) consideration.[17]

In the event that it slipped by unnoticed or too quickly, the non-religious case is a parallel to standard human rights strong enough to question the earlier near-dismissal of a Kantian/Enlightenment framework. I add and summarize the arguments of Taylor, who stands firmly in this tradition and argues its extension to include a wider range of moral subjects than it has so far. First, if inherent worth is attributed to any creature by virtue of its membership in a biotic community, then the creature has status as a moral subject to which duties are owed by moral agents. Second, each creature is not to be treated as a mere means to human ends, since this would contradict its status as a bearer of inherent worth. Third, the promotion of the good of non-human creatures follows, for the sake of the being whose good it is. Fourth, while the foregoing means moral respect for non-human nature, and this can issue in the promotion of its well-being apart from the instrumentality of legal rights, internationally codified human environmental and/or biotic rights are preferable to instrumentalities that lack legal standing and clout.[18]

Incidentally, neither Paul Taylor nor James Nash argues that inherent value or worth means equal value. Nor do they, together with Sallie McFague and Holmes Rolston, believe that human environmental and/or biotic rights are without material conflict in practice. The predator, for example, values the life of the prey for the predator's own life, and the prey, fleeing, value the good of their own lives! Choices, even life and death choices, need to be made and will be made on the basis of some effective gradation of value, even where inherent value is present and considered.[19] Differently said, even if rights were extended on the basis of inherent value of life beyond human life, those rights may well conflict with one another and with human rights. Choices would need to be made. This does not diminish the case for such rights. It simply means that life as we know it provides no way of avoiding moral conflict and decision.

In passing we should note that a significant modification of rights language may occur now in the wake of warnings from the burgeoning ecological sciences and their narratives (recall the opening comments about the importance of the narrative context of rights). Potentially a revolution of sorts in ethics, ecological perspectives soften the line between inherent and instrumental worth while strengthening the former and understanding the latter in more complex ways. Ecological thinking implicitly scolds those who overemphasize the intrinsic or inherent worth of the individual, whether human or non-human, as an end in him/her/itself. The reason is that individuals and their worth cannot be decoupled from the communal biotic system.

Stated differently, any "skin-in" perspective is essentially meaningless apart from the "skin-out" location in which any individual creature lives and moves and has its being. To return to Rolston: "Concern about populations, species, gene pools, habitats, ecosystem health, integrity, and sustainability" always requires a corporate sense where value is invariably "good in community."[20] Inherent value is real. But it is value as part of a whole and cannot be abstracted by valuing populations in isolation.[21] Individuals are "ends in themselves," yes. But they are not "themselves" except as belonging to communities that create and sustain them, biotic communities among them. In Buber's famous terms, "I-It" and "I-Thou" are "primary" words. The "I" of each term is inseparable from the reality on the other side of the hyphen.

From an ecological perspective, then, value is a "systemic interweaving" of "instrumental and intrinsic value."[22] Or perhaps it is, as I am inclined to argue, a systemic interweaving of value beyond the distinctions of inherent and instrumental, a value for which we do not yet have the name because we do not yet have the narrative and cosmology. In any event, this membership in Earth as, in the end, common membership in a community enhances the status of all that contributes to the Community of Life. This fosters inherent value, or at least precious value, where rights discourse has generally not bothered to look. At the same time the relational nature of reality softens distinctions between inherent and instrumental value, and describes the latter in complex ways that the earlier stance of the human self vis-à-vis the rest of nature did not. Nothing is what it is apart from all else, and all else is intrinsically relational, infinitely complex, dynamic, and open to change.

The consequences of this "nothing-is-what-it-is-apart-from-all-else" angle should be drawn for human environmental rights in particular (as distinguished from the more inclusive biotic rights). Human environmental rights advocates sometimes reject the inherent worth of non-human life as grounds for non-human rights. Rather, claims for nature's welfare—and for nature's rights—rest in nature's instrumental value for human well-being. The larger courses of nature are to be respected, and the requirements of nature for its own regeneration and renewal translated into the coin of legal rights, because our own well-being and that of future human generations is otherwise damned. In other words, a kind of biospheric Golden Rule must be observed for self-interested reasons: we must necessarily give back to the biosphere what we take, and do it on terms the biosphere can accept, or we do ourselves in.

Here again ecological cosmologies soften what, in other frameworks, might be starker contrasts, the contrasts between rights based in, say, a Schweizerian, Buddhist, or Hindu ethic of respect for all life, and rights in anthropocentric Western traditions. If reality is by nature relational, and the well-being and redemption of each creature is required for the well-being and redemption of all (to remember Thomas Aquinas's teaching), then borders between anthropocentric and biocentric ethics leak. If ecocide is homicide, the biophysical and geoplanetary state-of-the-union is as crucial as the socio-communal to which it is integrally linked, and equally the domain of ethics and rights. A strictly anthropocentric argument for environmental rights thus becomes a forceful one. It can, in fact, carry much the same rights content as the arguments of inherent value more typically made by advocates of biotic rights. Hence, my formulation, "environmental rights and/or biotic rights."

The Human and Nature

In the final section of this chapter we will entertain a convergence of anthropocentric and biocentric grounds for environmental rights. Before then it is necessary to return to the comment that an Enlightenment accommodation of environmental rights will likely need either transformation or another framework. The heart of such transformation or substitution is a recasting of the human–rest-of-nature conceptual matrix. While this has already been broached, more discussion is in order. It will move back and forth between religious and empirical discourse.

Earth, so far as we know to date, is the only planet with the display of vibrant life. It is also the only known place fine-tuned for our exuberant species. We are at home nowhere else, we belong nowhere else. If we are alienated from our native *oikos* ("house" or "home" in Greek, and the root word for economics, ecology, and ecumenics), then we are necessarily alienated from our own being and its welfare.

The present threat of modernity's institutional arrangements to planetary life systems is, in fact, a measure of severe systemic alienation. It is a massive dysfunctioning in which ways of life run against the grain of the very nature upon which they utterly depend. This is the case most of all for the hyperconsumption of richer nations and peoples, whose ways are responsible for approximately three-quarters of presently known environmental damage. Such nature-defying living is "an identity crisis [and institutional crisis] in our own home territory."[23]

In an effort to combat the global peril of such errant identity and behavior, science and religion have recently sought alliances with one another in order to foster reverence for the fragile Life Ark we inhabit. Both have underscored the planet's uniqueness, just as they both have underscored the uniqueness of the species responsible for both the damage and the stewarding of life's possibilities from this time forward. (At least as that stewardship bears upon humankind. Much of the rest of life can get along quite well without the predatory species at the top of the food chain!)

Science and religion have also been in accord of late in arguing that human responsibility assumes spiritual as well as moral dimensions. The memorial service for a "non-believer" at the Cathedral of St. John the Divine, the scientist Carl Sagan, is a nice symbol. Sagan was one of the distinguished scientists issuing an "Open Letter to the Religious Community." After detailing environmental degradation—which the scientists said might, in religious language, be called "Crimes against Creation"—the letter says this:

> Problems of such magnitude, and solutions demanding so broad a perspective must be recognized from the outset as having a religious as well as a scientific dimension. Mindful of our common responsibility, we scientists ... urgently appeal to the world religious community to commit, in word and deed, and as boldly as required, to preserve the environment of the Earth.[24]

The point is not to track the pilgrimage of science and religion. It is to record the present common effort to articulate a cosmology and ethic adequate to a notion of environmental rights. This effort embraces the Community of Life as a whole and gives voice to a cosmology and ethic in which nature is charged with the numinous and elicits a reverence affecting the exercise of our agency in all domains, not least our day-to-day institutional and personal habits.

The case can be made on empirical grounds as well—that life exists because it is provided for in the biospherical Earth system. Earth is "a kind of providing ground," a slow and continuous womb where the life epic is lived out "in the midst of its perpetual perishing."[25] An awesome creativity is here, and sufficient simplicity, complexity, and wonder to leave even articulate scientists "stuttering about the mixtures of accident and necessity out of which we have evolved."[26] One need not call this holy ground, in the manner of everyday mystics. But this strange creation, stranger than fiction, is sufficiently bone of our bone and flesh of our flesh to warrant the protection that rights proffer. From a strictly descriptive point of view, Earth is the only land of promise we know, the only place where the lives we wish to lead can be had. That, amid the wonder that is life, constitutes preciousness without qualification or substitution.

Others will argue religiously. "Nature is grace, whatever more grace may be."[27] There is a splendor and primordial creativity in nature that drives many, perhaps most, either to spell nature with a capital N, or to pass through nature to nature's God. The spiritedness in living things, and the majesty of much that is non-living, bespeaks the ineffable, an Encompassing Mystery surpassing the burning mysteries of our own lives. To consider ourselves planetary "managers," the crew of Spaceship Earth, or the end for which all else is one big bank of "information" and "resources," as well as a bottomless sink, is only to indulge the hubris that religious and cultural wisdom has consistently identified as our supremely foolish and fatal flaw. Genuine wisdom includes the creation of an ethos that guards against collective arrogance and destructiveness. Universally binding environmental rights are one medium for such an ethos of appropriate humility and the recognition of limits and proper human reach.

"The Community of Life," a phrase from Paul Taylor used widely now, is yet another meaningful way to describe a cosmology supportive of human environmental and biotic rights. "Community," often reserved for human groupings and settlements, is an apt term for Earth itself. Persons are nested in cultures and cultures are nested in nature in such a way that the socio-communal, biophysical, and geoplanetary are radically interrelated and interdependent. Moreover, living systems well beyond human constructions are self-organizing, self-generative, self-healing, and self-renewing. Indeed, these qualities, together with dynamic interplay and interdependence, are the distinctive features of living systems generally, not human systems only. "Agency" as the capacity to effect change and respond to it in interlocking ways belongs to far more than Homo sapiens.

"The Community of Life" thus seems yet another way to describe the context of rights discussions. In fact, one wonders whether "rights of nature" would not have long been on the agenda if the mechanical assumptions of the Enlightenment and modernity—human as subject, nature as object; culture as active, nature as passive; human as above, nature as below, with each half of these pairings separate one from another—had not been the cosmology of rights discourse. What would have been the case if the organic assumptions of dynamic, interrelated reality as a comprehensive community had framed the discussion of rights?

Convergence?

All this said, a meeting ground for human environmental rights and biotic rights may in fact already exist, despite different arguments with different assumptions and narrative frameworks. The meeting ground looks something like this, à la Pedersen and McFague.

Practical differences of anthropocentrically based rights and biocentric ones narrow with the realization that for the former, economic, political, and social issues must be seen in environmental terms, and for the latter, environmental issues must be seen in economic, political, and social ones.[28] After all, human actions—of some humans far more than others!—are the cause of the eco-crisis. No severance of the societal from the biophysical and geoplanetary is therefore possible. Obligations to present and future generations, to sentient life generally, to organic life, to ecosystems, and in fact to all that is necessary to life, from atmospheric gases to deep ocean processes, are of a piece. Human responsibility will of necessity have to be parceled, channeled, and rendered accountable, in part through rights and their enforcement, but it is indeterminate.

Responsibility is indeterminate because the shared reality is Earth, nature, and human society together, as a comprehensive community. When rights are considered in this perspective, it may matter little whether the starting point is anthropocentric or biocentric. What matters is whether community informs the notion of rights and rights inform the functioning of community. When comprehensive community informs rights, it fights any notion of rights resting on the faulty understanding that we are individuals who construct our world through relationships we freely create and discard. Such a notion generates a society that, in a saturated and complexly interdependent world with a globalizing economy and a single biosphere, simply does not work well: "A society of haves and have nots, of violence between the victors and the losers, of a deteriorating natural world that has minimal rights and hence is mainly a resource for humans."[29]

At the same time, a community model for life together that does not include a strong establishment of extended rights does not work well, either. Without rights, there are insufficient means for engendering and enforcing human responsibility. "Care" and "respect" and the voluntarism of sound civil society is too little and too episodic to address systemic issues fairly and justly. If the notion of community is no more than the sum of citizen initiatives, even healthy citizen initiatives, it is too soft. The rights/justice tradition keeps such community from relying upon the vagaries of changing social moods and motivations arising from changing hearts and minds. In the rights/justice tradition obligations are pinned down and find their way into the routines that policy and structure provide. What may have begun with citizen initiatives and movements in civil society has become a matter of contract, law, institutional arrangement, and habit. "Tough-minded, dispassionate, and properly impersonal" are the words McFague uses for the contribution the rights/justice tradition brings to community care as an ethic.[30]

In short, both of the frameworks we have entertained for extending rights to nature—anthropocentric and biocentric or geocentric—could share common ground in a working perspective that is essentially communitarian. The well-being of the whole is both the assumption and the goal, but this can be reached only by attending to the needs of the many subjects, human and others, that make up the Community of Life. In addressing both the differing needs and the well-being of the whole, rights are powerful means of institutionalizing responsibilities protective of all.

The further advantage of this communitarian framework is its capacity to bridge a wide span of peoples and cultures. There is common conceptual ground for North, South, East, and West here, just as there is support for religious and secular rationale.

Conclusion

This chapter does not assume, despite this plea for institutionalized responsibility, that everything ethically desirable should find its way into the domain of rights and law. Much that is both morally desirable and necessary is not appropriately located there; the relationship of morality and law is unidirectional to the peril of each. But this chapter does wave a banner for a new generation of rights, the rights of nature, whether construed as human environmental rights or as biotic rights. It argues for nature's rights as rights with international standing, a parallel to the Universal Declaration of Human Rights. Simple respect for nature and innumerable voluntary actions, or even laws, regulations, and negotiated treaties, will fall short of the necessary protection that interwoven, border-crossing planetary life systems require in a world of six, then eight, then probably ten billion people, all within the lifetime of a child born today. The health of these planetary life systems is the precondition for all other rights and human life itself. The children of the next century will likely find it very odd that we did not sooner consider this precondition worthy of universal rights.

The contribution of religious communities to all this is threefold. Religious communities are grass-roots communities in every neighborhood on the planet. As such, they can be significant communities of moral deliberation and formation on matters of extended rights. Religious communities are also international institutions. In that role, they can be present as advocates in international policy-making fora, as well as local, regional, and national ones. And religious communities are, perhaps above all, shapers and keepers of overarching meaning and value as mediated across ages and generations through ritual, instruction, and concrete practices, all in the context of community understood as cosmic in scope.[31]

A fitting closing, then, is this list of shared religious content that reaches across diverse religious communities, and that these communities can bring to their roles of formation and advocacy. This is shared content supportive of rights extended across the Community of Life. I use Kusumita Pedersen's summary and cite it verbatim.

1. The natural world has value in itself, and does not exist solely to serve human ends.
2. There is significant ontological continuity between human and non-human living beings, even though humans do have a distinctive role. This continuity can be felt and experienced.
3. Non-human living beings are morally significant, in the eyes of God and/or in the cosmic order. They have their own unique relations to God, and their own places in the cosmic order.
4. The dependence of human life on the natural world can and should be acknowledged in ritual and other expressions of appreciation.
5. Moral norms such as justice, compassion and reciprocity apply (in appropriate ways) to both human beings and to non-human beings. The well-being of humans and the well-being of non-human beings are inseparably connected.
6. There are legitimate and illegitimate uses of nature.
7. Greed and destructiveness are condemned. Restraint and protection are commended.
8. Human beings are obliged to be aware and responsible in living in harmony with the natural world, and should follow the specific practices for this prescribed by their traditions.[32]

Of course, a list such as this is not powerful on its own. It must be culturally and institutionally embodied in community practices. Innumerable religious communities obstruct an effective movement toward rights for nature more than they promote it. Wendell Berry's harsh condemnation of Christianity's adaptation to the industrial paradigm and modernity as a "conniving in the murder of Creation"[33] could be leveled against other faiths as well. A fateful splitting of spirit from matter, mind from body, and humankind from the rest of nature, all within a continuing patriarchalism that devalues women and nature together, runs deep in many traditions. In short, religious resources such as the tenets listed above are frequently frustrated by the practices that are to express them.

At the same time, religiously motivated groups are often among those in the forefront of progressive change, and often in conflict with others in their own religious communities. This is as true of the rights/justice movement as any other, not least in the Southern Hemisphere.

None of this should catch us by surprise. The reason for religion's presence rests deep in our being as a species. Humans seem almost incorrigibly religious. We yearn to see things whole and sacred. We insist on telling a cosmic narrative and being a part of it. We desire assurance that the same powers that threw the galaxies into orbit buoy us up as well. We insist on naming with the name of God, or some other intimation of divine reality, the grand mystery that surrounds the mysteries of our own fleeting lives. Not least, we want to make a difference that is not simply lost or rendered meaningless.

All this yields a certain tenacity and ardor rightly associated with religious motivation and behavior. It makes for convictions and commitments with staying power, fueled by what David Ben-Gurion once called a "moral-spiritual energy" that resides in the "mysterious, uncompromising, unfathomably, and divinely inspired" souls of human beings.[34] If this is so, a simple conclusion follows. Religious and moral dimensions of campaigns for the rights of nature are crucial, both as a matter of conceptual and motivational support and as a matter of eventual implementation.

Notes

1. Immanuel Kant, "Duties to Animals and Spirits," in *Letters on Ethics*, Louis Infield, trans. (New York: Harper and Row, 1963), 239, cited by Sallie McFague, *Super, Natural Christians* (Minneapolis: Fortress Press, 1997), 156.

2. René Descartes, *Discourse on Method and Meditations*, Laurence J. Lafleur, trans. (Indianapolis: Bobbs-Merrill, 1960), 8, cited in David Hollenbach's excellent discussion, "Social Ethics Under the Sign of the Cross," *The Annual of the Society of Christian Ethics 1996* (Georgetown: Georgetown University Press, 1996), 4.

3. This sketch is indebted in part to the paper by Reinhard Huetter, "Christian Freedom and God's Commandments: The Twofold Center of Lutheran Ethics," prepared for the Lutheran Ethics Project of the Evangelical Lutheran Church in America, Division of Church in Society, 4–7.

4. See the excellent work of Elizabeth M. Bounds, *Coming Together/Coming Apart: Religion, Community, and Modernity* (New York: Routledge, 1997), 30–31.

5. See Larry Rasmussen, *Earth Community, Earth Ethics* (Maryknoll, NY: Orbis Books, 1996), 31–34.

6. Cited by Paul G. Risser, Jane Lubchenco, and Samuel A. Levin in "Biological Research Priorities—A Sustainable Biosphere," *BioScience* 47 (1991): 625–27.

7. Ibid.

8. Thomas Berry and Thomas Clarke, S.J., *Befriending the Earth* (Mystic, CT: Mystic Twenty-Third Publications, 1991), 97.

9. James A. Nash, *Loving Nature: Ecological Integrity and Christian Responsibility* (Nashville: Abingdon Press, 1991), 171–72.

10. The Brundtland list of states' responsibilities can be cited as a kind of minimum that numerous NGOs also favored: "To maintain ecosystems and related ecological processes essential for the functioning of the biosphere; to maintain biological diversity by ensuring the survival and promoting the conservation in their natural habitats of all species of flora and fauna; to observe the principle of optimum sustainable yield in the exploitation of living natural resources and ecosystems; to prevent or abate significant environmental pollution or harm; to establish adequate environmental protection standards; to undertake or require prior assessments to ensure that major new policies, projects, and technologies contribute to sustainable development; and to make all relevant information public without delay in all cases of harmful or potentially harmful releases of pollutants, especially radioactive releases." Ibid., 172.

11. For a comprehensive treatment of this in the world's religions, see the excellent chapter by Kusumita P. Pedersen, "Environmental Ethics in Interreligious Perspective," in *Comparative Religious Ethics and Interreligious Dialogue: Studies in a Collaborative Effort,* Bruce Grelle and Sumner B. Twiss, eds. (Boulder, CO: Westview Press, 1998). I have borrowed here from Pedersen's discussion, pages 1–2.

12. My personal assessment of modernity is more multivalent than these pages allow, and I focus here on one of its aspects only, the relationship of us "moderns" to the rest of nature. That, too, is complex in ways I have tried to reflect in both *Moral Fragments and Moral Community* (Minneapolis: Fortress Press, 1993), and *Earth Community, Earth Ethics* (Geneva: World Council of Churches, 1996). The comment by Marshall Berman is as good a one-line assessment as I know: "To be modern is to find ourselves in an environment that promises adventure, power, joy, growth, transformation of ourselves and the world—and, at the same time, that threatens to destroy everything we know, everything we are." From Marshall Berman, *All That Is Solid Melts into Air* (New York: Simon and Schuster, 1982), 345, cited by Bounds, *Coming Together/Coming Apart,* 9.

13. Holmes Rolston III, "Ecology: A Primer for Christian Ethics," prepared for the Environmental Ethics interest group of the Society of Christian Ethics, 14.

14. Ibid., 14–15.

15. Ibid., 15.

16. See James A. Nash, "Biotic Rights and Human Ecological Responsibilities," in *The Annual of the Society of Christian Ethics* (Georgetown: Georgetown University Press, 1993): 154–157. The broader argument is congruent with Sallie McFague's in *Super, Natural Christians,* especially her discussion of "the arrogant eye" and "the loving eye" in Chapters 4 and 5.

17. Paul W. Taylor, *Respect for Nature: A Theory of Environmental Ethics* (Princeton: Princeton University Press, 1986), 71–80.

18. See ibid., 78–79. Taylor makes the case for non-human life having legal rights while arguing that the case for their moral rights is weaker. He does not think it conceptually confused or logically absurd to grant moral rights to non-human life. But it is a "weak" notion of moral rights, since moral rights are usually associated with agents of moral choice and responsibility. Thus Taylor's preference for legal, rather than moral, environmental rights. The point above, however, is that for both Taylor and Nash and, I would argue, anyone else, the case for legal rights requires moral grounding. The moral warrants for biotic rights as legal claims is a separate issue from non-humans having, or not having, moral rights.

19. For an extensive effort beyond those of Taylor and Nash to make meaningful distinctions that aid policies and decisions when there is conflict among entities who enjoy inherent worth, see the work of biologist Charles Birch and theologian John B. Cobb, Jr., *The Liberation of Life: From the Cell to the Community* (Denton, TX: Environmental Ethics Books, 1990).

20. Rolston, "Ecology: A Primer for Christian Ethics," 16.

21. We cannot here entertain the consequences of this kind of abstraction of human and non-human populations from their environments. I consider it a basic fault line that has wreaked enormous destruction. See my *Earth Community, Earth Ethics,* especially the chapter, "The Big Economy and the Great Economy."

22. Rolston, "Ecology: A Primer for Christian Ethics," 16.

23. Ibid., 20.

24. Carl Sagan, "An Open Letter to the Religious Community," National Religious Partnership for the Environment, 1047 Amsterdam Ave., New York, New York 10025, 3.

25. Rolston, "Ecology: A Primer for Christian Ethics," 21.

26. Ibid.

27. Ibid.

28. Pedersen, "Environmental Ethics in Interreligious Perspective," 5.

29. McFague, *Super, Natural Christians,* 156.

30. Ibid., 157. This discussion of community and the rights–justice tradition draws from McFague.

31. Pedersen, "Environmental Ethics in Interreligious Perspective," 6.

32. Ibid., 26.

33. Wendell Berry, *Sex, Economy, Freedom, and Community* (New York: Pantheon, 1993), 115.

34. Cited in Daniel Hillel, *Out of the Earth: Civilization and the Life of the Soil* (Berkeley: University of California Press, 1991), 8.

5

REPLY   PATRICIA A. DALY

Rights of Creation to Rites of Revolution

What will it take for the human species to see itself as part of creation and not the perfection of creation? What needs to occur for us humans to experience ourselves as one dimension of life, rather than entitled to jurisdiction over all life? How will we be invited to see ourselves as simply one element of the "Community of Life"? Of greater concern, how may the economic and political systems of this planet be converted to include the priority of all life systems? Is this even possible?

In his response to the crisis of our planet Professor Rasmussen hopes to move us to action. He has clearly presented the options for our motivations: our commitment to human environmental rights or our commitment to all life: biotic rights. The clarification of this motivation not only shapes and moves the dialogue, but also helps those developing the strategies to cease and maybe reverse the decimation of life systems. If these strategies are to be effective in any way, they must generate energy in people no matter what their perspectives or motivations may be.

The Prophetic Role of People of Faith

As one voice speaking from a primarily religious perspective, I am confronted by the complicity of religious institutions in the perpetuation of the theology of the primacy of the human. Yet religious institutions are well ahead of other power systems on this planet in calling all people of faith to both personal and corporate responsibility for all creation. While complicit in many shadow moments both historically and in contemporary times (slavery, subjugation of women and indigenous peoples, and so on), religious institutions have played a prophetic role calling for the conversion of powers.

For almost three decades now, religious institutions in the United States, Europe, and Canada have worked in an interfaith network to address ethical issues as investors and shareholders in transnational corporations. Along with concerns for international human rights, militarism, rights of women and men in the workplace, the burden of international debt on poor people, and health issues, the interfaith investment community also forces corporations to address ecological issues. Responses are as varied as each corporation. There are executives who are attentive to the crises of the planet and who use their influence to bring about serious change within companies. Yet there are too many executives who cannot move beyond maximization of profits and who continue to pour resources into fighting environmental regulation. Rather than taking responsibility for reversing contamination, those executives consider monies better spent in delaying environmental clean-up; rather than investing in research for cleaner technologies, corporations invest in lobbying against such initiatives.

Religious institutions and other socially responsible investors also invest internationally in smaller businesses and community development initiatives. Many of these investments or microcredit loans are granted specifically because of these businesses' commitment to sustainability. The new models of appropriate technology and sustainability need to be encouraged and financed along with any critique of transnational corporations. Yet these initiatives are few and may be considered token when one considers the crises facing this planet. At a recent international conference on microcredit lending, only 35 of over 2,000 participants attended a meeting dealing with the ecological ramifications of development. We are wise to be attentive to the first-world nature of this discussion; while 50 percent of the people of this planet are malnourished, other priorities are addressed.

Ecological Priorities? A Case in Point and a Moment of Truth

While for many decades voices have been clear about the dangers before us, ecological concerns did not move into the mainstream until the early seventies. Even as situations worsen, earth issues are just not as "sexy" as they were in the late eighties and early nineties. In the spring of 1997 members attending the United Nations Conference on Sustainable Development were confronted with a depressing evaluation as little had been accomplished since the 1992 Earth Summit in Rio, and with the fact that many countries were now backtracking on the commitments they made in 1992.

In 1997 U.S. citizens began to catch up with the rest of the population on the planet in their understanding of the dangers of climate change. As an international treaty is negotiated we see the resistance of developed countries to return to 1990 levels of heat-trapping gases by 2012. This is a token effort when we consider that in order to stabilize the atmosphere at current (1998) concentrations, emissions would have to be cut 50 to 70 percent immediately.

This climate change issue exemplifies many of the dynamics that add to the resistance of any meaningful change. The United States and other first world countries are insisting that every country be obliged to the same emissions standards. Rasmussen points to the "hyperconsumption of richer nations and peoples, whose ways are responsible for approximately three-quarters of presently known environmental damage." Tens of millions have already been effectively spent in the United States by the fossil-fuel–related industries to finance a campaign of disinformation and fear. Rather than taking up the challenge to initiate new and cleaner technologies and products, most corporations spend their resources defending the status quo. In many ways, we in the developed countries are happy to be concerned about the environment, until that concern questions our lifestyle and patterns of consumption. As long as political systems are controlled more by corporations rather than by citizens, it is no surprise that the priority of the planet will not be reflected in juridical or policy changes.

The Power of Sacred Images and Institutional Actions

Many theologians are convinced that the inequality of women will continue as long as we believe in a male god. Likewise, one may wonder if the domination of life forms by human beings will continue as long as we imagine and teach anthropocentric images of God. Larry Rasmussen looks to encourage a new generation of the rights of nature, and admits it may matter little whether we begin as human-centered or biocentric. He is right to seek the contribution of religious communities. There is a need for reflection on how religious symbols and rituals may contribute to the crises of creation. Imagine the impact if religious institutions asked the forgiveness of the natural world in continuing the heresy of dualisms: the priority of spirit over matter. Imagine religious leaders confessing their complicity in ecological destruction for the sake of maintaining a first-world lifestyle; confessing their role in colonialism, industrialization, and modernization in order to retain their power in political and economic arenas.

The Sacred Scriptures of most faiths hold the truth of the primacy of all life. These truths need to be reclaimed. Individuals and communities who share a deep critique of religious, educational, economic, and political systems will be the ones to imagine and employ the strategies for their conversion and their participation in bringing about profound change. For these same holy people see themselves as part of the mystery and sacredness of all creation and know the responsibility of the human species.

6

Margaret E. Crahan

Religion and Societal Change: The Struggle for Human Rights in Latin America

Introduction

Remarkably, some of the most arresting developments within churches in recent years have occurred in Latin America, an area long regarded as religiously conservative. This is a consequence, in part, of denominations responding to high levels of human rights violations in the region. Given the resultant increased ecclesial support for societal change, the role of religion has become more controversial. This has increased generalized ferment, which has been augmented by a quickening tempo in the growth of non-traditional religions, particularly fundamentalist and spiritist. As a result the religious scene in Latin America has become more varied, at the same time that the historically predominant Catholic church is experiencing a revitalization.[1]

In addition, claims that economic and political modernization are facilitated by reducing the influence of religion in society are falling by the wayside as denominations, particularly Catholic and mainline Protestant, have become more directly involved in promoting societal change. This has involved them in political and ideological struggle, which has precipitated sharp conflict in some countries. Meanwhile, the churches themselves are changing and undergoing transformations, particularly with respect to the

---

Some material in this chapter was previously published in Margaret E. Crahan, "Religion: Reconstituting Church and Pursuing Change," in Alfred Stepan, ed., *Americas: New Interpretive Essays* (New York: Oxford University Press, 1992), 152–77, and "Catholicism and Human Rights in Latin America," in Irene Bloom, J. Paul Martin, and Wayne L. Proudfoot, eds., *Religious Diversity and Human Rights* (New York: Columbia University Press, 1996), 262–77.

definition of their mission, both spiritually and temporally. While evangelization for salvation continues to be a priority, salvation is not limited to the afterlife, but includes the re-creation of the Kingdom of God on Earth, that is, societies characterized by that level of enjoyment of justice and human rights conducive to societal concord.

To better understand the role of religion in the struggle for human rights in Latin America today, this chapter will analyze evolving ecclesial agendas and their impact on the nature and behavior of religious institutions, as well as individuals and society in general. The capacity of churches and church people to be effective agents for societal change and promoters of human rights will be examined using the Catholic church as the prime example. This will include analyzing competing strategies for change and impediments to change. This chapter is intended to analyze the capacity of religious institutions to promote societal change rather than simply describing one church's efforts.

Several caveats should be kept in mind. Religions are often more internally diverse than their images suggest. Over time, they have developed a considerable capacity to adapt to historical circumstances and can be more flexible than has sometimes been supposed. For example, the widely held image of the Catholic church in Latin America as monolithically supporting the status quo is clearly challenged by the dynamism of its evolution in this century, as well as by the degree to which it has become a major actor in the struggle for human rights.

In evaluating the role of any religion in society, it is useful to remember that for complex organizations to effectively promote change, certain conditions are generally necessary.[2] These include a relatively high degree of internal consensus on goals and means of attaining them, sufficient autonomy to legitimate the latter, the resources necessary to convince a critical mass within society to accept change or at least not to be strongly opposed, the expertise to devise tactics and strategies adequate to the effective promotion of changes and their implementation, as well as the maintenance of commitment to a change-oriented agenda over the long term in the face of fluctuating circumstances both within and without the institution.

The Agenda of the Catholic Church

The Catholic church in Latin America has set as its task nothing less than the restructuring of society to ensure the common good, defined as "that combination of specific conditions which permit all people to reach standards of living compatible with human dignity, thus the essential characteristic of the common good is that it be common for everyone, without discrimination of any kind whether it is cultural, social, religious, racial, economic, political or partisan."[3] Such an undertaking implies major political, economic, and social change that could undercut the interests of some sectors of society. This appears to be somewhat at odds with the church's desire to maintain the universality of its appeal. As a consequence, it has attempted to promote change, while reasserting the importance of building community, solidarity, and reconciliation within society. The difficulties involved make the maintenance of a fair degree of consensus within the Catholic church critical to achieving its objectives.

The Catholic church's current agenda was hammered out at the Second Vatican Council (Vatican II), 1962–1965, held in the aftermath of World War II and the Holocaust, and amid a growing sense that the church was not well equipped to meet the challenges of the modern world. These included the arms race, increasing conflict generated by poverty and other disparities within and between nations, and escalating repression by authoritarian governments in response to popular pressures resulting in part from economic development, urbanization, and social mobilization. Prelates from Asia, Africa, and Latin America, while in the minority at Vatican II, did succeed in increasing the focus on poverty and human rights violations, as well as on unequal relations between industrialized and industrializing nations. The Brazilian bishops, in particular, lobbied their colleagues for more attention to social justice issues. In part, as a consequence, the prelates gathering in Rome concluded that the Catholic church should have as priorities the promotion of peace, justice, and human rights, together with the modernization of their institution theologically, bureaucratically, liturgically, and pastorally. In 1968 the Latin American hierarchy met in Medellín, Colombia, for the Second General Conference of Latin American Bishops (CELAM II) to translate Vatican II for Latin American realities.[4]

Influenced by position papers often drafted by progressive theologians and social scientists, the bishops concluded at Medellín that the promotion of peace, justice, and human rights required a preferential option for the poor, that is, greater involvement in the struggle of the majority of Latin Americans for liberation from economic and social exploitation and political repression.[5] The Medellín conclusions, cast in the general terms of consensus statements, stimulated a great deal of debate both within and without the church and were interpreted by some as justifying support for revolutionary movements, including Marxist ones. Prelates with strong reservations began to organize, coalescing around the Colombian bishop Albinos López Trujillo, who succeeded in being elected Secretary General of CELAM, albeit by a narrow margin. From 1972 until the 1979 General Conference in Puebla, Mexico, there was intense debate focusing on the implications of the preferential option for the poor, the utilization of Marxist concepts and analysis in the emerging theology of liberation, new pastoral forms such as Base Christian Communities (CEBs), and the direct involvement of priests in politics.[6] Puebla reasserted the church's commitment to a preferential option for the poor, avoided taking a stand on liberation theology, supported CEBs as a useful tool for evangelization, and condemned clerical involvement in politics, held to be the responsibility of an evangelized laity. Since Puebla, debate has continued, stimulated in part by the attempted imposition by John Paul II (who became pope in 1978) of greater theological and doctrinal orthodoxy and of more centralized authority. This was apparent at the 1992 Latin American Bishops Conference in Santo Domingo, Dominican Republic (CELAM IV). The conference again affirmed support for that level of change necessary for societal justice and human rights. But the precise means to achieve that change continued to be debated. Given this, it is remarkable that the Catholic church has maintained the degree of consensus it has concerning its overall goals. To achieve this consensus, however, the church has asserted it at a level of generality that has created some problems in terms of mobilizing support. The church has also communicated ambiguity concerning the means to achieve change, further complicated by the existence of very visible champions of neoliberal and socialist options within the church.

The Struggle to Promote Societal Change

Ambiguity concerning the means to accomplish change can impede any church from reaching that level of internal consensus and commitment sufficient to convince a critical mass of the populace, not necessarily a majority, of the necessity and desirability of its goals. If the agenda involves major structural changes that are perceived by some influential sectors of society as prejudicing their interests, then implementation will obviously be difficult. Some of these sectors may be within the church or have allies within the church, owing to the tradition of ecclesial cultivation of political and economic elites. Opposition may also come from non-elites who perceive their interests as more likely served by achieving greater influence over existing structures. Given the complexity of modern societies, opposition to any agenda for substantial change will probably cut across class, as well as other categories. Such an agenda may also be impeded by recalcitrant socioeconomic conditions. Churches must, as a consequence, calculate the impact on their institutional well-being, as well as their capacity to maintain consensus over the long term. This may give the appearance that ultimately a church's commitment to change is limited or waning.

Opposition to a church's promotion of change often takes the form of challenges to its authority. While churches such as the Catholic have historically had substantial roles in influencing normative values, this has not necessarily generated definitive support for a change-oriented agenda, particularly since many churches historically promote non-conflictual societies as an ideal. To achieve its current goals the Catholic church, as well as some mainline Protestant ones, must therefore transcend part of their own heritages. Churches root their authority in a divine mandate, as well as a commitment to the salvation of all. This makes the definition of the latter of critical importance. The reformulation of the concept of salvation at Vatican II and Medellín to emphasize more strongly communal and temporal elements has given rise to sharp debates. Many of these have been focused on new theologies, such as liberation theology, which has been criticized for allegedly placing the temporal over the spiritual. Such challenges require the church to expend considerable energy on defending reconceptualizations that underpin the change-oriented agenda. Given the complexities of the theological, political, and ideological issues involved, differences of opinion are critical and have given rise to diverse positions being taken by church leaders at all levels. Since the 1960s there has been a greater sense of multiple voices speaking for the church, allowing for individuals and groups within and without the church to opt for the view that reinforces their stance. There has been, as a consequence, some erosion of hierarchical authority. This has undercut the internal cohesion of the church, thereby weakening its ability to maintain a high degree of consensus on the means to promote societal change.

For a church's agenda to transcend this, together with class and other interests, it must have a clear analytical grasp of historical processes and the complexities of socioeconomic and political realities. This necessitates resources and expertise not only to adequately diagnose the roots of societal problems, but also to understand societal dynamics. It also requires that the church's analysis, as an institution, be accepted by a cross-section of society. In the post–World War II period and particularly since the 1960s, church personnel have become more highly educated and cognizant of specialized disciplines, including those in the social sciences. Indeed, some have become adept in such areas as public opinion research and become more focused on influencing public consciousness. In addition, since the 1960s the Catholic church has concentrated on conscientization, a method originally aimed at empowering the poor by assisting them in analyzing the causes of their condition and means to change it. CELAM III in Puebla, Mexico, insisted in 1979 that the whole of society needed to be conscientized if society were to become more just. While the Catholic church has developed more professionalized cadres and technical expertise to accomplish this, it has also had changing, and, at times, conflicting policy and programmatic emphases. Some groups and programs have even appeared to be working at cross-purposes. There has also been competition for resources, credibility, and influence on the part of church personnel that affect the achieving of ecclesial objectives. In addition, it must be remembered that policy makers frequently tend to opt for what is feasible, rather than pursuing stated goals. Even when an objective is aggressively pursued, it may not be achieved, or may have unintended consequences. These factors place a premium on consistent administrative control, the loyalty and skill of officials, and access to substantial resources, including financial ones, in a region where churches have limited incomes. This generally requires financial assistance and personnel from outside the region, who may introduce additional agendas. Overall, it necessitates a steady supply of capable recruits who are retained and able to transcend, to a degree, their own specific interests. They also need to be able to revise and jettison policies and programs when necessary. This is not always easy for individuals imbued with a high degree of moral certainty within institutions that tend to encourage their personnel to avoid rocking the boat if they are to advance in the ranks. Obviously such institutional issues help determine a church's capacity both to change society and to be changed.

The Catholic church does have some advantages in spite of increasing internal debate; it has a tradition of incorporating diverse sectors and adapting to fluctuating circumstances. The very ferment and pressures for change affecting it, as well as Latin American society more generally, sometimes serve as a stimulus to its leaders to take the initiative and thereby increase the institution's influence. Crises can also incite actions that transcend traditional ecclesial behavior, as well as supplant the roles of temporal actors unable to exercise effective leadership roles. With the emergence of authoritarian regimes in such countries as Brazil (1964), Chile (1973), Uruguay (1973), and Argentina (1976) and the intensification of repression in others, particularly in Central America in the 1970s, the church helped fill the vacuum created by the repression of political parties, labor unions, and civic organizations. In this respect the church was favored by the stability of its leadership and bureaucracy, as well as its willingness to incorporate some displaced secular leaders. This helped create a critical mass of experts and policy strategists who, under the protection of the church, challenged authoritarian governments with a view toward establishing more democratic systems.[7] The incorporation of individuals from the secular sphere cannot help but have an impact on a church's analysis of society and modus operandi, thereby contributing to more internal dynamism with modernizing and democratizing results. In highly repressive situations it also tends to increase trust in a church among diverse actors, including some who were previously irreligious or anti-clerical. On the other hand, the role of a church in opposing authoritarian governments can alienate sectors benefiting from the latter's policies, leading to secular challenges to the authority of the church's leadership and the legitimacy of its policies. In general, crises in Latin America since the 1960s have tended to mobilize the Catholic church, and some Protestant churches, to formulate policies and strategies that have promoted change.

A dilemma remains, however. By mobilizing church resources to promote change within secular society, especially aimed at democracy, a church increases pressures for its own democratization. This can result in greater caution in promoting societal change reflected in a continuous refining of the church's positions, and giving the appearance of backsliding. Pressures increase on the loyalty of bureaucrats and line personnel and may lead to serious institutional struggles and divisions. In this context challengers from radical clerical elites on both the right and the left or from sectors of the laity take on increased weight. This can undercut consensus, as well as generate fears concerning the stability of the institution.

The Catholic Church and Change

What is noteworthy is that up to the present the Catholic church in Latin America has continued to support societal change in the face of such problems, limitations, and impediments. In so doing, it has become a more visible political actor with all the inherent risks. Recognizing this and the fact that religious institutions are not substitutes for secular organizations that represent class and other interests, the Catholic church has generally attempted to retire to a less partisan role when crises have subsided. This has been regarded by some as evidence of a reassertion of conservatism within the church, particularly in view of the partisan alliances that it has sometimes supported in its efforts to eliminate authoritarian regimes.

In Brazil, for example, as the military government liberalized in the 1970s and early 1980s and political and civic activity became more possible, the Catholic church encouraged secular organizations to provide services it had previously offered, particularly to workers and community groups. The defeat of General Augusto Pinochet in a 1988 Chilean plebiscite and the return to civilian government in March 1990 stimulated church agencies, such as the archbishopric of Santiago, to increase emphasis on popular education for human rights, rather than the direct provision of legal, medical, and other services to human rights victims as it previously had.

Some within the Catholic church feel it should also engage in partisan politics during transitions to democracy or the creation of revolutionary regimes thought to be more beneficial to the common good. The church's official position has been that to effectively promote peace, justice, and human rights it must function in a non-partisan and politically neutral fashion in order to be true to the universality of its salvific mission and maximize the appeal of its temporal agenda. Ecclesial leaders argue that only by convincing all sectors of society of the legitimacy of its goals will it have impact. For those who believe that no universal agenda is possible, the official church is regarded as failing to live up to its commitment to a preferential option for the poor.

The reality, however, is more complex. In fact, the Catholic church has, particularly since the late 1960s, demonstrated multiple tendencies with respect to evaluating contemporary societal structures and the need to change them. At times over the past thirty years the church has strongly challenged political, economic, and social systems, and at other times helped defuse revolutionary movements. It continues to attempt to transcend class, ideological, and other interests, while at the same time asserting a preferential option for the poor, as well as salvation for all.

How to implement a preferential option for the poor has been the subject of considerable debate and involves a substantial rethinking of ecclesial conceptualizations and strategies. As the Canadian social scientist Michael Gismondi notes:

> [R]eligion does not shift, paradigm-like from an oppressive to a liberative social force in some apocalyptic moment. Rather, it is a temporal, and processual struggle by which the poor add a new, more radical content to the same values cherished and generated by that more conservative hierarchy. Because the poor also believe in the church, and seek to preserve it, this is a process of negotiation and renegotiation over values, and definitions of social order. Nevertheless, this is a process that takes place within the church; it is not a schism.
>
> In more abstract analytical terms, this struggle over values sees different religious groups emphasizing different referents for the same signifier. But, contrary to claims of discourse analysis, this struggle is not merely a struggle over language, or social meaning, or the multivocality of religious symbols. Instead, these struggles take place in history, and this demands we pass the insights of discourse analysis through the analytical prism of the socio-historical context. For me, these struggles over meaning occur, in fact, as a result of this new call by the hierarchy for more democracy in the church. But it is the inconsistency, conflict and contradiction between 1) the values a modernizing church hierarchy offers the poor, and 2) the socio-historical experience of the poor of their particular material conditions of life, that creates the tension in this process, and generates a burst of new religious meanings from below.[8]

Failure to develop a paradigm founded on a solid awareness of historical context and processes can lead to confusing conflict over religious values within broader social struggles.[9] Furthermore, it encourages analysts to regard developments such as popular churches as outside the Catholic church rather than within. It also results in the diminution of consideration of the role of belief in the action of grace as a motivator of the faithful of all theological, political, and ideological persuasions, helping them maintain their loyalty to the institution even when they may oppose some of its official positions.

The vision of the church enunciated at Vatican II and Medellín as a community of believers struggling for salvation here and in the hereafter led to the conclusion that the Christian was morally obligated to act in the face of sin, including that resulting from societal structures. To challenge the status quo and identify with the poor was to discharge one's moral responsibility. On that there was widespread agreement, but not on the means to effect change, or on the nature of the new political and economic structures. Such disagreement was highlighted by the initial acceptance by liberation theologians such as Leonardo Boff, Gustavo Gutierrez, and Juan Luis Segundo of class struggle and socialism. Others strongly disagreed and the 1970s and 1980s were characterized by considerable political and ideological conflict within the Catholic church, giving rise to the image of it being divided between a left and a right. The reality was somewhat more complex, as the majority were between the two and even the most vociferous paladins of the right and the left generally evinced a strong commitment to their faith. Indeed, the desire to maintain the Catholic church intact was pervasive even among those ideologically and politically opposed, and helped maintain support for its overall goals of promoting peace, justice, and human rights.

The increased conceptualization of the Catholic church as a community of believers recalls Max Weber's view that congregational religion is change oriented and encourages the integration of one's religious values into one's daily life. An additional similarity is the emphasis on personal interpretation of the scriptures and increased participation of the laity.[10] However, there are some important distinctions. These include the incapacity of Weber's formulations to take into account the degree of internal change that can occur within institutional churches. Weber clearly did not foresee the extent to which change-oriented elites might join with the base in contributing to ecclesial and societal change. His work does, however, help explain some of the institutional impediments to ecclesial change.

Impediments to Change

Historically, religion has not been regarded as a motor of change. Classical theorists such as Durkheim, Marx, and Weber viewed churches largely as impediments to it and those views are shared, to a degree, by some contemporary scholars including Vallier, Houtart, Pin, Rousseau, Dussel, and Maduro.[11] The sociologist Ivan Vallier insisted that as a religious system, Roman Catholicism

> blocks, restrains, and otherwise handicaps a country's capacities to generate and institutionalize modernizing forces. By virtue of its conceptions of religious accomplishment, its sacramental procedures for restoring religious confidence, its assent to fixed orders of hierarchical calling, and its tendency to both devalue the world and to separate ethics from mass religiosity, Roman Catholicism inclines men toward a passive acceptance of the status quo. Certain specific doctrines and beliefs also lend positive value to behaviors that would work against socioeconomic change, e.g., norms governing sexual relationships in the family (the fertility problem and its demographic implications), the emphasis on charity as a noble solution to the problems of the needy (thus fixing attention on symptoms, rather than causes), and the assumption that theology stands at the apex of the educational curriculum (thus infusing many aspects of professional and technical training with religious principles). All of these configurations help to assign Catholicism a negative role in the broad processes that go by the names of "development" and "modernization."[12]

Such assertions have some basis in fact, but do not fully take into account increased emphasis, since the late nineteenth century, on socioeconomic justice within Catholic social doctrine, the presence of a critical mass of change-oriented personnel within the church, and the impact of societal pressures. This is not to deny the existence of church people resistant to change or the institutional weight and traditions of Roman Catholicism that serve to restrain change at times. On balance, however, there has been a noticeable shift in Latin American Catholicism, as well as mainline Protestantism and even some fundamentalist groups, in support of societal change. Churches have accomplished this, in part, through reconceptualizing their views of salvation, community, and justice. The frequent issuance of critiques of existing political and economic systems, together with state abuse of power and violations of human rights, has stimulated reformist and revolutionary movements. Intensified political and ideological conflict within and without the church has also raised fears for institutional survival. Nevertheless, there is evidence that historical churches are generally more trusted by the majority than they were in the past and hence are more influential, precisely because of their increased identification with justice and human rights.[13]

The consequences for the Catholic church of its support for greater democracy in Latin America included a heavier focus on public welfare and the means to promote it, which involved more specific positions on temporal issues. This resulted in the church's appearing more political, particularly since the 1960s, at the same time it was insisting that it was neutral and non-partisan. It also encouraged questioning of secular authority and support for broader popular participation. By so doing, the church stimulated pressures for change in the exercise of ecclesial authority, thereby adding to institutional stresses. The interplay of secular and ecclesial pressures for change reflected the historical context of the post–World War II church with accelerated industrialization, urbanization, technification, and socioeconomic dislocation.

Faced with challenges posed by such developments, the Catholic church held that the church was in and of the world, and hence it was incumbent on it to speak out on temporal as well as spiritual issues. By regarding itself as a community of believers, engaged in a struggle for salvation via the promotion of the common good, the church raised the issue of the criteria for the legitimate exercise of political and economic power. Those systems that resulted in exploitation, repression, and poverty, for example, were considered immoral. Both socialism and capitalism were criticized for contributing to these evils. It was argued, however, that there were individuals of good will in both the Marxist and capitalist camps with whom the church could work to promote reform and the common good.

The general nature of the conclusions of Vatican II, Medellín, Puebla, and Santo Domingo have allowed for considerable latitude in interpretation. At Medellín, for example, capitalism, colonialism, and underdevelopment were sharply criticized. This made the church appear somewhat partisan at the same time the hierarchy was attempting to establish itself as a neutral actor. The utilization of Medellín by some church people to legitimate specific movements, theologies, or ideologies contributed to controversy over the actual intent of the conclusions. They became the object of intense debate in the period prior to Puebla, at the same time that the institutional reforms of Vatican II were being implemented. The creation or activation of national bishops' conferences, national associations of members of religious orders, and a variety of lay groups provided numerous arenas for debate. This raised questions concerning the magisterium or teaching authority of the hierarchy, as well as theological and ideological orthodoxy. The impact on the public was mixed—disquieting some and energizing others. Attempts at Puebla and Santo Domingo to clarify the role of the Catholic church, particularly with respect to politics, resulted in some analysts' concluding that it had become more conservative.

Insistence at Puebla and elsewhere that the preferential option for the poor was intended to be inclusionary rather than exclusionary, and referred not just to the materially poor but also to the poor in spirit, did not eliminate the fears of those who saw in it an acceptance of the inevitability of class conflict. In response, the liberation theologian Gustavo Gutierrez held that recognition of class struggle did not mean advocacy of it but rather:

> Those who speak of class struggle do not "advocate" it—as some would say—in the sense of creating it out of nothing by an act of (bad) will. What they do is to recognize a fact and contribute to an awareness of that fact. And there is nothing more certain than a fact. To ignore it is to deceive and to be deceived and moreover to deprive oneself of the necessary means of truly and radically eliminating this condition—that is, by moving toward a classless society. Paradoxically, what the groups in power call "advocating" class struggle is really an expression of a will to abolish its causes, to abolish them, not cover them over, eliminate the appropriation by a few of the wealth created by the work of the many and not to make lyrical calls to social harmony. It is a will to build a socialist society, more just, free, and human, and not a society of superficial and false reconciliation and equality. To "advocate" class struggle, therefore, is to reject a situation in which there are oppressed and oppressors. But it is a rejection without deceit or cowardliness; it is to recognize that the fact exists and that it profoundly divides men, in order to be able to attack it at its roots and thus create the conditions of an authentic human community. To build a just society today necessarily implies the active and conscious participation in the class struggle that is occurring before our eyes.[14]

In spite of such disclaimers, the utilization of concepts as class struggle aroused fears of church identification with Marxism and armed struggle in some quarters. This gave rise to efforts to modify some of the conclusions of Medellín as well as liberation theology.

These efforts were directed, in part, against such groups as the priests for the Third World in Argentina, the National Office for Social Information in Peru, and Christians for Socialism in Chile, as well as against priests participating directly in politics and some liberation theologians. Also targeted were some foreign missionaries whose numbers had increased substantially in the 1960s and 1970s.[15] Disagreements between those who supported reformist modernization paradigms and those who supported socialism intensified in church organizations, theological schools, and within dioceses, parishes, and CEBs.

Puebla attempted to restate the church's agenda by reaffirming support for peace, justice, and human rights, but cautioned that they should be promoted via evangelization rather than direct political action on the part of the church or its personnel and without identification with a particular system. The language of Puebla was sufficiently general to allow considerable latitude in interpretation and hence little was changed in terms of ecclesial debates. The legitimation of change by Vatican II and Medellín had already had its impact and there was no strong anti-change lobby within the church. The debate involved essentially how to accomplish it, whether through conflict, including revolution, or through gradual reforms.

Efforts to reduce the political vulnerability of the Catholic church, particularly in the late 1970s and 1980s, by attempting to rein in some of the more radical sectors, were interpreted by some as evidence of a waning commitment to change. However, the institutional weight of the church, and the values it propounded, were already identified with change. Hence, while the hierarchy may not have fully realized all the possible impacts of their decisions at Vatican II and Medellín, their support for peace, justice, and human rights encouraged already existing societal processes that would make abandonment of the church's agenda difficult. Much of the debate focused on the authority of those arguing for specific strategies for change. As a consequence, the actions of a good number of agents for change became highly controversial.

Agents and Strategies for Change

There have been a variety of attempts to identify and categorize agents for change in contemporary Latin America.[16] They include those that accept the necessity for limited change, in part, to avert violent confrontations in highly inegalitarian societies. Others support more substantial transformations and include some of the democratic left and the military. Their objective is the creation of a type of welfare state via evolutionary change. They reject violence and emphasize building consensus through dialogue with influential sectors. A third group includes those who believe in the need to radically transform society through revolution, but differ especially between those who counsel waiting for the propitious objective conditions and those who argue for hastening revolution via armed struggle. Clerics and members of religious orders are most often found in the second, non-violent group, although some highly visible church people have advocated armed struggle and revolution, particularly in the 1960s, 1970s, and 1980s. Indeed, even bishops have been known to favor insurrection in the face of long-standing repressive governments, such as the Somoza dynasty in Nicaragua.

Today the majority of church people appear to favor gradual reform to achieve pluralistic welfare states and competitive politics. The experience of the violence of insurrection, revolution, and counterrevolution in Nicaragua and El Salvador in the 1970s and 1980s, as well as increasing conflict in other countries, contributed to a decrease in ecclesial support for armed struggle. Ultimately, it has been the actual involvement of church people, rather than their specific strategies, that appears to have had the most impact. As agents of change church people have had the advantage of their moral authority, as well as their faith-imbued commitment, which has helped them transcend some, if not all, institutional and other impediments. A principal constraint on promoting societal change has been division between those who believe that change can be accomplished by transforming individuals and their values and those who believe it can only occur by changing societal structures. This difference exists not only within the Catholic church, but also within society. At Puebla, attempts were made to clarify the limits of ecclesial political involvement by asserting that the role of the church was to animate the laity to participate politically, not to act itself. The maintenance of the distinction is extremely difficult, especially in highly unequal and repressive societies. While the church regards religious beliefs as politically neutral, their definition since Vatican II encourages political activity given objective conditions in many societies. The Catholic church has always attempted to mold the normative values and communal reactions of the faithful toward the institutional bases of society. This can encourage political partisanship. Attempting to exclude clergy and members of religious orders from such partisanship is virtually impossible.

Some analysts have seen the distinction as between activation and activism. Activation focuses on evangelization to inspire lay people to do justice, while activism involves all church people, including priests, nuns, and brothers, acting to achieve justice. Studies have shown that ecclesial leaders regard activation as more consonant with the proper role of the church.[17] In terms of institutional or individual practice, where activation ends and activism begins is not clear. In crisis situations, exceeding the limits of activation has often been morally sanctioned. At the Santo Domingo Conference in 1992 evangelization was emphasized as the principal means for societal transformation, causing some to regard the Catholic church as retreating from a more activist stance, particularly that championed by liberation theology.

Liberation theology had helped encourage activism through its methodology, which encouraged the individual to analyze reality, reflect upon the biblical message, and act. The Christian was required to participate in the struggle for liberation within a historical context, thereby reducing the traditional separation between the sacred and the secular. The methodology of liberation theology also reinforces the vision of the church as a community of believers, thereby legitimizing new pastoral forms such as the CEBs and challenging highly centralized decision making. Promotion of societal change, together with the concomitant emergence of such innovations as liberation theology and CEBs, has raised several critical issues: the morality of violence to accomplish liberation and societal restructuring, the democratization of the church, and the politicization of the church.

Although liberation theology has been criticized as promoting revolutionary violence to accomplish change, one of its chief proponents, Gustavo Gutierrez, denies the charge. He argues that "to be committed to struggle for justice is not to advocate class struggle or some form of social conflict. On the contrary, it tries to eliminate this confrontation."[18] In spite of such denials liberation theology has been used to justify class and armed struggle. That, and its utilization of elements of Marxian analysis, led to its being officially criticized by the Vatican's Congregation for the Doctrine of the Faith in 1984 and 1986. The Vatican censured it for its alleged partisan conception of truth and for confusing the spiritually poor with the proletariat of Marx. Liberation theology was also seen as challenging the magisterium of the hierarchy. The Congregation did, however, admit some positive aspects of the theology, endorsed CEBs, and confirmed the church's historical position that armed struggle was legitimate in the face of long-standing tyranny.[19]

The impact of liberation theology on contemporary Latin America is difficult to measure, although there are a good number of commentators who assert that it has been substantial. A multinational survey commissioned in the late 1980s by the United States Information Agency concluded that it was not as widely disseminated as had been supposed and had influenced primarily clerical and lay intellectuals, as well as students.[20] In addition, research has shown that reactions to liberation theology have been varied. In some instances it has stimulated more attention to pastoral work, rather than political activism. In addition, there are in Latin America many generalized liberationist impulses which make the measurement of the specific impact of the theology difficult. It does appear to have helped reinforce the attention that the institutional church has paid in recent years to popular sectors, which has resulted in a proliferation of grass-roots activities and greater identification with the church. The utilization of lay deacons and preachers in an area where there has been a chronic shortage of clergy and religious has also opened up the church to more popular input. Such individuals bring to the church some of their own strategies, which may bear little resemblance to ecclesial ones, including those of liberation theology. Grass-roots religious work has taken on a dynamic in the last decades that suggests that the agents for change are not limited to innovating elites or their strategies. Hence, liberation theology, and other such innovations as CEBs, are less pervasive than the more generalized commitment of the Catholic church to peace, justice, and human rights.

Realities of Religiously Inspired Change

Impediments to religiously stimulated change are obviously related to both the institutional and transcendental nature of churches. The Catholic church is a complex bureaucratic institution with a hierarchical superstructure. As such it finds it difficult to make those internal modifications necessary for the effective promotion of substantial societal change. Even with the influx of young ecclesial "technocrats," the devising of adequate programs and strategies, together with the generation of resources for them, has been difficult. When policies or programs are perceived as threatening by secular authorities, church leaders may downplay them out of fear for the long-term survival of the institution and the security of its personnel. In practice, however, since the 1960s the Catholic church has acted, particularly in crisis situations, with remarkable disregard for institutional concerns. But such pressures do occasionally erode internal consensus in support of change, exacerbating the usual gap between stated objectives and their implementation. Although the Catholic church is committed to distancing itself from secular authorities and elites, it has not abandoned its desire to incorporate them into its salvific mission. As a consequence, the church has been insistent in recent years that its message is inclusionary rather than exclusionary. This has been reflected in increased attempts at societal conciliation and the elaboration of a theology of reconciliation that emphasizes the need for cross-class accord. The Santa Domingo Conference reflected this and emphasized evangelization as the principal strategy for change by transforming people's hearts and minds, as well as the political will of elites.

Ideological and political divisions within Latin American society make such reconciliation difficult. Since they are reflected within the church, they have given rise to considerable ideological and political tension and have made the maintenance of the church's commitment to universality problematic. Since Medellín there has been a competition between the universality of the salvific mission and the preferential option for the poor. Irrespective of repeated assertions that the option is inclusive rather than exclusive and relates to both the spiritually and materially poor, the reality of socioeconomic cleavages in Latin America has made it difficult to pursue both.

This has been particularly true given the survival within the church of some inclination toward elite insertion and cultivation, as well as the church's continuing desire to play a mediating role in society. The hierarchy, at times, tends to formulate policy in the context of its participation in elite circles. While alternative or dissident elites have emerged, they generally have less direct control over the church as an institution. Competition between these elites has focused on questions of ideological and theological orthodoxy, as well as authority, ultimately centering on strategies for the promotion of change. The utilization of Marxist concepts in some of these strategies has revived historical fears among some in the church. This has challenged the church's ideal of society as non-conflictual and has contributed to the promotion of a theology of reconciliation that prioritizes conflict resolution over class struggle. Increased political violence in the 1970s and 1980s further reinforced doubts about strategies that accepted class conflict. Hence the emphasis at Santa Domingo on the evangelization of all, rather than the preferential option for the poor.

The preoccupation of Pope John Paul II with the radicalism of some change-oriented sectors of the church has also had some impact, particularly in moderating the utilization of Marxist analysis and clerical involvement in partisan politics. The positions of the national churches in Latin America vis-à-vis change, however, appear to be more influenced by local conditions than by pressures from Rome. This is also true with respect to other pressures from abroad, whether from the right or the left. Dependency on foreign resources, particularly from Western Europe and North America, has sometimes given rise to allegations that external actors are determining the church's positions concerning change.[21] In reality a good number of external sources of aid, as well as missionary groups, have been strong promoters of change.

Responding to Neoliberalism

The end of the Cold War and the spread of fragile democracies have presented churches with new challenges. In particular, the spread of neoliberalism and increased global integration have precipitated considerable concern among some leaders of the Latin American churches. For example, calculating in 1996 that "at least 180 million people in Latin America and the Caribbean live in poverty and 80 million of them survive in misery," the Jesuit Provincial Superiors from Latin America and the Caribbean concluded that neoliberal economic policies had "left multitudes in poverty without the possibility of participating in the construction of a common destiny, [which] threatens cultural identity and destroys natural resources."[22] Specifically, the Jesuits criticized governments following neoliberal policies for cutting back on basic services and social programs, precipitous privatizations, lack of protections for small domestic producers, implementation of structural adjustment programs without sufficient attention to social costs, reduction of labor rights, damage to the environment, and stimulating greater concentration of wealth. They foresaw increased societal tension, conflict, and violence as a result. The provincials claimed that they did not favor a particular economic system, but rather wanted a just society in which no one was excluded from work and that satisfied people's basic needs, such as nutrition, health care, housing, education, and personal security.[23] In order to accomplish this they insisted that society had to be more participatory. Such positions are fairly widespread among Catholic and mainline Protestant churches.

Such concerns on the part of church leaders exist at the highest levels, as demonstrated by a meeting in June 1997 between leaders of CELAM and the managing director of the International Monetary Fund, the president of the World Bank, and the president of the Inter-American Development Bank. At the meeting the prelates expressed their preoccupation over the growth of poverty and the maldistribution of wealth and income in Latin America, as well as the impact of foreign debt on appropriations for social welfare programs. The heads of the international organizations reportedly attempted to reassure them by demonstrating that some countries had already begun to make some progress in reducing poverty by increasing economic growth. They also solicited the prelates' assistance in increasing transparency and accountability in government and in reducing corruption. A follow-up meeting was held in October 1997 at which the prelates reasserted the destabilizing consequences of the growth of poverty in Latin America.[24] Such initiatives reflect not only the level of concern of the leadership of the Catholic church, but also the degree of consensus that continues to exist about the need to confront the ongoing denial of basic rights.

This consensus is not limited to Latin America, but was also expressed at the first-ever synod of prelates from throughout the Americas in late 1997 in Rome, where socioeconomic issues, particularly the consequences of burdensome foreign debts, became a prime focus. Recognizing that the church did not have the expertise to propose specific solutions, prelates from both the North and the South discussed the need for the Catholic church to serve as a catalyst in the search for moral technical solutions to such problems. Attention was also focused on working together to respond to such problems as endemic poverty and the consequent denial of basic rights. Again, more intensive evangelization was seen as a prerequisite for the societal change needed to achieve more just societies.[25]

Conclusion

Granted that the leadership of the Catholic church, particularly since Vatican II and Medellín, has supported peace, justice, and human rights via political and socioeconomic change, the precise impact of the church's agenda for change is unclear.[26] Official statements emanating from Rome, CELAM, national bishops' conferences, religious orders, and a variety of other groups seem to indicate considerable consensus, but few studies have documented the specific impact. Some prelates at Medellín, for example, signed the conclusions without fully realizing their implications or the degree to which they would be used to legitimize radical activism. This helps explain efforts to clarify Medellín at Puebla and Santa Domingo. Even with a strong consensus in favor of an agenda for change, there is the question of whether or not the Catholic church had sufficient resources to effectively promote it, particularly given internal and external impediments. A wide variety of real limitations within the church, as well as strong disagreements that cut across status, class, and generation, have obviously made it difficult to mobilize the institution, and society in general, in a specific direction. Nevertheless, many feel that there is greater consensus concerning the need to promote change to achieve more enjoyment of justice and human rights than there was thirty years ago.[27]

Responding to the debate over reformist modernization versus revolutionary socialism, the Catholic church has reacted in a variety of ways. Although the official stance has been that the church does not favor a particular political or economic system, its distaste for violence and Marxism has inclined it toward reformist gradualism. Within the church, however, influential sectors have claimed class struggle to be a necessity and socialism more moral than capitalism. The church's attempts to mold normative values and to encourage societal transformation have clearly been hindered by its immersion in such debates. Perhaps its greatest contribution has been to legitimize change in general and to foster the expansion of political spaces in which to debate and accomplish change. The church has also provided opportunities for previously unorganized sectors of society to mobilize.

The attempts since the 1960s on the part of the Catholic church to extricate itself from its identification with elites have tended to reduce its influence with some governments. On the other hand, support for the church appears to have increased not only at the grass-roots level, but also among some of the bourgeoisie. The church has had some success in encouraging such sectors to become active in favor of peace, justice, and human rights in such countries as Brazil, Chile, and El Salvador. This has modified the church's view of its role in society, as well as the public's perception of it.

One of the most interesting developments resulting from the Catholic church's involvement in promoting change has been the creativity unleashed within the church, which has stimulated considerable experimentation. This has contributed to the revitalization that was part of the agenda of Vatican II and Medellín. Some innovations, particularly liberation theology, have, however, undercut the stated universality of the church's mission. Furthermore, a good number of liberationists do not appear to have fully recognized the degree to which the poor may have their own agenda.[28]

As the process of change has evolved in the last thirty years in Latin America, there has been an intensification of societal conflict that is inimical to the religious ideal of society as non-conflictual. This has caused some to question any involvement of churches in the promotion of change. Nor have churches always foreseen the consequences of some of their positions and actions. At times they set in motion processes that they were unable to control. Churches have also generated pressures for greater involvement in secular politics, raising the contentious issue of whether the commitment to change required the partisan participation of churches. Related to this are debates over the morality of revolutionary violence and redistribution through forcible expropriation. Religious leaders have attempted to deal with these by justifying armed struggle only in extreme cases of tyranny and the sanctioning of both private and social property so long as they were supportive of the common good and human rights.

The repression leveled at church people, particularly in the 1970s and 1980s, raised the question of whether the active promotion of change should be abandoned because it jeopardized church survival. The evidence suggests that repression helped fortify Catholic and Protestant churches in crisis situations, reducing internal divisions and increasing their moral sway. In Central America and Chile, for example, participation in and esteem for churches appear to have increased. Certainly, the Catholic church has succeeded in accomplishing one of its Vatican II objectives, namely the assertion of stronger moral leadership.

All this makes the growth of religious competitors particularly challenging. The very ferment within church and society has stimulated some of the growth, particularly among fundamentalists and spiritists who may offer greater certainty and psychological release than a change-oriented Catholic church. Competition has generated some preoccupation within the Catholic church, undercutting ecumenism. The growth of religious competitors is a further indication of more autonomous behavior of some sectors of Latin American society. Throughout Latin America all religions have been strongly affected over the last fifty years by escalating pressures for change. Churches have not been the sole or even the principal cause for such pressures, which have deep roots in the long-term historical struggle for justice by the poor majority.[29] Rather, religions have been pressured to join the intensified social mobilization of previously marginalized sectors of society including indigenous peoples, Afro-Latins, women, and the poor in general, as well as reformist and radical sectors of the bourgeoisie. This trend has combined with demands from within churches to respond more directly to societal problems, especially those arising out of critical socioeconomic disparities. As a consequence, some religions in Latin America have repositioned themselves in order to respond more effectively to the spiritual and temporal needs of their members, as well as to society in general. The very process of doing so has been, to a degree, transformative, resulting in churches being more closely identified with the ongoing struggle for justice and human rights. This has contributed to greater involvement of Latin Americans in religious activities of all sorts and increased the credibility of religious institutions. It has not, however, resulted in a high degree of consensus on the strategies required to create more just societies. As a consequence, political and ideological struggle involving religion will continue.

Notes

1. Because of constraints of space, this essay will emphasize the Roman Catholic church, with which over 80 percent of Latin Americans identify. Since the 1950s groups such as the Assemblies of God, Church of the Open Door, Jehovah's Witnesses, Seventh-Day Adventists, and the Four Square Gospel Church have grown substantially, as have African and European-derived spiritist groups, particularly in Brazil and the Caribbean. Catholic and mainline Protestant congregations that have strong leadership and are responsive to community needs have also experienced growth. Accurate statistics on current denominational membership are difficult to obtain, in large measure because they are often based on claims rather than actual censuses. In addition, there is considerable variation as to what constitutes a member, which is sometimes defined as anyone who may have participated in any of the activities of a church, including visiting a soup kitchen or clinic. Furthermore, research on fundamentalist growth suggests that there are substantial retention problems, with many "members" leaving the congregation within a year or two. See, for example, Timothy E. Evans, "Percentage of Non-Catholics in a Representative Sample of the Guatemalan Population," paper presented at the XVI International Congress of the Latin American Studies Association, April 4–6, 1991, Washington D.C. More optimistic estimates of fundamentalist growth are contained in David Martin, *Tongues of Fire: The Explosion of Protestantism in Latin America* (Cambridge: Basil Blackwell, 1990); and David Stoll, *Is Latin America Turning Protestant? The Politics of Evangelical Growth* (Berkeley: University of California Press, 1990). On spiritists, see Diana DeG. Brown, *Umbanda: Religion and Politics in Urban Brazil* (Ann Arbor: University Microfilms International Research Press, 1986); David J. Hess, *Spirits and Scientists: Ideology, Spiritism and Brazilian Culture* (University Park: Pennsylvania State University Press, 1991); Jim Wafer, *The Taste of Blood: Spirit Possession in Brazilian Candomblé* (Philadelphia: University of Pennsylvania Press, 1991); Peter H. Fry, "Reflexões sobre o crecimento da conversão à Umbanda," *Cadernos do ISER,* 1, 29–40; Paulo Montero and Renato Ortiz, "Contribuiçao para um estudo quantitativo da religião Umbandista," *Ciência e Cultura,* 28, no. 4: 407–16; and América Moro and Mercedes Ramírez, *La Macumba y otros cultos afro-brasileños en Montevideo* (Montevideo, Uruguay: Editora Oriental, 1981). Sources commonly used for general statistics

on religion in Latin America are the World Christian Encyclopedia, as well as the Anuario Pontificio and Statistical Abstract for Latin America.

2. These conditions are derived, in part, from analyses of how other actors promote change. See, for example, H.E. Chehabi and Alfred Stepan, eds., *Politics, Society, and Democracy: Comparative Studies* (Boulder, CO: Westview Press, 1995); Ruth Berins Collier and David Collier, *Shaping the Political Arena: Critical Junctures, the Labor Movement, and Regime Dynamics in Latin America* (Princeton: Princeton University Press, 1991); Peter B. Evans, Dietrich Rueschemeyer, and Theda Skocpol, eds., *Bringing the State Back In* (New York: Cambridge University Press, 1985); Albert O. Hirschman, *The Rhetoric of Reaction: Perversity, Futility, Jeopardy* (Cambridge: Harvard University Press, Belknap Press 1991); Peter Katzenstein, *Corporatism and Change: Austria, Switzerland and the Politics of Industry* (Ithaca: Cornell University Press, 1984); Scott Mainwaring and Timothy R. Scully, eds., *Building Democratic Institutions: Party Systems in Latin America* (Stanford: Stanford University Press, 1995); Angelo Panebianco, *Political Parties: Organization and Power,* Marc Silver, trans. (New York: Cambridge University Press, 1988); Theda Skocpol, *States and Social Revolutions: A Comparative Analysis of France, Russia, and China* (New York: Cambridge University Press, 1979); Alfred Stepan, *Rethinking Military Politics: Brazil and the Southern Cone* (Princeton: Princeton University Press, 1988), and *The State and Society: Peru in Comparative Perspective* (Princeton: Princeton University Press, 1978); and Charles Tilly, *Big Structures, Large Processes, and Huge Comparisons* (New York: Russell Sage Foundation, 1985).

3. Brazilian Episcopal Conference (CNBB), "Christian Requirements of a Political Order," February 17, 1977, *LADOC 'Keyhole' Series,* 16 (Washington, DC: United States Catholic Conference, nd), 57.

4. For the Catholic theology and social doctrine that informed Vatican II, see Donal Dorr, *Option for the Poor: A Hundred Years of Vatican Social Thinking* (Maryknoll, NY: Orbis Books, 1992); and Joseph Gremillon, *The Gospel of Peace and Justice: Catholic Social Teaching Since Pope John* (Maryknoll, NY: Orbis Books, 1976). On Vatican II see Peter Hebblethwaite, *Pope John XXIII: Shepherd of the Modern World* (New York: Doubleday, 1985); Thomas F. O'Dea, *The Catholic Crisis* (Boston: Beacon Press, 1968); and Austin Flannery, ed., *Vatican Council II: The Conciliar and Post-Conciliar Documents* (Northport, NY: Costello, 1975). On Medellín and Puebla see Latin American Episcopal Council (CELAM), *The Church in the Present Day Transformation of Latin America in the Light of the Council,* 2 vols. (Bogotá, Colombia: General Secretariat of CELAM, 1968); Philip Berryman, "What Happened at Puebla," and Renato Poblete, S.J., "From Medellín to Puebla: Notes for Reflection," in Daniel H. Levine, ed., *Churches and Politics in Latin America* (Beverly Hills: Sage, 1979), 41–86.

5. The Peruvian priest Gustavo Gutierrez drafted the principal position paper on theology for Medellín, which constituted the core of his book *Teología de la liberación: Perspectivas* (Lima, Peru: CEP, 1971). In it Gutierrez was highly critical of capitalism and liberal democracy as they had developed in Latin America, and was supportive of socialism. His analysis made use of some Marxist concepts, including class struggle. It also proposed a three-part methodology for Christians; namely, analyzing reality, reflecting on it particularly in light of the gospels, and acting in accordance with the gospels. This served to legitimate activism and identification with the poor and oppressed. In his more recent works, particularly *La verdad los hará libres: Confrontaciones* (Lima, Peru: Instituto Bartolomé de las Casas, 1986) and *A Theology of Liberation: History, Politics, and Salvation,* rev. ed., Sister Caridad Inda and John Eagleson, trans. and eds. (Maryknoll, NY: Orbis Books, 1988), Gutierrez has moderated some of his criticism of liberal democracy, as well as his support for socialism. For the

evolution of liberation theology see Phillip Berryman, *Liberation Theology* (New York: Pantheon Books, 1987); Arthur F. McGovern, *Liberation Theology and Its Critics: Towards an Assessment* (Maryknoll, NY: Orbis Books, 1989); and Paul E. Sigmund, *Liberation Theology at the Crossroads: Democracy or Revolution?* (New York: Oxford University Press, 1990). On Pope John Paul II's views see Giovanni Caprile, *Karol Wojtyla e il Sinodo del Vescovi* (Rome, Italy: Editrice Vaticana, 1980); Peter Hebblethwaite, "Changing Vatican Policies, 1965–1985: Peter's Primacy and the Reality of Local Churches," in Thomas M. Gannon, S.J., ed., *World Catholicism in Transition* (New York: Macmillan, 1988), 36–53; J. Bryan Hehir, "Papal Foreign Policy," *Foreign Policy,* 78 (Spring 1990): 26–48; Thomas J. Reese, S.J., *Inside the Vatican: The Politics and Organization of the Catholic Church* (Cambridge: Harvard University Press, 1996).

6. Base Christian Communities (CEBs) began emerging in Latin America in the 1950s as an alternative to formal parishes, particularly in areas where there was a scarcity of priests. These small faith communities generally gathered together ten to thirty people to discuss the application of the gospels to everyday problems, both spiritual and temporal. Once thought likely to become ubiquitous, CEBs have been limited in their impact and vary widely in their political, ideological, and pastoral orientation. See, for example, John Burdick, *Looking for God in Brazil: The Progressive Catholic Church in Urban Brazil's Religious Arena* (Berkeley: University of California Press, 1993).

7. The role of the Vicariate of Solidarity of the Archbishopric of Santiago, Chile, and the Commission on Justice and Peace of the Archbishopric of São Paulo, Brazil, are examples.

8. Michael Gismondi, "Conceptualizing Religion from Below: An Approach to Popular Religious Values," paper presented at the XIV International Congress, Latin American Studies Association, March 17–19, 1988, New Orleans, LA, 47–48.

9. Ibid., 50.

10. Max Weber, *Economy and Society,* E. Roth and C. Wittich, eds., 2 vols. (Berkeley: University of California Press, 1978).

11. Emile Durkheim, *Elementary Forms of Religious Life* (New York: Collier, 1947); T.B. Bottomore, ed., *Karl Marx: Early Writings* (New York: McGraw Hill, 1963); Max Weber, *The Sociology of Religion,* Ephraim Fischoff, trans. (Boston: Beacon Press, 1963); Ivan Vallier, *Catholicism, Social Control and Modernization* (Englewood Cliffs, NJ: Prentice Hall, 1970); François Houtart and Emile Pin, *The Church and the Latin American Revolution* (New York: Sheed and Ward, 1965); François Houtart and André Rousseau, *The Church and Revolution* (Maryknoll, NY: Orbis Books, 1971); Enrique Dussel, *Historia de la Iglesia en América Latina* (Barcelona, Spain: Editorial Nova Terra, 1972); Otto Maduro, *Religión y lucha de clases* (Caracas, Venezuela: Editorial Ateneo, 1979).

12. Vallier, 156–57.

13. CERC, *Informe preliminar sobre primera encuesta nacional* (Santiago, Chile: CERC, 1988).

14. Gutierrez, *A Theology of Liberation,* 274.

15. In response to requests from Latin America between 1963 and 1965, U.S. priests, brothers, and nuns in the area increased 50 percent to some 4,000. Missionaries from Canada, Italy, Spain, France, and Ireland also increased as did financial support, especially from Germany. Luigi Einaudi, Richard Maullin, Alfred Stepan, and Michael Fleet, *Latin American Institutional Development: The Changing Catholic Church* (Santa Monica: Rand Corporation, 1969), 33–34.

16. See, for example, Isaac Cohen and Gert Rosenthal, "International Aspects of the

Crisis in Central America," paper presented at Workshop on Central America, Wilson Center, April 2–3, 1981, Washington, DC; Satya R. Pattnayak, ed., *Organized Religion in the Political Transformation of Latin America* (New York: University Press of America, 1995); William H. Swatos, Jr., *Religion and Democracy in Latin America* (New Brunswick: Transaction Publishers, 1995).

17. Daniel H. Levine, "Church Elites in Venezuela and Colombia: Context, Background and Beliefs," *Latin American Research Review* 14, no. 1 (1979): 62.

18. Gustavo Gutierrez, "Liberation Theology: Gutierrez Reflects on 20 Years Urging Option for the Poor," *Latinamerican Press* 20, no. 26 (July 14, 1988): 5.

19. Congregation for the Doctrine of the Faith, "Instruction on Certain Aspects of the 'Theology of Liberation,' " *Origins: NC Documentary Service,* 14, no. 13 (September 1984): 193–204; and "Instruction on Christian Freedom and Liberation," *Origins: NC Documentary Service* 15, no. 44 (April 17, 1986): 714–28.

20. The survey was undertaken largely because of a sense that liberation theology was encouraging Marxist revolutionary movements in Latin America. It found that liberation theology was not necessarily contrary to U.S. interests and concluded that "practitioners of liberation thought had actually aided the U.S. agenda throughout the region, as well as the transition in many Latin American countries to democracy." William Bole, "Conclusions of 1987 U.S. Information Agency Study Contradicted Official Government Line on Liberation Theology," *Religious News Service,* June 25, 1990, 1. See also N. Patrick Peritore, *Socialism, Communism, and Liberation Theology in Brazil: An Opinion Survey Using Q-Methodology* (Athens: University of Ohio Center for International Studies, 1990).

21. For example, Dan C. McCurry, "U.S. Church Financed Missions in Peru," in Daniel A. Sharp, ed., *U.S. Foreign Policy in Peru* (Austin, TX: University of Texas Press, 1972), 402–3. For a more complex view, see Claude Pomerleau, "The Missionary Dimension of the Latin American Church: A Study of French Dioscesan Clergy from 1963–1971," Ph.D. dissertation, nd, University of Denver; and Brian H. Smith, *More than Altruism: The Politics of Private Foreign Aid* (Princeton: Princeton University Press, 1990).

22. Jesuit Provincial Superiors of Latin America and the Caribbean, "Reflections on Neoliberalism in Latin America," *LADOC* 27, no. 6 (July/August 1977): 23.

23. Ibid., 26.

24. Personal communication from CELAM official.

25. The General Secretariat of the Synod of Bishops, *Encounter with the Living Jesus Christ: The Way to Conversion, Communion and Solidarity in America: Instrumentum Laboris* (Vatican City: Libreria Editrice Vaticana, 1997); John Thavis and Cindy Wooden, "Foreign Debt Synod's Central Issue; Fifteen Chosen to Write Final Document, " *National Catholic Reporter,* December 19, 1997, 18.

26. Cornelia Butler Flora and Rosario Bello, "The Impact of the Catholic Church on National Level Change in Latin America," *Journal of Church and State*, 31 (Autumn 1989): 527–42.

27. Bishop Jorge Hourton, "Comment," 500 Años del Cristianismo en América Latina Conference, July 19, 1990, Santiago, Chile.

28. Scott Mainwaring, "Grassroots Catholic Groups and Politics in Brazil," in Scott Mainwaring and Alexander Wilde, eds., *The Progressive Church in Latin America* (Notre Dame: Notre Dame University Press, 1989), 176–83.

29. Ofelia Schutte, *Cultural Identity and Social Liberation in Latin American Thought* (Albany: State University of New York Press, 1993).

7

REPLY   JAMES F. JOYCE

Religion and Societal Change: The Struggle for Human Rights in Latin America

In opening, I should thank Professor Crahan for all her research and involvement in these issues over the course of many years. As to her comprehensive analysis in this chapter, little remains to be commented upon, but a few thoughts come to mind.

First, we should acknowledge that when we speak of the "church," even the Catholic church, we oftentimes use a form of shorthand. The official and authoritative definition of the church is "the people of God." The wording of this definition by the Second Vatican Council was quite significant.

Often, however, we slip into using the term "church" as denoting one of several realities. Harvard professor and former director of the U.S. Catholic Conference Office of Social Development and World Peace Father Brian Hehir, in a recent lecture at Columbia University, suggested three different ways in which the church could be regarded as influencing the promotion of human rights: by the institutional and hierarchical church structures; by Catholic social thought in its various expressions; and by the community or people of God, "the body of Christ," which coincides in some areas with the "body politic." In further study of perceptions in Latin America about the efforts of the church, it might be useful to be aware of which strain has been most operative in the various national situations and during the various eras.

On the level of the hierarchy, the bishop is taken to be the authoritative voice of the church within his particular diocese. The emergence of national (or regional international) conferences of bishops is a new phenomenon. Some question how much "authority" to give the pronouncements issued in conjunction with them. Of course, there is the issue of how consensus is reached, by democratic vote or otherwise. This in turn raises the issue of how bishops are appointed, with what consultation and by what criteria as to their personal opinions and abilities. I raise this as an area for further research because the appointment of bishops in "developing countries" will impact efforts on behalf of human rights for the coming decades.

At the level of Catholic social thought, Professor Crahan cites the documents of the Second Vatican Council and, naturally enough, those developed by or with Latin Americans. These documents did not evolve in a void, however, as regards the progression of events in Latin America or Catholic social thought emerging from the Holy See in Rome. A relationship must be acknowledged to the pronouncements that came, with varying degrees of authority, from the popes.

Since John XXIII's *Pacem in Terris,* Paul VI issued the encyclical *Populorum Progressio* in 1967 and an apostolic letter entitled *Octogesimo Adveniens* that deals with socio-political issues (he issued no more Encyclicals after *Humanae Vitae*). Also of note are Paul VI's addresses given at Yankee Stadium and the United Nations during his visit to the United States.

From John Paul II have come several remarkable addresses given during visits to various areas of the world that deal extensively with social issues. But most noteworthy are his encyclicals *Laborem Exercens* in 1981 and *Sollicitudo Rei Socialis* ("On Social Concern") in 1987. More recently, John Paul II issued *Centesimus Annus,* which touches obliquely on issues that arise from the unfettered market and international trade, particularly the need for the poor to be protected.

To my mind, *On Social Concern* is one of the best-kept secrets and one of the most relevant documents to our topic. It deals directly with the concept of "sinful structures" in economics and in society. Space limits preclude going into detail, but the progressive nature of some of the ideas in *On Social Concern* might surprise the reader. Also, this document has the authority of an encyclical, and must therefore be taken into account by those developing social theory.

At the third level of the church community as "body politic," Professor Crahan notes the Christian Base Communities and their role in Latin America. The concept is currently in use in other parts of the world as well.

In her essay, Professor Crahan acknowledges divisions within the church in Latin America besides those evident in our three categories. Particularly, she refers to fears among some of the hierarchy over the development of popular organizations, groups formed by Latin Americans themselves, but often with a faith dimension. Chilean Christians for Socialism and what developed as a "popular church" in Nicaragua are examples. Fears that these organizations might be identified with the political left was due in part to the recent pasts of Eastern Europe and China where "national" or "puppet" churches were set up in an attempt to co-opt the power and influence of the Catholic church. Concern within the hierarchy arose not only from the perceived need to exert control over what might appear as church-related, but also from practical concern about the consequences if they were to follow an Eastern European model.

Mention should also be made of efforts by right-wing groups, sometimes with the connivance of the right in the United States, to co-opt religion for their own purposes in Latin America. In an attempt to discredit religious people whose faith called them to actively oppose oppression, plans were made and efforts were funded to enhance authoritarianism in Latin America. One example is the Banzer Plan.[1] Named for the current president of Bolivia, the Banzer Plan called for wedges to be driven between the "progressive clergy" (who are deemed political), the bishops, and the harmless dispensers of charity to widows and orphans (many of whom were made orphans by right-wing government policies). CIA involvement has been alleged, as well as financial support from right-wing U.S. Catholics.

A second example is the support of fundamentalism. Fundamentalists who would preach an individualistic concept of one's relationship with God and would emphasize obedience to civil authority were subsidized with large sums. The funds came from outside "mainline" Protestant channels because those churches were generally quite progressive and concerned with human rights. Attempts to alter the attitudes of Christian believers and to co-opt religion for right-wing purposes were a particularly obvious ploy in Guatemala, but this has occurred in other Latin American countries as well. Pejorative stereotypes of the Catholic church abounded in these fundamentalist crusades, but particularly denigrated was the concept of social action as a part of one's faith.

I found Professor Crahan's description of the two meetings in 1997 between Latin American prelates and high-ranking officials of the IMF, the World Bank, and the Inter-American Development Bank fascinating. Professor Crahan has attributed her information to "personal communication" with a CELAM official. We shall see what results from these meetings. Following on the Latin American Jesuit Provincials' letter outlining the detrimental effects of "neoliberal" economic policies, it is unclear whether the meetings will be perceived as a sort of backsliding by the hierarchy in its commitment to economic justice.

It is a situation that bears watching. The heart of the matter may come down to trust. One has to wonder in this context whether the decision makers really understand the nature of the poverty in the developing world, particularly Latin America, and whether they genuinely intend to afford protections for the poor.

In a sense these final comments by Professor Crahan deal with the current situation rather than historical development. Perhaps they can be taken as food for thought to spur on people of faith in the developed world, the United States especially, to investigate ways that we might practice the virtue of solidarity with those who struggle for human rights, particularly economic justice, in Latin America and the developing world. In the past, some areas for action were obvious: opposition to U.S. aid for the military in El Salvador, opposition to funding for the Contras, and the like.

An issue that remains is what is going on at the School of the Americas in Georgia, where Latin American military leaders have received training in the art of counter-insurgency warfare. Advocacy continues, along with bills in Congress to restrict funding for what is described as the "School of Assassins." Graduates of the School include the soldiers who murdered six Jesuit priests and two women in El Salvador, and Colonel Julio Alpirez, responsible for the murder and torture of Guatemalan and U.S. citizens.

Professor Crahan's exposition of the inter-relation of Catholicism, human rights, and economics in Latin America provokes thought and challenges us to investigate other appropriate areas for activism, particularly around the impact of international agreements, "fast track" proposals, and the policies of international financial actors. My greatest concern about this academic treatment is that probably fewer than 1 percent of the U.S. population even know what is meant by "neoliberalism." (It would probably be good to work toward a simple, agreed-upon definition to allow for a more recognizable synonym.) Some might groan at what they perceive as "sloganeering" or "rhetoric" and miss the crucial economic concerns behind documents being drafted in Latin America that decry "neoliberalism."

Terms for ideologies have tended to induce knee-jerk reactions. Anti-communism was an ideology that emphasized being against a "godless" system, and ignored the possible benefits to the poor of some socialized structures. (Of course, the limitation on personal freedoms, human rights violations in themselves, was one obvious problem.) One of the best examples of Catholic social thought that avoids such stereotyping is *On Social Concern.* Here John Paul II severely criticizes both economic systems in existence at the time, but notes:

> The church does not have technical solutions to offer for the problem of underdevelopment as such.... For the church does not propose economic political systems or programs, nor does she show preference one for the other, provided that human dignity is properly respected and promoted.... The church's social doctrine is not a "third way" between liberal capitalism and Marxist collectivism, nor even a possible alternative to other solutions less radically opposed to one another: rather, it constitutes a category of its

own. Nor is it an ideology, but rather the accurate formulation of the results of a careful reflection on the complex realities of human existence, in society and the international order, in the light of faith and of the church's tradition. Its main aim is to interpret these realities, determining their conformity with or divergence from the lines of Gospel teaching. It therefore belongs to the field, not of ideology, but of theology and particularly of moral theology.[2]

John Paul II then goes on to comment particularly on the reform of the international trade system, the reform of the world monetary and financial system, the exchange of technology and its proper use, and the need to review the structures of existing international organizations.

With this background, an alternative and possibly more effective approach than speaking strongly against the ideology of "neoliberalism" might be found by detailing the down-to-earth, practical results of bad decisions—quantifiably approaching "structural sin"—by the neoliberal structures.

Have the World Bank and the IMF just recently taken up making bad decisions based on the perceived goods of the market economy and fiscal responsibility in "developing" countries"? Or have they always been and do they continue to be, by their capitalistic nature, "sinful structures" that actually promote evil effects—poverty, indeed death—among the poor majorities of those countries? Allegedly, not only have the poor in Latin America suffered the consequences, but the poor in Africa have fallen victim as well, perhaps even more grievously.

Are these institutions reformable that were intended themselves as reform? Could it be that their considerable influence (or coercive capability) in developing countries is now too intimately based on an ideology of free-market unregulated "neoliberalism"? Will NAFTA, free trade zones, *maquiladora* schemes, recent global arrangements such as the General Agreement on Trades and Tariffs, and the establishment of genuine powers for the World Trade Organization improve things for the vast majority of the world's poor, or will they be made even worse off? Have the beginning, middle, and end results of these proposals been directed toward the good? Perhaps not, if we invoke the idea of the "common good." Have technical "fixes" intended as reforms become norms in themselves at the same time that the external debt of many nations continues to suffocate the poorest and, in fact, increase their suffering exponentially?

At one point during the most difficult times in El Salvador, the Jesuit University in San Salvador (UCA) published a study under the name of Father Ignacio Ellacuria, then president of UCA. The study detailed a trade union dispute with a utility company (privately owned by a general, I believe). Evidently not wanting to be bound by the terms of a contract negotiated with a genuine, duly elected workers' union, the company formed a "dummy" union and produced a "sweetheart" contract. The UCA study documented chapter and verse.

When the "dummy" union requested recognition by its respective international organization of trade unions (which would have meant a great deal of support and some financial assistance), the vote of the AFL-CIO affiliated union was crucial. Concerned labor and church activists were able to demonstrate to the union leadership in the United States that this was not an ideological dispute (as the company had portrayed it), but a dispute over a traditional trade-union right that their forebears had fought dearly to obtain. Although they were not persuasive enough to have the legitimate union recognized, they were able to block recognition of the "dummy" union. The carefully researched facts were used to swing the day on traditional principles.

Some of these same activists have obtained agreements with U.S. retailers to conform their "sourcing" practices in poor countries to principles that may have international impact at the "grass roots," for the real working people on the ground. If ever humanitarian principles on child labor, wage scales, and workers' rights were applied universally, it would thwart the "neoliberals" and "unfettered capitalists" from playing one poor country off against another to increase their profits by exploiting cheap labor.

The National Labor Committee based in New York City has embarked on a campaign to investigate and reveal the working conditions in the apparel industry worldwide. Their approach has not been one of protecting U.S. jobs (though some job security may well be a by-product), but of trying to ensure, by independent monitoring, that workers are in safe, nonthreatening environments, that they are treated with human dignity and paid a fair wage, and that conditions are not those of a sweatshop. If manufacturers flee from one country to another in search of the cheapest possible wage, activists of the National Labor Committee pledge to follow and expose them. Much of their good work in the developing countries is made possible by organized church groups and networks of "people of faith."

With support from people of faith, the body of the church as defined by Vatican II, international solidarity might become a reality and have genuine results for the poor. If the poor who are directly involved in the developing countries and the religiously inspired activists in the developed world are able to truly communicate and to work together, by established means of procuring social justice, genuine solidarity would exist. It would be difficult for any element of the church to stand opposed to the religious virtue of international solidarity. To strive toward solidarity might prove a long, difficult (and not mainly ideological) struggle, but one well worth undertaking. Professor Crahan's reflections are most helpful in understanding the history and nature of such a struggle as it has progressed in Latin America.

Notes

1. As quoted in William J. O'Malley, S.J., *The Voice of Blood: Five Christian Martyrs of Our Time* (Maryknoll, NY: Orbis Books, 1980), 31–32, the Banzer "plan of action" includes the following:

   1. Never attack the church as an institution and even less the bishops as a group. Rather attack the part of the church which is most "progressive."
   2. Attack, above all, the foreign clergy. Insist continuously that they are preaching armed warfare, that they are connected with international communism and have been sent to this country with the exclusive goal of moving the church toward communism.
   3. Control certain religious orders.
   4. The CIA has decided to intervene directly in this affair. It has promised to give us information about certain priests (personal documents, studies, friends, addresses, publications, foreign contacts).
   5. Control certain religious houses.
   6. For the present, do not repress religious houses since this will stir up too much controversy.
   7. Confront the hierarchy with deeds already done.
   8. Arrests should be made in the countryside, on deserted streets or late at night. Once a priest has been arrested, the Minister should plant subversive material in his briefcase and, if possible, in his room or home, and a weapon, preferably a high caliber pistol. Have a story prepared disgracing him before his bishop and the public.
   9. By any means of public communication, publish loose, daring, compromising material in order to discredit priests and religious who represent the tip of the progressive element in the church. Demand an official signature for any communique so that we can control where they come from and who writes them.
   10. Maintain a friendly relationship with some bishops, with certain members of the church, and with some native priests. In such a way we will assure that public opinion does not believe that there is a systematic persecution of the church, but only of a few of its dissident members. Insist on the authenticity of the national church (as opposed to the church in other countries).
   11. Reward the agents who best work at enforcing this plan of action by giving them the belongings confiscated from the homes of priests and religious.

2. John Paul II, *On Social Concern* (Boston: St. Paul Books, 1987), chapter 6, v. 41, 78–79.

8

CARRIE GUSTAFSON

Gandhi's Philosophy of *Satyagraha*: Cautionary Notes for the International Penal Lobby

> In the end we see that it is better to tolerate the thieves than to punish them.... But whilst we may bear with the thieves, we may not endure the infliction.... Since we regard the thieves as our kith and kin, they must be made to realize the kinship. And so we must take pains to devise ways and means of winning them over.... The thief is bound in the end to turn away from his evil ways and we shall get a clearer vision of truth.
>
> —Mahatma Gandhi[1]

For the true believer, the one who sees human rights activism as always directed *against* power, as always operating on behalf of those who dwell "on the bottom," the intersection of international law and criminal law merits close inspection. As for the accused, there is no lower bottom. As for mechanisms to wield power, there is none more potent than the power to punish, save that of war.

As human rights activists lobby daily for a permanent international criminal court (ICC), their oratory is eerily reminiscent of former cold warriors, and hints at an emerging class of global interventionists bent on "doing something" to stem the world's horrors. Regarding human rights atrocities as the work of an evil few operating apart from the ordinary Us, they propose a simple solution: hunt Them down, put Them away, and peace will again be ours.

Those who strive to expand the carceral network may be overlooking a higher sensibility—a middle option between moral inertia and moral hysteria, indifference and an increase in human-inflicted suffering. Gandhi's philosophy of *satyagraha** provides such an alternative.

In combination with social theory, *satyagraha* offers an ethical and practical response to disorder, suffering, and injustice that eschews inflicting or threatening to inflict violence on others. Further, it serves to remind us that violence and power are inherent features of any system of criminal justice; that an expanded power to punish is not universally regarded as a sign of moral progress or the achievement of "justice"; that punishment is not the inevitable or the pre-eminent response to deviant behavior; and that strategies to resolve conflict and to strengthen social norms should reflect the inherent dignity and potential for moral responsibility in all persons—they should humanize, rather than degrade their participants.

For those who would dismiss *satyagraha* as "religious," a few brief remarks about the part played by religion and religious belief. Many of the world's organized religions aspire to truth and non-violence, the central values of *satyagraha*. Yet few endorse the principled renunciation of coercive threats at its core, and their dogmatic, exclusionary tendencies made them frequent targets of Gandhi.[2] Gandhi wrote and said a great deal about religion, yet *satyagraha* cannot be ascribed to any particular orthodoxy. Indeed, a great strength of *satyagraha* is its universality—neither religion nor religious belief is sufficient or necessary. To the extent faith enters in, it is a faith rooted in non-violence and truth that even an atheist could endorse. Yet Gandhi's life-work, like that of Bishop Dinis Singulane in Mozambique, Martin Luther King in the United States, Aung San Suu Kyi in Burma, and Nelson Mandela in South Africa, is a testament to the religious values that inspire these and other individuals working to combat injustice without violence.[3]

For those who would dismiss *satyagraha* as "womanly," a few brief remarks. Much could be said about the prominence of women in the practice of non-violence in India, Japan, Eastern Europe, Latin America, and elsewhere.[4] As a strategy to fight injustice that requires human commitment rather than military might, that aims to transform rather than to subvert human relations, that distributes power away from traditional centers to "ordinary" persons, non-violence is often associated with "feminine" val-

---

*Satyagraha is the term Gandhi coined to describe his philosophy of active non-violence. Comprising the words *satya* (truth) and *agraha* (holding firmly), it literally means the firm grasping of or holding on to the truth. The core elements of *satyagraha* are truth, broadly defined to encompass factual and moral or metaphysical truth, and *ahimsa*, meaning not injuring and, more broadly, doing good even to the evil-doer.

ues.[5] Conversely, systems of criminal justice—hierarchical, adversarial, remote, rule-oriented, and dispassionate—are commonly associated with men and "masculine" values. Yet human beings and human values are not so easily divided into gendered camps. Men have figured prominently among non-violent theorists and practitioners, and women have at times been vocal supporters of punitive justice. Moreover, for those aiming to reverse the historical tendency to marginalize "feminine" values like care and empathy in conflict resolution, such compartmentalization is of dubious value.[6]

Violence, Power, and Systems of Criminal Justice

As a practicing lawyer in colonial South Africa and India, Gandhi well appreciated that violence *and* power inhere in systems of criminal justice.[7] Punishment must involve pain, suffering, deprivation, or other unpleasant consequence or it ceases to be punishment. Often veiled in the garb of non-violence, the nature of criminal justice is unmistakable to those on the receiving end—whether a suspect gunned down by arresting authorities, an individual "put away for life," or an abandoned spouse or child.

The ICC lobby has been remarkably candid about law's violence. It is not uncommon to hear casual talk of the number of lives worth sacrificing for a criminal prosecution, calls for a commando force to "hunt down" alleged criminals, and declarations that "the only way to be decisive is to take casualties."[8] To this must be added reasonably foreseeable deaths that result from retaliatory strikes and the murder of prosecution witnesses and their families, so tragically familiar in Rwanda.

For those who would cite among the virtues of ICCs a splendid isolation from power politics, Gandhian thought and ongoing crises in Bosnia offer a reminder that systems of criminal justice are inextricably linked to strategies of power. By definition, the balance of power rests with those who do the punishing. In the words of peace activist Thomas Merton, the example of criminal justice is based on force, and it carries the message that "you get what you have the power to take."[9]

It has been said that a standing ICC holds the promise of universal justice—that permanence will take power politics out. This is myth. For any foreseeable future, the permanent five members of the UN Security Council cannot be forced and will not submit to an effective, independent mechanism to enforce international criminal law. No matter how an ICC is established—by Security Council resolution, by treaty, or by the UN General Assembly—without the enforcement powers of the Security Council and its members, it would be an impotent entity. The gatekeeper and lead role played by the "permanent five" is and will remain secure no matter how an ICC is packaged.

The Burden of Legitimizing Law's Violence

Precisely because an expanded power to punish involves certain suffering and violence, the architects of ICCs are morally obliged to identify the specific aims they expect to achieve, and the mechanisms by which their progress will be assessed. Without a clear conception of appropriate and achievable aims, a firm basis in reality, and a critical understanding of their endeavor, ICC proponents risk costly failure. For Gandhi, who viewed ethics and politics as equally and fundamentally concerned with the pragmatic, the delict is double.[10] The apparent risk of doing more harm than good makes blind guesses and laundry lists of speculative ends unacceptable. The supposed aim of "achieving justice," having no empirical referent, is also a wholly inadequate response.

Deterrence Theory

Virtually all theories of criminal justice can be characterized as either retributive or utilitarian. Among utilitarian schemes, the ICC lobby relies particularly on deterrence theory, and does so with a level of confidence matched only by theorists' disaffection.[11] Positive criminology has accumulated masses of evidence testifying to the failure of deterrence. Described by Karl Menninger, it is an "utter failure," "primitive," "antiquated, expensive, and disappointing."[12] For James Miller, our deterrence-based system is "distinguished mostly by its failure to make communities safer and its alienation of large segments of our population."[13]

According to deterrence theorists, persons commit atrocities when the expected value of doing so exceeds the cost of punishment. Their solution? Simply raise the price for committing them by imposing certain and harsh penalties. Harvard psychologist James Gilligan identifies four problems with this model in the real world: "It is totally incorrect, hopelessly naive, dangerously misleading, and based on complete and utter ignorance of what violent people are actually like." The U.S. imprisonment fiasco shows how misguided the behaviorist faith of ICC advocates is in times of ostensible peace. How the findings of myriad scholars on the exaggerated part played by rational calculus in deviant behavior translate in humanitarian crises remains, lamentably, wholly unexamined.[14]

Retributive Theory

The liberal vision of reducing crime by attacking its social causes was all but supplanted in the 1980s by retributive schemes reflecting the belief that it is morally fitting that offenders be made to suffer, that something "in the souls of men" requires vengeance, and that society ought to respect and provide an institutional home for that urge. ICC discourse is imbued with like sentiment and the characteristic self-righteous tenor of those striving to secure the "deserved" punishment of others.

Before its renaissance, retribution was widely considered a dead letter, particularly among liberal theorists like H.L.A. Hart.[15] In the words of Hannah Arendt, "We refuse, and consider as barbaric, the propositions that 'a great crime offends nature, so that the very earth cries out for vengeance; that evil violates a natural harmony which only retribution can restore; that a wronged collectivity owes a duty to the moral order to punish the criminal.'"[16] At the domestic level, the pendulum is again swinging *slowly* away from politically expedient appeals to vengeance. That historically progressive human rights advocates now move contrariwise is startling. If our true aim is to restore order and human dignity, *satyagraha* offers an approach vastly superior to the proverbial pound of flesh, as evidenced daily in transitional South Africa.

Reprobative Theory

What ICC proponents ultimately seek through pain infliction is an authoritative expression of moral condemnation. They propose that life be risked—elsewhere, of course—so that we might emphatically demonstrate our abhorrence of the *unlawful* destruction of life. H.L.A. Hart, among others, assailed such expressive justice, depicting it as "uncomfortably close to human sacrifice as an expression of religious worship."[17] Reprobation and denunciation are important aspects of social ordering. But remote, atomized, violence-based international penal institutions are a dubious means to this end.

Gandhi, like Primo Levi and others, observed that evil in the world results largely from humanity's tendency to deny and disregard injustice and suffering *in toto*.[18] In the words of Auschwitz survivor Sarah Berkowitz, "silence is the real crime against humanity."[19] To recite Hitler's reputed quip—"Who after all remembers the Armenians"—to legitimate prosecutions is thus inapt. Far from a failure to initiate criminal proceedings, the world largely ignored the Armenians' plight. Ongoing revelations about World War II indicate how tragically unexceptional such indifference was. Then and now, the absence of *any* response to human suffering, not simply a punitive one, demands our attention.

Equating Criminal Prosecutions with Justice

No claim of ICC lobbyists is more common or questionable than their equation of punishment and justice. Gandhi, like Plato, recognized that criminal punishment signifies *not* the triumph of justice and morality, but its antithesis.[20] Any so-called peace attained through punitive measures, Gandhi regarded with disdain, dismissing an international police force as "a concession to human weakness, not by any means an emblem of peace."[21] It may be pragmatic to punish wrongdoers, but doing so is an act of violence that no amount of justification can make intrinsically good or indicative of virtue.

Above all, a puritanical equation of justice and punishment is conducive to violence. The wisdom of *satyagraha* rests in its recognition that when ideals pertaining to ends gain ascendancy—when lives are to be sacrificed in the name of an abstract principle like justice—violence is more probable. Attempts to achieve justice or to undo injustice, whether pursued by individuals or groups, constitute *the one and only universal cause of violence.*[22] Once associated with movements for *social* justice, the slogan "no peace without justice" has been transformed overnight by ICC advocates into a recipe for perpetual war. Based on twenty-five years' work with the most violent individuals in U.S. penal institutions, James Gilligan concludes:

> The purpose of both forms of violence—crime and punishment—is the same: to restore justice to the world by replacing shame with pride. And the means by which that is accomplished is the same. The very same acts of violence and mutilation (by which one prevents one's victim from shaming oneself further) serve to shame one's victim.... [F]or it is shameful to suffer violence (regardless of whether it is called crime or punishment), just as it is a source of pride and honor to be the one who dispenses violence to others.[23]

The concept of justice is inextricably contextual and presupposes a local set of conditions and considerations. Different societies have distinct notions of what is fair and "right," as do their members.[24] It is not uncommon, therefore, for a verdict in a criminal trial to ameliorate one group's sense of injustice while provoking that of another. The varied responses given by Hutu and Tutsi to the question "Was justice served?" hours after a Rwanda court sentenced a Hutu to death provide a classic illustration.[25]

Should there be any doubt whether former warring parties are likely to consider ICCs productive of justice, a simple thought experiment should suffice. Imagine that defendants before ICCs are entitled to have their guilt determined by a jury of peers representative of their community, whether Chilean, Bosnian, Chechen, Canadian, or Nicaraguan. At present, and contrary to U.S. jurisprudence, they have no such right. Were it otherwise, we might at least get a clear, if discomforting, glimpse at the underlying reality not unlike that bared in the O.J. Simpson proceedings, where "blacks 'got' the criminal verdict and the whites 'got' the civil one."[26] Due partly to the ubiquity of situationally rooted expectations and norms prevalent in armed conflict, "ordinary" members of an offender's community are best suited to understand and to judge deviant conduct alleged to have been committed in this context.

In a deeply divided society—arguably the only type of society likely to produce the types of crimes for which ICCs are intended—criminal prosecutions do not have a conciliatory effect; rather, they manifest and exacerbate division. This follows in part because those who occupy the dock are inevitably and widely seen as symbolic representatives of their group. As Court TV anchor Raymond Brown remarked of the trial of Dusko Tadic, such proceedings are *nothing but metaphor*. The association is even greater when "big fish" like Maurice Papon, P.W. Botha, General Pinochet, or Winnie Mandela are to be judged. Given their significance as metaphor, one can hardly expect ICCs to ameliorate collective guilt. On the contrary, they actually revive and inflame antagonistic sentiment, as Chancellor Adenauer foresaw of the Eichmann trial.

Disinterring Community, Decentering the Monstrous Few

Despite a veritable cottage industry of ICC literature and conferences, there is scant evidence of serious thought being given to *specifically who* is the intended beneficiary and target audience of international prosecutions. The omission bolsters suspicions voiced by a Rwandan delegate to the UN that they exist to appease the conscience of the international community, not to provide enduring value to a ravaged community.[27] For reasons given below, the subject and object of humanitarian efforts in the wake of human rights disasters must be the community directly affected by and implicated in the events. It is what Alex Boraine presumptively meant by "common," when he spoke of the "common good" of South Africa.

If champions of ICCs rather intend the amorphous "international community," they have yet to examine, even to identify, myriad derivative questions. If, for instance, a government's prerogative to punish rests, as some claim, on the reciprocal benefits and burdens constituting the social contract, on what does the international community base its prerogative? Individual Kurds, Bosnian-Serbs, Greek-Cypriots, and Palestinians would likely be hard-pressed to name the benefits they receive from the international community for which they are obliged. The mere occurrence of serious human rights violations is itself indicative of the inadequacy of international recourse and remedies.

what units, individual or groups, should be the targets of efforts to restore order to a badly fractured society? individuals? or rural moral communities?

GANDHI'S PHILOSOPHY OF SATYAGRAHA

ICC proponents also overlook the central question of what *units*, individuals or groups, should be the target of efforts to restore order to a badly fractured society. Backing a remedy designed to socialize *individuals*, they envisage a society disintegrated into an amoral, Hobbesian war of all against all, rather than *rival moral communities*. Deftly noted by Dennis Wrong, for group-level conflict to occur, the individual group members must already have been socialized to correctly gauge the expectations of others, to internalize at least some norms, and to possess selves sensitive to the appraisal of others.[28]

Like justice, crime is embedded in community and it is the ultimate concern of community. Gandhi well appreciated this and other commonplaces of modern criminology, like the need to focus on the character of society that engenders depraved acts, rather than fixating on a supposed base few. Repudiating the fashion of ascribing crime to isolated individuals, Gandhi declared:

> It hardly becomes us to take refuge in that moral alibi. Who are the hooligans after all? They are our own countrymen and, so long as any countryman of ours indulges in such acts, we cannot disown responsibility for them.[29]

Familiar to students of Nazi Germany, a Hitler—like a Stalin, a Karadzic, a Tudjman, a Mao—is only as strong as the power of mass obedience and support.

However, it is a mistake to confuse the notion of corporate responsibility with collective guilt or excusable impulses. As Gandhi reiterated time and again, life circumstances do not remove individual responsibility. Indeed, to hold otherwise is tantamount to denying the very foundation of human dignity.

this can become the terrorists' argument — innocent civilians can be killed because the gov. simply enacts their policies.

The Heart of Normative Order: Punitive Sanction or Social Embeddedness?

Durkheim —

The ICC lobby presupposes that formal institutions are integral to uphold group life and to stem deviant behavior. Reminiscent of presociological thought, this view overlooks the informal network of social ties that spontaneously create expectations and norms that predate and exist independently of legal institutions.[30] *Satyagraha* presupposes otherwise. The cooperation and consent of the governed is a sine qua non of long-term crime control and good government; soldiers or police may be able to "retake" a community, but they cannot hold it without the assent of its members. For lasting peace, Nelson Mandela proclaimed, "we do not rely on laws, we rely purely

Should be clear that govs. may enact policies that many of their citizens may oppose —

on persuasion."[31] For Gandhi, where society instead depends on law, law ceases to be law and society ceases to be society.[32]

To understand why people commit heinous acts, it helps to appreciate what motivates combatants to face the threat of death and mutilation in battle and to perform familiar heroic acts in gratuitous defiance of fate. Time and again, military historians and professionals dwell *not* on the coercive power of the army or state, but on what Dennis Wrong calls the "merely mental stuff that binds like chains of steel."[33] Like heroic deeds, deviant behavior stems from expectations of what is acceptable, even laudable behavior, which are borne out because others are aware of and live up to them. As modern Israeli soldiers attest, what most concerns combatants is "what others would think of them, or what their families or friends would feel about them when they came home."[34]

In conflict or cooperation, the major spring of human action is the desire to win the good opinion of family, friends, and close associates.[35] Indeed, the priority human beings place on honor and self-respect (our own and that of our group) over survival may be our most unique and our most dangerous attribute.[36] If we understand that fear of shame or ridicule is *the most common reason* human beings engage in violent behavior, the advantages of *satyagraha* over penal threats as a means to elicit right conduct become manifest.

Supporting and Yielding to Local Initiatives

Because the determinative response to deviancy occurs locally, communities that treat crime as something best left to institutions and professionals at far remove risk costly error. The requests of Cambodian and Burundi officials for an international tribunal to try certain of their nationals exemplify a dangerous abdication of responsibility that international mechanisms ought not to condone, let alone encourage. In the spirit of *satyagraha,* such requests ought to be rejected in favor of constructive, local action. Where, for instance, a state's judiciary is in such disarray that fair and impartial trials are not possible, rather than spending scarce resources on a stop-gap measure of dubious efficacy, the overriding aim should be to assist and encourage local efforts to remedy that situation as expeditiously as possible.

All but ignored in Cambodia, Bosnia, and Rwanda, the development of an effective and impartial local judiciary is vital to stabilize society. In Cambodia, an inept and corrupt judiciary remains after an unprecedented amount of humanitarian funds were spent on other projects. In Rwanda, limited capital (tangible and otherwise) expended on a comparatively opulent and ineffectual ICC should have been invested in local judiciary devastated by genocide and overwhelmed with approximately 120,000 individuals awaiting trial in squalid prison conditions.[37]

Where local leaders are *unwilling* to pursue a national remedy, and the international community is unwilling to spend the needed blood and treasure to assume de facto control à la Nuremberg, the best that can be done is to systematically collect and catalogue evidence. Whether "justice" comes quickly or not at all in such cases, events in Indonesia, Argentina, Ethiopia, South Korea, France, Cambodia, and so on indicate that changes in government, venue, and popular opinion disqualify the pat answer.

Punishing for Peace: The Unity of Means and Ends

A signal challenge to the ICC enterprise is the core precept of *satyagraha* that ends pre-exist in the means. In Gandhi's words,

> It is a great mistake to believe that there is no connection between the means and the end. . . . The means may be likened to a seed, the end to a tree; there is just the same inviolable connection between the means and the end as there is between the seed and the tree.[38]

Gandhi's insistence on the inviolability of means derived in part from man's ability to exercise control over means, but never to command results. For transitional societies in particular, an ethically responsible policy is one that reflects a world where unintended consequences are the rule. An ends-oriented strategy like criminal justice, however well-intended, falls short of the mark.

The indivisibility of means and ends follows also from the axiom that violence, even where seemingly justified, only leads to more violence.[39] Hunting down "international criminals" does not deter violence. Rather, as an example of violence, it teaches what it would deter. The destructive strategies and war mentality integral to the pursuit of criminal justice only fuel revolt, engender martyrs, and harden resistance in the defeated "enemy" as confirmed by events in Somalia, Rwanda, and Bosnia. By choosing not to retaliate, *satyagrahis* undermine the target and throw him off balance in what is described as "moral *jia-jitsu*."[40]

Above all, means are expressive and fused with values like human dignity and respect that signal the type of society we envision and presage the outcome we seek.[41] Here, the ICC enterprise is inapposite. Profoundly undemocratic, it is antithetical to responsible, local self-determination and accountability; it communicates that threats are considered constructive of social order, that the dominant party is willing to use force to achieve that end, and the imbalance of power that enables it to do so.[42] Like the Hegelian man who lifts a stick to his dog, to "civilize" others by force is to treat human beings as innately antisocial, amoral calculators, and to deny the spiritual unity of humankind envisioned by Gandhi.

A great strength of *satyagraha* is its inherent appeal to the Other as a moral agent endowed with reflective consciousness and concern for justice and other people's needs. No matter how depraved a person might appear to be, *satyagraha* reflects the dignity and potential for good in him or her. In the words of Gandhi, "Who can dare say that it is not in their nature to respond to the higher and finer forces? They have the same soul that I have."[43] The unparalleled success of Nelson Mandela, who "pinned the label 'man of integrity' to de Klerk's breast," demonstrates the efficacy of treating an adversary as a morally responsible agent capable of responding to reasoned normative appeals.[44]

Lasting stability is possible only when both sides to a conflict recognize they cannot *force* the other to submit, whether on the battlefield or the courtroom. For this, hope rests with those situated in the middle. Unlike a threat-based strategy, which dissipates the will of otherwise indispensable, well-intended persons, *satyagraha* is practiced *with* the opponent and avoids methods likely to humiliate, harass, or engender opposition. So that "ordinary" persons are given every chance for a decent response, *satyagrahis* ensure that the case is set out as clearly as possible, and that there is ample opportunity for the opponent to reflect and to respond. Here again, a punitive approach is inapt.

Practical Discourse and the Search for Truth

For Gandhi, truth was but another name for God, envisaged by everyone "in fragment and from different angles."[45] "Truth is my religion," he declared, "and *Ahimsa* [non-violence] is the only way of its realization."[46] Gandhi's insistence on non-violence and man's incompetence to punish derived from his belief that no human being is capable of knowing absolute truth. Conflict, he observed, is the result of misperceptions and competing relative truths, and its resolution requires a willingness to hear and to consider the opponent's position and to communicate one's own.[47] In particular, those on the margins of society—"criminal" and otherwise—must have an opportunity to be heard.

A core strength of *satyagraha* rests in the harmonizing, socializing, educative power of dialogue, increasingly recognized by contemporary social theorists. Like the Navajo strategy of "talking things out," *satyagraha* treats crime and conflict as a starting point for dialogue, wherein all are given an opportunity to express the truth as they see it and to offer solutions.[48] Like Willem de Haan's conception of practical discourse, it is an open, elaborative process that begins with the admission that there are no simple or categorical answers.[49] In contrast, administering "justice" by judicial fiat from above is anathema to the republican sense of a shared, participatory life.

A particularly misguided claim of ICC proponents is that criminal prosecutions are productive of "the truth." Nothing so belies this as the paucity of information about the Rwandan genocide generated by *hundreds* of criminal prosecutions, relative to the wealth of information about apartheid South Africa uncovered through non-prosecutorial means. Manifest in the trial of O.J. Simpson, criminal trials are anything but a search for the truth. On the contrary, their reductionist, bipolar logic and inherent barriers to the truth conceal, distort, and even reinvent history.[50] Remarked by Hannah Arendt following the Eichmann trial:

> [J]ustice for the accused necessitates that all the other questions of seemingly greater import—of "How could it happen?" and "Why did it happen?," of "Why the Jews?" and "Why the Germans?," of "What was the role of other nations?" ... be left in abeyance.[51]

In post–World War II Germany, Japan, and France, judicial processes effectively absolved the general populace and overlooked the mass collaboration and institutional support by *unavoidably* ascribing responsibility to a select few individuals. Instead of stimulating serious moral deliberation and self-scrutiny, Mark Osiel concludes on the basis of exhaustive research that the trials hindered an open debate on the far more complex reality.[52]

Causal Understanding, Exculpations, and Forgiveness

Once a hallmark of conservative thinking, the degree of disinterest ICC proponents show in causal theory is striking. Of equal concern are their related efforts to steer thinking about complex conflicts into criminal stereotypes, exemplified by one journalist's recent appeal to portray "news" from Africa in criminal terms.[53] Declining his invitation, BBC correspondent Lindsey Hilsum observed:

> We refuse to allow conflicts in Africa to have any politics. We always report them as "crimes." They are not crimes. It's politics. We have to understand that, and if we don't we're nowhere.

Not unlike religious dogma Gandhi scorned, the popular appeal of criminal stereotypes emanates from the security of binaries—good and evil, guilt and innocence, right and wrong, Us and Them—that shield us from the uncomfortable and complicated realities that yield atrocities. Criminal prosecutions serve as substitute for understanding—a way to label, think, and talk about the adversary, rather than having to listen to her. The wisdom of *satyagraha* rests in a commitment to understand why people commit heinous acts. If our aim is prevention, nothing is more important.[54]

The popular notion *tout comprendre, c'est tout pardonner*—to understand everything is to forgive everything—is a moral fallacy and the bogeyman of every serious effort to understand violence. Primo Levi, occasionally cited as its key proponent, repeatedly acknowledged the importance of understanding, for "what could be perpetrated yesterday could be attempted again tomorrow."[55] The aim of causal understanding is not to obliterate, pardon, or justify the past, but to achieve primary prevention. As a witness to genocide in Rwanda avowed, "you have to try to understand, because if you don't try to understand, you get nowhere."[56]

Those who counsel against vengeance and retaliation are also often labeled "forgivers." Yet evident in the work of Gandhi, retaliation and forgiveness are not inversely related, nor do they exhaust the world of possible responses to injustice. Clearly one may forswear retaliation, but withhold forgiveness. Forgiveness, on the other hand, presupposes that any plans to punish or otherwise retaliate have been forsworn—for, once one has retaliated, what remains to forgive? It is nonsensical to assert that "unless justice is done it's difficult to think about forgiving,"[57] if by "justice" one means punishment.

For policymakers concerned with prevention and restoring order, the question of forgiveness may simply be beside the point *except* to the extent that they may not wish to foreclose individual acts of forgiveness. Above all, forgiveness is a matter of individual conscience that no institution or authority can demand or effect in another's name. It is thus not surprising to hear expressions of dissent when Desmond Tutu, for instance, offers forgiveness on behalf of all South Africans.[58]

Working to Identify and Satisfy the Particular Needs of Victims and Survivors

Any serious effort to deal with a legacy of human rights violations must include a commitment to confront and constructively respond to victims' suffering and sense of injustice. The extent of modern society's failure in this regard has been widely remarked by Gandhi and innumerable others. Given the profound and varied experiences of victims, as well as the disparate coping mechanisms within and across cultures, any singular "right" approach is untenable.[59] *Satyagraha* appropriately demands constructive remedial action, but abjures a one-size-fits-all managerial solution.

To the extent it is humanly possible to mitigate the suffering of survivors of atrocities, this can be accomplished as effectively, if not more, without inflicting or threatening to inflict suffering on other human beings. To the extent persons derive solace from seeing an enemy-oppressor "get what they deserve"—defeated or humiliated in the courtroom, if not on the battlefield—it is an end at which criminal law should not aim. The notion that penal institutions provide an essential outlet for innately violent and vengeful human beings has been thoroughly debunked by modern social science as dangerously unhelpful, pseudo-biology.[60]

The punishment as collective therapy model—the idea that peaceful coexistence requires a clean slate that only punishment can deliver—has been similarly discredited as bad socio-psychology and based on an exaggerated and misguided fear of vigilantism.[61] Despite outrageous acts and levels of crime throughout history, vigilantism and vengeance remain extremely rare. In post–Civil War America, post-Stalinist Russia, post-Maoist China, post-Vichy France, colonial Congo, as well as present-day Cambodia, El Salvador, Argentina, Nicaragua, and Chile, victims and victimizers have coexisted in relative peace.[62]

There is perhaps no greater canard than the idea that punitive justice provides needed therapy for individuals—that nothing can assuage anger or restore dignity like punishment. Accounts of scholars who have worked extensively with survivors reveal that the urge for vengeance is far from universal.[63] Empirical studies indicate further that the emphasis on victimhood, blame, and powerlessness may actually undermine recovery from violent crime.[64] In Gandhi's experience, confirmed in the work of Bruno Bettelheim and Viktor Frankl with Holocaust survivors, individuals who neither submit passively nor retaliate to violence find in themselves a new sense of strength, dignity, and courage.[65]

What victims typically seek is the restoration of order, meaningful restitution and rehabilitative services, a thorough inquiry into the events that is recorded and publicly acknowledged, and an opportunity to participate in decision making and to recount their experiences. Echoed in the words of emancipated slaves—"Give us some land and you can keep your apology"—restitution and rehabilitation are especially vital, yet wholly ignored by the criminal justice model. Above all, meeting the day-to-day emotional challenges that result from the sheer terror of being victimized may be the greatest need, and the most daunting task. Faced with such pressing needs, the expenditure of untold sums *merely debating* the mechanics of prosecuting a handful of culpable elites perilously approaches malfeasance.

Avoiding Blueprints, Accommodating Indigenous Values and Needs

For the sake of appearing resolute, we risk putting an iron grip on diverse problems that demand local solutions. International criminal prosecutions exclude myriad values like mercy, shaming, recompense, forgiveness, compassion, and repentance that may be regarded locally as valuable, even imperative, to alleviate suffering and to restore order. By assuming that a serious disturbance of social order is first and foremost a criminal matter that demands a legal solution, we overlook and underrate indigenous values and practices like *satyagraha* or *ubuntu,* as practiced in South Africa.[66]

The cautionary words of Justice Richard Goldstone, former prosecutor of the International Yugoslav Tribunal, spoken at a time when the fate of *his* native South Africa was at stake, are instructive:

> A solution successful in one country may fail in another. The correct approach to the past will depend upon myriad political, economic, and cultural forces.... The manner in which violations are handled, whether perpetrators are punished, lose office, or are granted indemnities are issues will depend on political considerations which will differ from country to country.[67]

After the fashion of economic developmental assistance, will decades of costly error pass before the international community reawakens to the value of decentralization, discretion, and local initiative? Rather than indulge the notion that we have a corner on the universal meaning of justice, we should seek out and support local initiatives to restore human dignity and a semblance of order in the wake of human rights disasters. In striking contrast with events in Latin America and Southern Africa, those in the Balkans and the Great Lakes region of Africa suggest that a fixation on formal justice may be irrelevant *at best* to the ends of peace and stability.

Notes

1. Mahatma Gandhi, *The Moral and Political Writings of Mahatma Gandhi,* Volume 2: *Truth and Non-Violence,* Raghavan Iyer, ed. (Oxford: Clarendon Press, 1986), 229.

2. *Harijan,* May 30, 1936. Quakers and Anabaptists provide notable exceptions. Mike Yarrow, *Quaker Experiences in International Conciliation* (New Haven: Yale University Press, 1978); *War and Its Discontents: Pacifism and Quietism in the Abrahamic Traditions,* J. Patout Burns, ed. (Washington, DC: Georgetown University Press, 1996).

3. The role of spiritual and religious factors in conflict resolution is discussed in *The Missing Dimension of Statecraft,* Edward Luttwak, ed. (Washington, DC: Center for Strategic and International Studies, 1994); and *Justice Without Violence,* Paul Wehr, Heidi Burgess, and Guy Burgess, eds. (Boulder, CO: Lynne Rienner, 1994).

4. For example, see *Bringing Peace Home: Feminism, Violence, and Nature,* Karen Warren and Duane Cady, eds. (Bloomington: Indiana University Press, 1996); and *Reweaving the Web of Life: Feminism and Nonviolence,* Pam McAllister, ed. (Philadelphia: New Society, 1982).

5. This distinction was most notoriously drawn in Carol Gilligan's *In a Different Voice* (Cambridge: Harvard University Press, 1982).

6. Of note, studies on non-violence are ongoing at the U.S. Institute for Peace, the Albert Einstein Institution, the Center for Strategic and International Studies, and the Program on Nonviolent Sanctions at Harvard University.

7. "The *Satyagraha* Way with Crime," in *Satyagraha (Nonviolent Resistance),* Bharat Kumar, ed. (New York: Schocken, 1951).

8. See, for example, "Finding an Unlikely Ally in Bosnia," *Washington Post National Weekly,* September 8, 1997, 14; "New Line in Bosnia? Raid to Seize Serbs Bolsters NATO Image," *Herald Tribune,* July 14, 1997.

9. Thomas Merton, *Faith and Violence* (South Bend, IN: Notre Dame University Press, 1968), 246.

10. George Orwell, "Reflections on Gandhi," in *The Collected Essays: Journalism and Letters of George Orwell,* Sonia Orwell and Ian Angus, eds. (New York: Harcourt, Brace and World, 1968), 84.

11. For scholarly critiques of deterrence theory, see John Brathwaite and Philip Pettit, *Not Just Deserts: A Republican Theory of Criminal Justice* (Oxford: Clarendon Press 1990); Adrian Howe, *Punish and Critique: Towards a Feminist Analysis of Penality* (London: Routledge, 1994); Barbara Hudson, *Justice Through Punishment: A Critique of the 'Justice' Model of Corrections* (New York: St. Martin's Press, 1987); and Andrew Rutherford, *Criminal Justice and the Pursuit of Decency* (New York: Oxford University Press, 1993).

12. Karl Menninger, "Therapy, Not Punishment," in *Philosophy of Punishment,* ed. Robert Baird (New York: Prometheus, 1988), 48–49.

13. James Miller, *Search and Destroy: African-American Males in the Criminal Justice System* (Cambridge: Cambridge University Press, 1996), 136.

14. James Gilligan, *Violence: Our Deadly Epidemic and Its Causes* (New York: Grosset-Putnam 1996), 94–95.

15. Brathwaite and Pettit, *Not Just Deserts,* 3, 6–7; Willem de Haan, *The Politics of Redress: Crime, Punishment and Penal Abdition* (London: Unwin Hyman, 1990), 115; Igor Primoratz, *Justifying Legal Punishment* (London: Humanities Press International, 1989), 70.

16. Hannah Arendt, *Eichmann in Jerusalem: A Report on the Banality of Evil* (New York: Penguin Books, 1992), 277.

17. Cited in Dan Kahan, "What Do Alternative Sanctions Mean?" *University of Chicago Law Review* 63 (Spring 1996), 591, 596.

18. Gandhi, *The Moral and Political Writings,* 624; Primo Levi, *Afterword,* trans. Ruth Feldman (New York: Collier-Macmillan, 1965), 214.

19. Sarah Berkowitz, *Where Are My Brothers?* (New York: Helios, 1965), 43.

20. V.S. Hegde, "The Practice of Law and Gandhi," in *New Dimensions and Perspectives in Gandhism,* V.T. Patil, ed. (New Delhi: Inter-India Publications, 1989), 411–25; Dennis Dalton, *Mahatma Gandhi: Nonviolent Power in Action* (New York: Columbia University Press, 1993), 127.

21. Gandhi, *The Moral and Political Writings*, 498.
22. Gilligan, *Violence: Our Deadly Epidemic*, 11–12.
23. Ibid., 185.
24. For example, whether a disaster qualifies as misfortune or injustice may be determined largely by local sensibilities and the proclivity to respond with indifference, blame, punishment, or relief. Judith Shklar, *The Faces of Injustice* (New Haven: Yale University Press, 1990), 38, 110.
25. Alan Zarembo, "Judgment Day," *Harper's*, April 1997.
26. See Laura Mansnerus, "Truth in the Simpson Trials: The Devil Is in the Details," *New York Times*, January 12, 1997, 4; David Shipler, "Living Under Suspicion: Why Blacks Believe Simpson and Not the Police," *New York Times*, February 7, 1997.
27. Xinhua News Agency, November 26, 1996. See also "Justice for Genocide: Rwandan-Style," *The Economist*, January 11, 1997; "Rwanda: Punishing the Guilty, Maybe," *The Economist*, October 12, 1997.
28. Dennis Wrong, *The Problem of Order: What Unites and Divides Society* (New York: Free Press 1994), 161, 176, 182.
29. Gandhi, *The Moral and Political Writings*, 252.
30. Wrong, *The Problem of Order*, 49, 170, 222.
31. Patti Waldmeir, *Anatomy of a Miracle: The End of Apartheid and the Birth of a New South Africa* (New York: W.W. Norton, 1997), 261.
32. V.S. Hegde, "The Practice of Law and Gandhi," 424.
33. Wrong, *The Problem of Order*, 45. See, for example, James McPherson, *For Causes and Comrades: Why Men Fought in the Civil War* (New York: Oxford University Press, 1997); *The Laws of War: Constraints on Warfare in the Western World*, Sir Michael Howard, ed. (New Haven: Yale University Press, 1995); Samuel Hynes, *The Soldier's Tale: Bearing Witness to Modern War* (New York: Penguin Books, 1997); Richard Holmes, *Acts of War: The Behavior of Men in Battle* (New York: Free Press, 1985).
34. Holmes, *Acts of War*, 283.
35. John Brathwaite, *Crime, Shame and Reintegration* (New York: Cambridge University Press, 1989), 21.
36. Gilligan, *Violence: Our Deadly Epidemic*, 77, 197.
37. Madeline Morris, "Trials of Concurrent Jurisdiction: The Case of Rwanda," *Duke Journal of Comparative & International Law* 7 (Spring 1997), 349; "Justice to Prevail?" *Washington Post*, February 2, 1997.
38. Dalton, *Mahatma Gandhi*, 9.
39. Johan Galtung, *Peace by Peaceful Means: Peace and Conflict, Development and Civilization* (Oslo: International Peace Research Institute, 1996), 7.
40. Orwell, "Reflections on Gandhi," 79. *Satyagrahis* are practitioners of *Satyagraha*.
41. H.J.N. Horsburgh, *Non-Violence and Aggression: A Study of Gandhi's Moral Equivalent of War* (London: Oxford University Press, 1968), 44.
42. Wesley Cragg, *The Practice of Punishment: Towards a Theory of Restorative Justice* (London: Routledge, 1992), 196.
43. Gandhi, *The Moral and Political Writings*, 488.
44. Waldmeir, *Anatomy of a Miracle*, 158.
45. Gandhi, *The Moral and Political Writings*, 252.
46. *Harijan*, April 30, 1938.
47. Madan Gandhi, "Metaphysical Basis of Gandhian Thought," in Patil, ed., *New Dimensions*, 197, 206.

48. Robert Yazzie, " 'Life Comes from It': Navajo Justice Conceptions of Criminal Justice," *New Mexico Law Review* 24 (Spring 1994), 175.
49. de Haan, *The Politics of Redress,* 159–60, 168.
50. Mark Osiel offers a comprehensive assessment of the efficacy of criminal trials to illumine events in the aftermath of human rights disasters in "Ever Again: Legal Remembrance of Administrative Massacre," *University of Pennsylvania Law Review* 144 (December 1995), 463.
51. Arendt, *Eichmann in Jerusalem,* 5.
52. Osiel, "Ever Again."
53. Roy Guttman, Reporting from the Killing Fields, conference at the University of California, Berkeley, May 1997.
54. Gilligan, *Violence: Our Deadly Epidemic,* 183, 258, 267.
55. Primo Levi, *The Drowned and the Saved* (New York: Summit Books, 1988), 53.
56. Lindsey Hilsum, Reporting from the Killing Fields, conference at the University of California, Berkeley, May 1997.
57. Tina Rosenberg, "Recovering from Apartheid," *New Yorker,* November 18, 1996.
58. Timothy Garton Ash, "True Confessions," *New York Review of Books,* July 17, 1997, 33–38.
59. Lynn Henderson, "The Wrongs of Victim's Rights," *Stanford Law Review* 37 (April 1985), 937, 997.
60. Gilligan, *Violence: Our Deadly Epidemic,* 210–11.
61. George L. Kelling and Catherine M. Coles, *Fixing Broken Windows: Restoring Order and Reducing Crime in Our Communities* (New York: Simon and Schuster, 1997), 108–56.
62. See, for example, "Cambodian Aesop Tells a Fable of Forgiveness," *New York Times,* June 28, 1997; David Rieff, "The Big Risk," *New York Review of Books,* October 31, 1996; Alan Zarembo, "Judgment Day," *Harper's,* April 1997.
63. See Thomas Buergenthal, "The United Nations Truth Commission for El Salvador," in *Transitional Justice: How Emerging Democracies Reckon with Former Regimes,* Neil Kritz, ed. (Washington DC: United Institute for Peace 1995), 292; Jose Zalaquett, "Confronting Human Rights Violations Committed by Former Governments: Applicable Principles and Political Restraints," in Kritz, ed., *Transitional Justice,* 3.
64. Henderson, "Wrongs of Victim's Rights," 955, 965.
65. Gandhi, *The Moral and Political Writings,* 293; Nina Sutton, *Bettelheim: A Life and a Legacy,* David Sharp trans. (New York: Basic Books, 1996), 61, 65, and 104; Viktor Frankel, *Man's Search for Meaning,* Ilse Lasch, trans. (New York: Simon and Schuster, 1984).
66. *Ubuntu* is a term shared by a number of African languages, meaning humanity in Xhosa and human nature in Zulu, for example. As described by one South African legal scholar

> Ubuntu is a culture which places some emphasis on communality and on the interdependence of the members of a community. It recognizes a person's status as a human being, entitled to unconditional respect, dignity, value and acceptance from the members of the community such person happens to be part of. It also entails the converse, however. The person has a corresponding duty to give the same respect, dignity, value and acceptance to each member of that community. More importantly, it regulates the exercise of rights by the emphasis it lays on sharing and co-responsibility and the mutual enjoyment of rights by all.

Cited in Peter N. Bouckaert, "The Negotiated Revolution: South Africa's Transition to a Multiracial Democracy," *Stanford Journal of International Law* 33 (Summer 1997), 375.

67. Richard Goldstone, "Exposing Human Rights Abuses—A Help or Hindrance to Reconciliation," *Hastings Constitutional Law Quarterly* 23 (1995), 607, 615.

---

1. Civil rights movement – remember – nonviolence did bring, in many cases, government intervention.
   - Even in the Montgomery Bus Boycott – it was a court ruling that settled the matter – not clear where more going – King was on trial himself – (see *Why We Can't Wait?* (King's book on Montg. Bus Boycott))

2. Justice and Peace shall kiss, Mercy and Truth shall be together – Psalm 82. – see John Paul Lederach – *Building Sustainable Peace in Divided Societies* – the issue of Reconciliation

   – And don't forget St. Paul – we all fall short if judged by the law –

9

REPLY KENNETH ANDERSON

Secular Eschatologies and Class Interests of the Internationalized New Class

Introduction

It seems quite certain that Carrie Gustafson and I are not alone in harboring skepticism about the enthusiasm evident in this decade for the formation of international war crimes tribunals (IWCTs) and a permanent international "criminal" court (ICC). Her article takes up criticism from the point of view of Gandhian philosophy and in particular a critique of the urge to punish that seems to so engage internationalists of all types. I do not propose to address her Gandhian critique, on which I am inexpert. Instead, I propose to extend in very sketchy form the critique she makes by linking it to a specifically Biblical religious tradition, and then suggesting that it, too, must be seen in light of class interests of those pressing forward the idea of tribunals. In so doing, I aim to discuss some of the deepest assumptions of "internationalism" that underlie the practical and policy discussions of the tribunals.

Secular Eschatologies

It must be noted from the beginning that the issue of international tribunals does not frontally engage the passions of most who are not international lawyers, international law academics, international journalists, international activists, international bureaucrats, and others who all share, at bottom and whatever else their disagreements, deep attachment by profession and, ultimately, by class to a frankly internationalist vision of the world. Those skeptical of that vision have relatively little motive to argue the other side, for in so many ways it is a divide of worldview in which the discussants would share few foundational premises. The consequence is that the assumptions and reasoning of the internationalism leading to IWCTs and the ICC (collectively, "tribunals") go untested, sustained by endlessly self-reinforcing discussions among the converted. Self-referential preaching to the converted is one reason why international public law so frequently flunks the test of being an intellectual discipline; rarely does it engage inside its precincts with serious intellectual adversaries. Less academic discipline than club of the like-minded, its very postulates practically preclude a debate over the first principles of Grotian international legitimacy that might put the question of the tribunals on the table in the first place.[1]

This internationalism is a faith, in other words, like any other. Its articles divide into two streams, each of which is central to the aspirations of the two existing IWCTs, one for the former Yugoslavia and the other for Rwanda, and of the proposed ICC. The first stream is, in broad terms, a claim that the development of an internationalist world order—in which the highest forms of power and legitimacy would be fused in international organizations, establishing the constitutional supremacy of international law over all national law, as though the world were a unitary society in which international law was directly its law or at least the ultimate legitimator of any local law, and in which nation-states would be subordinate to that order—is morally desirable, good, and right. The second is, in equally broad terms, a claim not only that moral progress is defined by that internationalism, but that historical progress, "globalism," *is* in fact evolving—slowly and at times scarcely perceptibly, to be sure, and requiring all assistance possible from those seeking progress defined as internationalism—but evolving toward it just the same. History, and not merely morality, is on the side of internationalism; internationalism is progress, and progress is good.

These two claims are central to the project of the tribunals, and the project of the tribunals is central to them. True, when pressed by those suspicious of their political pretensions—a Senator Jesse Helms, for example—the architects of the tribunals will artfully understate their reach and ambition. The war crimes tribunals, for example, exist merely to punish the most outrageous and obvious crimes that otherwise would have no redress anywhere. But this exercise in modesty (not merely superficial recourse to it) is, in my experience, more the exception than the rule.

The tribunals are explicitly and proudly seen by their creators as the establishment of the rule of law at the international level; the deliberate creation of institutions of flesh and blood from what began as smoke and mirrors; the creation of legitimacy from the merest shred of an appearance of legitimacy. The legitimacy sought for the tribunals is one of supremacy over national claims, first over the limited area of war crimes and then to extend over the whole field of human rights. And the extension to human rights is, to say, over everything since human rights is a field that today promiscuously pronounces on matters which might have been thought paradigmatically of local concern, standards, and control, such as the details of child-rearing, or anything else in which the international activist community takes an interest and for which it believes that appeals to the "higher" legitimacy of international law can provide an "end run" around inconvenient national law.

To deny that the aim of the tribunals' supporters is fully to reach all matters of human rights, in a way that binds national parties, would be intellectually dishonest. The legitimacy of the tribunals is not thought to be merely that the events of Bosnia and Rwanda are so awful that someone must prosecute the perpetrators. If that were the case, there is no lack of national courts with a vastly fuller range of procedural protections that would be capable of trying the accused. On the contrary, those pressing the tribunals have been desperately eager to ensure that no mere national courts—Germany's, for instance—conduct such trials for fear of upsetting the momentum that the tribunals represent for enshrining both the moral supremacy of the internationalist rule of law and the practical demonstration that it is in fact coming to be. It is not really possible to discuss the tribunals without addressing these two internationalist claims, nor is it possible to discuss internationalism without addressing the role of the tribunals as today's leading edge.

What, then, of these two claims, one moral and the other factual? Each has a lengthy intellectual pedigree going back not merely to Grotius and the Enlightenment, but still further to root sources in Western thought: Biblical eschatologies and later those first Catholic preachers of the unity, indeed *totality,* of Christ's world, Augustine and Aquinas. The contemporary claims of internationalism are in many ways merely a secularization of ancient Catholic thought as it was drawn from Biblical texts and then given a specifically medieval Christian cast. Now updated and revised for modernity, even without Christ they lack none of the trappings of faith. The implication of intellectual and spiritual continuity from ancient Christian thought is not merely that this internationalism has certain parallels with other religious movements but, both more speculatively and more provocatively, that it is the direct heir to *this* religious tradition.

But seen at any distance from the faith itself, without the comforting certainties of the faith, each of these claims must be seen as audacious, heroic, and wild. They are comprehensible only upon the religious worldview that boldly proclaims the good news of international organizations, differing from the view of the Psalmist—the "earth is the Lord's, and the fullness thereof; the world, and they that dwell therein"[2]—only with respect to whom the earth belongs to. Thus shall the UN, that duly noted steward of the Lord, inherit the earth.

But are there really no serious moral and intellectual contenders against the philosophy that political and moral legitimacy flows from international organizations, from the United Nations, from the Security Council, from the top of the world down? Is there no one to dispute that the content of the most basic human rights are mysteriously and rightly discerned at the level of international organizations, by those whose homes and hearts are in New York City and Geneva, whose professions are diplomacy and law, and which flow down to inform those at the bottom, who are more likely to make their homes in the streets of Calcutta, in the shadow of the mosque in Teheran, in the jungles of Peru? Is there no one to dispute that merely because an enterprise has planetary pretensions, it has special claims to legitimacy? Is there no one to dispute that the Security Council should be the practical arbiter not just of war and peace but, according to the logic of the tribunals, of the deepest principles of right and wrong, fundamental morality, for the whole world—*China,* busily executing alleged criminals by quota among all its other crimes, and *France,* whose arms transfers to Rwanda were by any serious moral standard part of the crimes of genocide? Need one continue with the United States in Vietnam, or Russia more recently in Chechnya and Tajikistan? Surely it is one thing to recognize the practical imperatives of war and peace, who has power and who does not, and to take the Security Council for the limited purpose of a talking shop among the great powers, but it is scarcely absurd to ask, as among this less than glorious collection, by what possible moral authority it would purport to do anything more.

It therefore may be grounds for excommunication from the internationalist faith, but it is not mad to point out that there are moral and political theories at least as intellectually powerful and morally compelling as that offered by internationalism that would deny anything like the development of a top-down political order, at least at the level of the *whole planet.* To many people in the world, it seems as silly as it is unfortunately necessary to point out that it is those philosophies, and not top-down internationalism, that have often seemed to be not only right but even "progressive." For the very idea of a "world order," as a disturbing remnant of Judeo-Christian eschatology, expresses a derivative Enlightenment eschatology that is, if anything, stronger even than its Biblical antecedents. It is a stronger eschatology because it imagines that it will be carried out in historical time and not merely in the City of God. It is more frightening, at least to those of us who are frightened by all dreams of political and social totality, than even the fevered Christian apocalyptic visions of Joachim of Flora, preaching a thousand years ago; Joachim, at least, was a pessimist. Whereas the Enlightenment eschatology that finds expression in today's internationalism is downright planetary in its optimism, how many evils have been authorized in history by those believing they have legitimacy to improve the human race, here on earth and not merely in heaven?

Does this seem unnecessarily extravagant? Unfair to saddle the dream of an international order "merely" promoting peace on earth and the protection of universal human rights through the application of international law with conspiratorial visions of totality? It is not a religion, but simply the efforts of ordinary human beings seeking to carry out the technical and professional task of bringing about order upon the earth. Upon being accused of an overweening pride, it asserts a touching modesty; "We want only," it is said, with downcast eyes and modest mien, "to save the world."

Yet not so many years ago, before the strictures of the multicultural ideal served conveniently to conceal the religious origins of internationalist eschatology, it used to be perfectly acceptable to quote, in support of this same internationalism, and indeed as the fulfillment of it, the famous passage from Isaiah, "they shall beat their swords into plowshares, and their spears into pruninghooks: nation shall not lift up sword against nation, neither shall they learn war anymore."[3] What went less remarked, perhaps, was the still more compelling passage preceding it, in which the prophet laid out *his* understanding of the necessary conditions for that happy state to come about:

> [T]he mountain of the Lord's house shall be established on the top of the mountains, and shall be exalted above the hills; and all nations shall flow unto it. And many people shall go and say, Come ye, and let us go up to the mountain of the Lord, to the house of the God of Jacob; and he will teach us of his ways, and we will walk in his paths; for out of Zion shall go forth the law, and the word of the Lord from Jerusalem. And he shall judge among the nations, and shall rebuke many people.

The order of "all nations," flowing together to a central place, receiving the law from a city and a mountain, exalted above all others, a single law and a single lawgiver, and a single judge of a people at last made one ... the dream of the unity of all human beings across the planet, all and everyone, everywhere, is an ancient and powerful dream. It is a genuine vision of the future of the human race. And even if I think it wrong in moral principle, unlikely to bring about a happy end in fact, and frankly as mad as Joachim, why apologize for it and pretend to a modesty of aim that is neither true to the vision nor does it honor? Today's dream fully partakes of those ancient sources, and its vision, while genuine, is genuine *because* it is religious in origin and religious in its contemporary content and religious in what it requires of believers, namely, belief.

Whereas I am no believer and see it as bearing, at least in the absence of an actual appearance by the God of Jacob and the Lord of Hosts, all the marks of hubris. And the development of global tribunals whose principal claim is not to political practicality, but instead the enunciation of fundamental and universal morality, whose reach, moral and practical, is contemplated to be planetary, and whose function, whether admitted or not, is to carry out Isaiah's project of judging among nations and rebuking many people, genuinely brings the dream—or the madness, as one will—one step closer.

The International New Class

Similar skepticism can be applied to the second grand claim. What is obvious about the historical claim that the world is in fact advancing incrementally toward unity of the kind put forth by internationalist doctrine? Once upon a time evidence of this claim would have been discerned in the size of the bureaucracies of international organizations, the size of their budgets, the resources they consume. Few today, of course, would dare to claim much in the way of progress out of the mere existence and size of the international civil service; ideological markers have changed, even for internationalist ideology. Not insignificantly, the internationalist faith that it will eventually envelop the world today rests principally on the hope that the growth of global capitalism will do the job for it.

There *is,* in other words, a vanguard party in the old Marxist sense; it turns out to be the voracious, restless, volatile market. The global market penetrates what remains of traditional societies with its irresistible consumer goods and saturates all places with the media message, its own form of the good news, that the world is one and cultural differences are nothing more than differences in consumer preferences. Or rather, more precisely, that no cultural differences are legitimate if they amount to more than differences in consumer preferences for what the global market puts on offer anyway.

This is the eschatology of the market and the mantra of globalism. There are reasons, certainly, to wonder whether this globalism is coming about in the way announced, as either an economic or cultural proposition. Economist Paul Krugman, among others, has raised many questions as to whether the economic postulates of globalism, premised on interlinkages of national economies, really result in the true erasure of economic borders.[4] Globalism, in the sense of the true unification of markets, of both producer and consumer, may turn out to be different than the phenomenon of expanded free trade or expanded bloc trading by national economies or globalization of finance capital; it may not turn out to be true that trading across boundaries leads to the disappearance of those boundaries.

Moreover, the *cultural* interpretation of spreading global consumerism is not necessarily what the West would assume. Several years ago, for example, wandering in Harrod's department store in London, I happened into the lingerie section, there to find hundreds of veiled Islamic women carefully purchasing the latest in Western sex appeal. It occurred to me to wonder who, indeed, was colonizing whom in this exchange. Whether or not the economic or cultural presumptions of global capitalism turn out as predicted, surely there is little doubt that public law internationalists depend upon it to do heavy lifting in creating the material conditions of economic interdependence and dependence, loss of traditional societal norms, and legitimacy of a global order based on the supposedly natural law of capital required to sustain the propositions of internationalism necessary to tribunals.

Nor is there anything inconsistent with depending crucially upon transnational capital to create the conditions of internationalism, by undermining other sources of legitimacy, while at the same time announcing that internationalism is needed to regulate precisely that same international capitalism. The aspirations of internationalism and global capital are not inconsistent at the level of the need for a unified global market crucially *to be regulated,* however much any particular set of regulations may be resisted by particular economic interests, whether on environmental, labor, or other grounds. As an entire system, capital and its regulators have no fundamental disagreement, because as a whole system, regulation is needed to ensure a set of global consumers. It is needed to stabilize that market, economically and even culturally; this is true of the system taken as a whole no matter how much resistance is given in particular circumstances.

Painting such groups as human rights organizations and the like as fundamentally in tension with transnational capital is simply an illusion. If the global nongovernmental movement, as a key agent of internationalism, sees itself as a kind of "Sunday School of the nations," schooling them in their moral duties, it is able to do so because it fundamentally accepts their legitimacy as the repositories of global power, economic and cultural. Global capital has duties, says the internationalist human rights movement, precisely because global capital is entitled to the power it holds, and it is so entitled because it serves as the battering ram to make societies accessible and malleable to internationalism itself.

By the time one has come so far as to suggest that the internationalism underlying the tribunals is premised upon the interests of global capital, however, it is time to ask whether those who make up the ranks of managers of global capital and the internationalist movement among activists, scholars, and so on do not have at least some loose characteristics of class. Much has been written in recent years about the so-called "knowledge class" and "symbolic analysts," to use Robert Reich's terms in *The Work of Nations,* or alternatively just the "New Class."[5] The internationalism of this class, uniting capital and public regulation of it, is inescapable. As the late Christopher Lasch, in his final book, *The Revolt of the Elites,* put it,

> [T]he market in which the new elites operate is now international in scope. Their fortunes are tied to enterprises that operate across national boundaries. They are more concerned with the smooth functioning of the system as a whole than with any of its parts. Their loyalties—if the term is not itself anachronistic in this context—are international rather than regional, national, or local. They have more in common with their counterparts in Brussels or Hong Kong than with the masses of Americans not yet plugged into the network of global communications.[6]

This seems to me, unsurprisingly, a fair description of the principal players, particularly the international human rights NGOs, in their struggle to create and legitimize international tribunals. Their self-proclaimed allegiance is to supposedly "universal" principles, rather than to the parochial traditions of any particular society, such as the Constitution of the United States and its particular conception of the rule of law, or any other place. The proudest traditions of the *actual* rule of law in *actual* places are always subordinate to utopianized conceptions of the universal. Moreover, it is the universal which commands loyalty, and it, apparently like God, has no location and no place.

This ideological formation is at once transcendental in Isaiah's terms— aiming at a transcendental victory of universal unity of law and lawgiver over all nations—and simultaneously a nearly exact mirror of the allegiances and preferences of global capital, of which it is a Siamese twin joined at the hip. I do not wish to put overemphasis on the concept of class, in any strong or technical sense; it would probably be enough to describe these social agents as "elites." Still, it seems to me that they share enough characteristics of material interest, given to them by global capital, to go beyond mere ideological or sentimental identity, so to give class analysis a certain utility.

And the crucial point that class analysis yields here is that this global New Class, this internationalized elite, asserts time and again that its goal is a transcendent universal order. The internationalized New Class claims universality, in the name of everyone, for the sake of everyone, regardless of whether they are participants in this New Class or not. What it actually pursues, however, is something different—globalism and internationalism. The international New Class, it seems to me, pursues its particular class interest by declaring it to be a universal interest; it is able to do so by deliberately exploiting the confusion between "global" and "international," on the one hand, and "universal," on the other. But they are not the same thing. The internationalized New Class pursues a class interest that does not depend on geographical location; its interests are transgeographic and beyond borders because its economic interests are transborder. Perhaps critics like Krugman are right and its interests ultimately depend not on the gradual erasure of borders *altogether,* but on the ability to maximize transactions across borders consistent with being able (as a class owning the monopoly on access to that border) to extract maximum rents for goods, services, and capital; but even so, the material class interest is not rooted in a particular place. An interest can be global without being universal; that, I would suggest, is the fundamental class position of the New Class.

Conclusion

And so, a first step to understanding the ideology behind the internationalism that believes so fervently in international tribunals is to understand its religious roots in such sources as Isaiah's dream of transcendental unity— its actual religious derivation, as well as its parallels with other religious belief systems. But the second step is to understand that, given the class interest of the internationalist class carrying out this agenda, the claim to universalism is a sham. The universalism is mere globalism and a globalism, moreover, whose key terms are established by capital.

This foundation is the ideological base upon which the tribunals have been established, leaving aside all the other practical concerns about due process, effectiveness, the political concerns of the Security Council, agreement on the law to be applied, and so on. It seems to me to be part of the solution of a class in desperate search for legitimacy, reaching out to create institutions from the whole cloth of credulity without foundations, traditions, or rootedness, that exploit the gap between globalism and universalism, and yet simultaneously are firmly convinced of their own transcendental value, just as the internationalized New Class is convinced of its own transcendental virtue.

This is hubris. And it is hard to imagine that Gandhi, who (in my own inexpert understanding) seemed always to be concerned to root the universal in the local, would be enthused.

Notes

1. I have tried (unsuccessfully, I think) to put it on the table as a panelist at the American Society of International Law 91st Annual Meeting, April 9–12, 1997, on International Law and Literature. See also David Rieff's remarkable essay, "The Humanitarian Illusion," *The New Republic* (March 16, 1998), 27–32, reviewing Michael Ignatieff, *The Warrior's Honor: Ethnic War and the Modern Conscience.*

2. Psalms 24:1. I have here used the King James version not for accuracy, of course, but by appeal to the Christian cultural tradition of which this figures in the course of Western thought and, frankly, for the beauty of language.

3. Isaiah 2:4.

4. For example, Krugman's essays in *Pop Internationalism* (Cambridge: MIT Press, 1996).

5. Robert Reich, *The Work of Nations* (New York: Knopf, 1991).

6. Christopher Lasch, *The Revolt of the Elites and the Betrayal of Democracy* (New York: Norton, 1995), 47.

10

ARATI RAO

Speaking/Seeking a Common Language: Women, the Hindu Right, and Human Rights in India

Multireligious societies pose a singular challenge to human rights inquiry into religion. Given the single-religion focus of the bulk of this human rights scholarship—rights in Islam, for example[1]—the stage is now set for a more extensive and nuanced comparative analysis. In light of growing global modernization, communication, and transfers of population (voluntary and involuntary, temporary and permanent), very few societies can claim unfamiliarity with multireligious existence. A comparative human rights approach optimally would be interested in the protection of the religious rights of not just one community but of all. Further, in their desire to ground peaceful coexistence in existing traditions while developing new ideas when faced with unjust traditions, human rights theorists and advocates search for a common language in which religions may "talk to" each other, and build common ground for peaceful interaction and coexistence in an unavoidably multireligious world.[2]

This means that human rights, in understanding and implementation, must interact in a mutually constitutive relationship with other frameworks of belief, including religion and culture, if it is to have relevance. Indeed, scholars and activists like Abdullahi An-Na'im hold that "since people are more likely to observe normative propositions if they believe them to be sanctioned by their own cultural traditions, observance of human rights standards can be improved through the cultural legitimacy of those standards."[3] Since religion is usually an influential component of cultural practices, a closer look at religion will invariably lead to a broader understanding of prevalent culture.

But what about social groups that are discriminated against by the religious authorities and religious tenets that influence their lives? Since women are most intimately connected with religious and cultural practices, what price cultural legitimacy where women's rights are compromised or violated in the name of religion? Complicating this picture are the differences between mainstream rights discourse and women's rights advocacy in approaching the relationship of human rights and religion. Generally speaking, the chief religious concern of mainstream human rights remains the protection of religious liberties. Indeed, feminist legal scholar Donna Sullivan notes, "states that implement religious law, and believers themselves, have contended that many practices that violate women's human rights are manifestations of the freedom of religion or belief, and as such are entitled to protection under international law."[4]

Women's rights advocates, however, approach the relationship differently. Here, all religions are subject to scrutiny for their discriminatory treatment of social groups such as women, in doctrine and ensuing practice. It is precisely An-Na'im's "legitimacy" criterion that comes under feminist fire. In this light, religion is one of the chief perpetrators of women's subjugation, inequality, lower social status, lack of equal treatment and equal protection, and internalized notions of inferiority. In this approach, a religion is examined not only as doctrine and practice, but also as an organization whose structures and hierarchies are frequently mobilized to discipline and control women through manipulation, threat, and punishment that is psychological, physical, and emotional. Religious rules and exhortations of women's roles and duties in the normative female sphere of activity, the home, compel women's rights advocates to expand the "public" focus of mainstream human rights to include and give priority to this "private" realm, thereby revolutionizing the very field of human rights.[5]

In this article, I will examine the ideological framework within which right-wing forces in India have appropriated Hindu religion and culture in strategic ways to achieve their goals. The dream of a "Hindu India" (in which the Right's idiosyncratic definition of Hinduism rules) requires all other religious groups, particularly Muslims, to acknowledge the superiority and supremacy of the Hindu majority. In the process, Hindus who do not accept the Right's formulations are viewed as not "true" Hindus. Of the many political parties and organizations that have espoused the ideology of *Hindutva* (Hindu worldview) over the past two decades, the Bharatiya Janata Party (BJP) remains the most prominent. Its political successes demand a closer examination of the ideas it stands for. However, any analysis of Hindu Right ideology is complicated by the differences between its announced worldview (for example, the BJP's political manifestos), the rhetoric of leaders who recently have given priority to issues other than *Hindutva,* and a variety of policy approaches ranging from moderate to hard-line among the Hindu Right's leadership. Whatever the political exigencies to which the Hindu Right responds from moment to moment, women remain an important component of its agenda, be it the Right's hijacking of feminist demands for a Uniform Civil Code (UCC), or the targeting of minority women for sexual violence, or the real neglect of the welfare of all women.

Women in State, Religion, and Culture

Floya Anthias and Nira Yuval-Davis have shown how "the central dimensions of the roles of women are constituted around the relationships of collectivities to the state." At the same time, the "central dimensions of the relationships between collectivities and the state are constituted around the roles of women."[6] Accordingly, women's centrality in structuring and maintaining religious law and practice makes any critical reference to their position a potential threat to the entire social structure and problematizes the state's interest in gender justice.

Religion-based law, which monitors the realm of the "private" so assiduously, has gendered consequences that extend far beyond its immediate subject, the woman. As many writers note, the subordination of women in the home is central to the maintenance of unequal power relations everywhere else in society.[7] Women are, of course, the most visible and significant embodiments of culture in their appearance, demeanor, and language. They are the primary socializers of children in the customs of their community. They are the first to be targeted in violence against a group's cultural particularity, whether in organized state violence as in ethnic war or genocide, or in domestic social conflicts, such as Indian "upper-caste" targeting of "lower-caste" women and girls for abuse. Complicating the situation is the reality that, "while women have been historically excluded from the formal processes of articulating and interpreting religious law, they are active participants in the formation of religious practice."[8]

Multireligious countries with a long history of coexistence as well as periodic confrontation, such as India, are constantly adjusting themselves to a plethora of still-powerful legacies, including a political history of different religious groups in power in different parts of the country at different times; the opportunistic manipulation of religion by the state (under colonial as well as post-Independence governments); the strictures of a secularizing Constitution in the midst of a variety of legally recognized distinct religious legal systems; and the heightened demand from all levels of society for a new, self-conscious clarification of the boundaries of legitimate doctrine and behavior in religion.

India has a long way to go in protecting and guaranteeing women's rights in many areas, particularly economic well-being, health and reproductive rights, education, domestic violence, and gender violence committed by authorities, such as rape and torture. Indeed, the very number of females in India is falling dramatically due to a variety of economic and cultural phenomena, including poor pre- and post-natal care, which results in high female morbidity and mortality; poor feeding of female infants and children (boys and men are routinely fed first at family meals); neglect of female health at all stages of life; and the abuse of reproductive technologies such as amniocentesis and abortion in the culturally sanctioned preference for sons. Consequently, India today has one of the lowest female–male population ratios in the world: 927 women to 1,000 men in 1991 (the lowest since the statistics began to be compiled—compare the 1991 figures to 972:1,000 at the turn of the century). Given the highly visible participation of women and girls in the freedom struggle and the emancipatory goals of the political leaders in independent India, the backslide of gender justice is a tragic irony. Many Indian observers like Kumkum Sangari and Sudesh Vaid feel that the recent rise in gender-specific abuses, such as poverty and economic marginalization, police atrocities, and dowry murders, has "shattered the post-colonial complacency about the improving status of women and with it has gone the legitimacy of nationalist models of reform and 'development.'"[9] In a similar vein, others have argued that the legitimacy of the post-colonial state itself is in crisis, in large part because it has been unable to tackle the proliferation of movements for regional autonomy, competition for economic resources, and decentralization of power, resulting from uneven regional development.[10]

Complicating this abysmal scenario for women's rights are recent upsurges of sub-nationalisms that unfavorably target women in symbolic and real ways. Since 1980, a strong new challenge to the nationalist hope of a united secular India has come from the communal demands of Hindu right-wing parties and organizations, whose exclusionary ideology of *Hindutva* is designed to establish a strong Hindu state for Hindus that would accept only those minorities that acknowledge Hindu supremacy.[11] The ideological coalition between the various political parties, political movements, cultural organizations, and other loosely defined groupings that constitute the Hindu Right (led by the BJP, the Rashtriya Swayamsevak Sangh or RSS, the Vishwa Hindu Parishad or VHP, and the Shiv Sena in the western state of Maharashtra) has survived various changes and realignments since the early 1980s. However, the roots of the Hindu Right, as both an ideology (designed to cleanse Mother India of the polluting British) and a political movement (which eventually assassinated M.K. Gandhi in 1948 for his neglect of Hindu supremacy), are deeply sunk in the soil of British colonial rule in India.

Religion and Jurisprudence Under British Colonial Rule

British colonialists in the eighteenth and nineteenth centuries mistakenly believed that complex and ever-evolving Hindu religious understandings and customs could be codified into law by relying on particular texts and schools of Hindu thought, and that the uppermost caste of *brahmanas* were the sole custodians and interpreters. This had "devastating consequences," as Richard Lariviere notes.[12] The insistence on one set of laws per religion encouraged cultural nativism among Indians, and rigidified those oppressive religious practices that adversely affected girls and women. While the relationship between government, elites, social reformers, and religious leadership is always complex, particularly when cast against the backdrop of lengthy colonial rule, women remain one of the social groups most affected by subsequent developments.[13]

Indeed, contemporary jurisprudence on religious matters in post-colonial India continues to simultaneously deny and manipulate the real flexibility of Hinduism to permit the justices to behave like the earlier *brahmana* experts, who cited texts that were "mere window dressing for the interpretations of Hindu law they [sought] to promulgate."[14] In divide-and-rule fashion, essentializing "law codes" were constructed by the British for other similarly complex religions.[15] These law codes or personal laws, as they are known in India, focus on those aspects of family life that disproportionately involve women in normative ways, such as marriage and divorce, property and inheritance, and adoption. Legislation over several decades has built up a network of personal laws within the Hindu, Muslim, Christian, and Parsi religious communities. The differences between the personal laws of Hindus and Muslims dominate the Hindu Right agenda as seen most recently in inflammatory rhetoric against Muslims, support of discriminatory policies, and deadly riots.

Religion and Rights in Independent India

Post-Independence politics permitted reformist legislation, such as the Hindu Women's Code Bill, but favored a hands-off approach to the other religions. While this was argued in the pious language of non-interference with minority faiths, the communal bloodbaths of the 1947 Partition and the creation of a

Muslim homeland, Pakistan, were on the minds of the framers of the 1950 Constitution. Rather than insist on a UCC that would, in the process, draw the teeth of the many personal laws and their gender-discriminatory provisions, the framers settled on merely declaring a UCC an eventual goal: "The State shall endeavor to secure for citizens a uniform civil code."[16] The recent debates over a UCC and the accompanying Hindu Right's manipulation of the idea of a UCC to tar Muslims (in what Ratna Kapur and Brenda Cossman call "the communalized dimension of the gendered discourse of Hindutva")[17] is the chief consequence of this fifty-year-old legacy of timidity.[18]

The Indian Constitution casts a very wide net of religious protections and guarantees. However, it subsumes Buddhists, Jains, and Sikhs under "Hindu" in an idiosyncratic reading of the three religions, which colors the government's understanding of the application of personal laws. This has generated strong opposition from neo-Buddhists (made up chiefly of converts from "lower caste" Hindus) and Sikhs, particularly during the rise of Sikh separatist movements in the 1980s. This legal understanding of the religious communities under personal laws makes all women particularly vulnerable under laws that put religious freedom far ahead of gender equality.

The framers of the Constitution included a wide range of rights and freedoms, including the freedom of thought, conscience, and religion, and the right to proselytize religion.[19] These rights are subject to certain specified conditions, such as public order, laws regulating practices that may pertain to religion, and other parts of the Constitution. Progressive and secular forces have protested the failure of the authorities to take these conditions into account and curtail the Hindu Right's excesses. Other religious freedoms enshrined in the Constitution include the right to manage religious institutions and property; tax relief for religious purposes; limits on religious instruction in educational institutions receiving state assistance; and protection of the rights of all minorities, including linguistic and religious, in the cultural and educational fields on a variety of issues.[20]

The link between religion and the status of women is recognized in the Constitution. Mindful of centuries-old religious, customary, and social complexities, the framers placed a positive duty upon Indians to "promote harmony and the spirit of common brotherhood amongst all people of India transcending religious, linguistic and regional or sectional diversities," and "to renounce practices derogatory to the dignity of women."[21]

To what extent the Constitution has been influential in the active promotion of women's rights is an open question. As Indian feminist Madhu Kishwar observes, "the present family structure in India ensures the subordination and exploitation of women in a way that puts them beyond the purview of most of the fundamental rights guaranteed by the Constitution."[22] Since the 1980s, the expanding women's movement has used the law wherever possible to further its goals, but has been frequently stymied by unresponsive judges, police, and bureaucrats. Feminist lawyers like Indira Jaising also find the conditions attached to the freedom of conscience set forth in Article 25 "patently unconstitutional" because they permit state enforcement of religion.[23] However, despite a collapsing national legal infrastructure of overworked courts and insufficient resources, the Constitution has become central again to the UCC debate and its impact on women of all religions.

The National Human Rights Commission (NHRC) was established by the government in 1993. To the extent that the NHRC is dependent on complaints being brought before it, it has not developed a record on the protection of women's rights, let alone minority women's rights. For example, in the 1995–96 fiscal year, only three cases of custodial rape (rape by police) were reported to the NHRC. Even the U.S. State Department recognizes that "although evidence is lacking, a larger number [of cases] appears credible, in light of other evidence of abusive behavior by police and the likelihood that many rapes go unreported due to a sense of shame."[24]

All Religions Equal, or *Sarva Dharma Sambhava*

The Constitution's meaning for religious rights has been further complicated by the prevalence of two strains of thought regarding the place of religion in a secular India: the Gandhian notion of equal respect for all religions or *sarva dharma sambhava* (by and large the dominant tendency in Indian legal practice), and the separation of religion from politics, best articulated by Jawaharlal Nehru and generally thought to be less applicable. And yet, whether the principle of *sarva dharma sambhava* means simply that all religions must receive equal treatment, or that the outcome of all religions must be equal, permitting the law to treat some religions differently to achieve equal results, is unsettled. In the case of women's rights, a UCC would challenge both principles by purposefully eliminating religion-based personal laws, and thereby the option to adjudicate between competing visions.

The philosopher and former president of India, S. Radhakrishnan, wrote that "secularism is not a positive religion.... We hold that no religion should be given preferential status."[25] The goal of secularism dominated Indian politics until the rise of the Hindu Right, which now labels the long-standing understanding of secularism as nothing more than a code word for favoritism of minority religions. Thus, the Right defines all legal and political consideration of disadvantages experienced by minorities as discriminatory and anti-secularist.[26] As the militant organization, Rashtriya Swayamsevak Sangh (RSS), proclaims: "The RSS demands no special rights for Hindus. At the same time, it is against giving any concession to other religious minority groups."[27] The concept "all religions equal" has drawn fire from several advocates of secularism. For them, as summarized by Kapur and Cossman, "*sarva dharma sambhava* as an approach to the way secularism operates reinforces the very categories of community and in turn the forces of communalism that ultimately threatens to undermine secularism."[28]

A number of Hindu Right ideologues from pre-Independence to the present have asserted a particular vision of *sarva dharma sambhava*. Despite their scornful dismissal of secularism as nothing more than politically weighted preferences, some Hindu Right leaders retain the term, albeit in an idiosyncratic redefinition. For example, one leader of the BJP quoted the party manifesto in 1990 to insist that "the BJP believes in positive secularism which, according to our constitution-makers, meant *sarva dharma sambhava* and which does not connote an irreligious state."[29] (The so-called moderate wing of the Hindu Right usually prefers not to engage in openly bloodthirsty anti-Muslim rhetoric, choosing instead to manipulate existing understandings to simultaneously disarm and warn its critics.) The BJP's insistence that the majority has no particular advantage leads to astonishing and contradictory syllogistic assertions such as the same leader's comment in 1994: "The Bharatiya Janata Party believes that Indian secularism has its roots in *Hindutva*. India is secular because it is essentially Hindu. Theocracy is alien to Hindu tradition."[30]

Role of the Hindu Right in a Secular India

Scholars offer several reasons for the rise in fundamentalisms in India since the early 1980s. In the political arena, Mrs. Gandhi's frank playing of the communal card to gain vote blocs after her return to power in 1980 was rooted in her administration of the 1960s. At the social level, in towns where Muslims had achieved some economic success, the majority Hindu communities searched for a sinister explanation of why minorities were expanding into traditionally Hindu occupations. Sikata Banerjee notes that women were doubly disempowered, as individuals and as relatives of disheartened men, and responded with alacrity to the Hindu Right's recognition and call to violent action.[31] The studied indifference of the government to the horrific anti-Sikh riots of 1984 following Mrs. Gandhi's assassination by her Sikh bodyguards, growing Hindu Right hatred of "the Muslim," and

Hindu Right contempt for all "proselytizing religions" (which simply meant all non-Hindu religions), in turn encouraged the growth of right-wing organizations in the minority religions with aggressively defensive agendas and back-to-tradition controls over women. These factors must be placed in the wider context of the breakdown of centralized government and decades of Congress Party dominance, the weakening of political organizations, and the emergence of new and politically hungry elites. Where the Hindu Right has significant social clout or political power, it has won over the police, judiciary, bureaucrats, and politicians. Instead of protecting the beleaguered minority populations, these authorities often openly encourage communal behavior and even violence.

Anthropologist Stanley Tambiah's assessment of communalism in his native Sri Lanka can be applied to India as well: the Hindu Right today is "a majority with a minority complex."[32] The Hindu Right claims to speak for India's Hindu majority, about 83 percent of the population. In reality, its primary support comes from the "upper" castes and urban bourgeoisie, although more recently it has made a concerted effort to reach out to hitherto-neglected groups such as the "lowest" castes and tribals. The Hindu Right sees all other religions as proselytizing faiths and therefore invasive and manipulative. Muslims, the largest minority group, comprise roughly 12 percent of the population, but are seen as "spoiled" by affirmative action policies and therefore overly demanding and too big for their boots. In an ironic twist on the Tambiah thesis, the BJP's 1990 Manifesto admonished the very minority groups the Hindu Right has targeted for exclusion and violence: "it is also imperative for national integration that minorities do not develop a minority complex."[33]

What is this Hindu worldview that the right wing fears is under attack by all other religions? To the extent that a religious text, and a clearly identified body of experts, are key components upon which the fundamentalist draws, Hinduism is the least conducive of major world religions to fundamentalism. There is no one word or one law of god (or gods), no single or key text, no authoritative priesthood, and no interpretive religious body. And yet, it is precisely the imprecision and lack of firm boundaries in Hinduism that the Hindu Right draws upon to its advantage in highly political ways. An expansive Hinduism also makes it difficult for secularist forces to combat the tough, stark simplicity of what the Hindu Right has constructed as "real" or "pure" Hinduism. The Hindu Right has picked a few tropes from the ever-expanding multitude of texts, deities, philosophies, and rituals that constitute the infinite sprawl of what the colonial British sought ineffectually to contain in the word "Hinduism," and deployed them to serve its political ideology.

These "traditional" symbols and rituals are an amalgam of selections from North Indian regional religious practices with uppercaste and upperclass slants, and reifications of colonial practices. Key tropes include the priority given to a handful of the innumerable festivals and holy days in the "high" Hindu tradition alone; saffron-colored flag and clothing to symbolize Hinduism; uniforms and rituals in the militant groups, such as uniform shirts and shorts, exercise drills and snappy salutes; and the invocation of Rama, a deity with regional and sectarian popularity, often to violent end, as in the criminal destruction of the sixteenth-century mosque in the northern town of Ayodhya in December 1992 and the subsequent riots.

"Hinduism in danger" is key to the right-wing understanding of Indian history as one long bloody march of Islamic oppression. Consequently, Hindu survival today is predicated on a preemptive strike against other religions, Islam in particular. This right-wing insistence on a "true" Hinduism, backed by violence, requires all those who call themselves Hindu in India today to measure themselves against this new conception of "the good Hindu," with its gender-specific attributes. To speak of Hinduism or of being Hindu today is, therefore, to speak about politics as well. Paradoxically, the right wing's desire to establish a common language through which all Hindus can unite has sifted through the exhilarating multiplicity and jumble of Hinduism and set up a handful of rigid practices and beliefs that exclude more than they include, in ideology as well as in adherents.

Hindu Religious Manipulation of Gender

Religious manipulation of gender is primarily a series of paradoxes. Among the political and social ideas that instrumentalized the "feminine" and brought women into the public sphere of protest and imprisonment in the mass movement to oust the British colonial power was Gandhian thought, which "evoked 'tradition' by ahistoricizing its tenets and mythological figures." This approach continues to be applied in increasingly anti-female ways. As Ketu Katrak comments, "the dangers of reifying 'traditions,' of treating them as the transcendent emblems of a culture, are felt most negatively by women particularly after Independence when the rationale of justifying traditions against the enemy is no longer needed."[34]

There is an awkward tension between the modernistic and the traditional patriarchal in the policies of the Hindu Right, with difficult consequences for women. Today's Hindu Right extends Gandhi's ideals of the long-suffering and self-sacrificing Hindu mythological heroines of Sita, Savitri, and Draupadi to the militant Durga and Kali—primarily as part of its fantastical, mythified, defensive responses against the evil Muslim male whose rapacious designs on Hindu women are an inevitable extension of centuries of Muslim political domination and accompanying religious brutality. Accordingly, the Hindu Right woman's "notion of the Feminine Self and the space of relative freedom that she carves out for herself *absolutely depend upon* constructing 'the muslim' as demonic [and] threatening."[35] This is supremely ironic and tragic in an India that contains what has come to be one of the most flexible and varied manifestations of Islam anywhere. Indeed, different religious communities all over India routinely share many characteristics, such as the caste system, marriage practices, religious rituals, and saints.

Similar retention of the old and manipulation of the new in social developments inform the BJP's key declarations and policies regarding women. Since the early 1980s, the BJP has asserted that "the BJP looks to womankind as *Matri Shakti* (the power of the mother)"—a striking religious image that imbues the sacrificing dutiful mother and wife with divine power. All strongly worded language of equality in policy statements is qualified by a particular understanding of "tradition": "The BJP pledges itself to restore to women the position of equality with men that the Indian tradition proposed and accepted." What this single "tradition" consists of is for the BJP alone to define through its continuing declarations and policies.[36]

The Right's policies on women focus on traditional roles, but in so doing they also provide women with a number of empowering options. Social reforms are pledged to poor and slum women in the areas of maternal and child health care, kitchen advances such as the smokeless stove, and sanitation. Local units of right-wing parties have established income-generating programs, daycare facilities, and cultural festivals. Extreme right parties and cultural organizations also give women physical training in self-defense, and strategically deploy symbolism of warrior goddesses and historical heroines from the Hindu pantheon who fought to maintain individual honor as well as social hierarchies. Hatred and contempt for the Muslim Other is an organizing principle, fusing personal female honor (against the lascivious Muslim male) with group identity and loyalty (threatened by minority protections in laws and public policies) to create a gendered nexus of Hindu domination, national integrity, and personal worth.

Patriotism, self-worth, and religious triumphalism color the Right's assertion of a uniquely Indian/Hindu woman. As early as the 1985 UN Conference on Women in Nairobi, the women's wing of the BJP expressed its disgust for issues too "vulgar" and "irrelevant" to India, like lesbian existence and pay for domestic work. The language of liberation is a threat to the "true" Indian woman:

> We conceptually differ from what is termed as the women's liberation movement in the west. We require a sort of readjustment in the social and economic set up. No fundamental change in values is desirable. Women in India ever had a pride of place within the household, and the society. This has only to be reestablished and reaffirmed.[37]

To urban middle-class women today who face increased daily harassment as they enter the workplace, take crowded public transportation, and shoulder multiple responsibilities, this language, which simultaneously reinforces accepted roles while suggesting avenues for improvement, is particularly seductive. Women are presented with a neatly logical and ultimately convincing set of connections between the good wife and mother, the good Indian, and the good Hindu, all within the overarching framework of a revered, powerful, glorious womanhood. As Kapur and Cossman observe, "the problems that women face in contemporary society are seen through this lens of a fall from grace—that the harmony that came of respect and honor of women's distinctive roles as wives and mothers in the past has been lost [to evil scheming Muslims] and must be restored."[38] These Hindu Right strategies also have given a number of women an outlet for their creative energies. There is a sense of liberation—an opportunity to enter the public realm, albeit under male-dictated terms. Some women have spoken of the self-confidence that martial training gives them. Many take pride in the ideal of the strong, chaste, fearless Hindu woman who must learn to protect herself from the uncontrollable lusts of predatory Muslim men.

And yet, this is situated within the framework of return to the home. Changes in the Hindu woman's life are designed to underscore and enhance already-entrenched roles and status. "An Indian woman will command the affection of the father, the love of the husband, and the respect of her son only when she has been provided with equal rights and opportunities."[39] Feminists are disturbed by these strategies because, instead of investigating traditional treatments of women, patriarchal institutions such as religion remain the beneficiaries of these women's heightened commitment to their Hindu identity: "the reference point for equal treatment is religion, rather than sex."[40]

The leadership of the Hindu Right is male. Its constituents are primarily from the urban middle and upper classes, "upper" castes, and educated and business communities. A handful of colorful women (ranging from former royalty to self-professed ascetics) have been allowed a certain amount of the spotlight; their rhetoric is even more hate-filled and bloodthirsty than that of their male counterparts. Women leaders make frequent pronouncements in support of male leadership positions—for example, that widow burning or *sati* is a noble Hindu tradition and the highest expression of a chaste female identity. Over the years, the male leadership has noted, variously, that battered wives must stay within their brutal marriages; that divorce is pointless because women inevitably remarry and have no guarantee that the next husband would not also be a brute; that feminism is a conspiracy to import promiscuity and rape into a pure India; that widow remarriage is a "Western" concept and unsuitable to India.

The Hindu Right also has appropriated the language of outrage on issues which traditionally have been the domain of feminists, such as media depictions of women, sexual violence, self-defense, and pornography. However, as illustrated by the example of obscenity, "the secular women's movement has framed the issue as one of women's rights—the right to equality, the right to be free from sexual harassment," while for the Hindu Right, "obscenity is framed as a violation of women's traditional identity." Consequently, the narrowly rendered "traditional" roles of women (primarily the modest and chaste wife and mother) protect only those women who adhere to them. For the right wing, then, "men cannot be held to be at fault."[41] In the Hindu Right's formulation of the origins of violence against women, the discipline of women, through external and internalized controls, is seen as ultimately necessary for the enhancement of women's status. Continuing the contradiction between a regimented morality and the plurality of democracy, the BJP's 1998 Manifesto, *Our Vision, Our Will, Our Way,* declares the necessity of "a normative moral code" in society without which "a healthy polity and democracy cannot survive."

Uniform Civil Code

Against this backdrop, the issue of the UCC continues to demonstrate the nexus between women's rights, legal protections, and religion. In the 1980s and early 1990s, the debate regarding a uniform legal code that would replace the various personal laws of the various religions galvanized all groups across the political spectrum, particularly political parties, cultural organizations, legal societies, and women's groups. Since the personal laws pertain to the realm of the private, women's groups feel they have the largest stake in the outcome. In all the personal laws, a particular religious vision of woman's life and purpose circumscribes all matters closest to women's interests: marriage and its dissolution, bride wealth and dowry, adoption, succession, property, and inheritance. The problem for women's groups is acute: If women are both subjects and agents of change, how can one disentangle the two oppositional agendas of the religious right and women's groups without losing sight of the goal?

The government faced a similar dilemma in the pivotal lawsuit that brought thousands out onto the streets, some protesting the secular assertion of women's rights and some applauding the secular trumping of discriminatory personal law by the courts. The 1985 Shah Bano case was a watershed for right-wing targeting of minorities in the name of uplifting minority women. The Supreme Court's ruling that Shah Bano, a divorced Muslim woman, was to receive a (paltry) maintenance payment from her ex-husband flew in the face of traditionalist readings of Islam. Indeed, the Court went so far as to interpret a Koranic verse on its own and without the aid of Islamic commentaries, thereby delivering a slap in the face to Muslim jurists in both procedure as well as interpretation.

Confronted with electoral defeat in the midst of this upheaval, the Rajiv Gandhi government submitted to the bullying of the All India Muslim Personal Law Board, composed of mullahs and conservative men. In so doing, the government chose to view them as representative of all Muslims, rather than listening to the wide variety of other Muslim voices that were less orthodox, more aware of the flexibility of Muslim personal law, and willing to acknowledge the status of Muslim women as a serious subject for informed debate. Consequently, the government passed the ironically named Muslim Women's (Protection of Rights in Divorce) Bill which violated the Constitution and abandoned the divorced woman to the mercy of local Muslim authorities without recourse to favorable non-religious law, such as section 125 of the 1973 Criminal Procedure Code. As a result of the Muslim Women's Bill, section 125 today remains available to all but a Muslim woman.[42] In addition to effectively denying protection of women's rights in divorce, this legislation permits Muslim husbands to divorce their wives with impunity because the Bill places the burden of providing economic support for the wife on the community, and not on the husband.

The Hindu Right, which had vociferously supported the Shah Bano judgment as reforming an oppressive Muslim legal system, protecting Muslim women from Muslim men, and eventually moving toward the goal of a truly Hindu India, was inflamed by the Muslim Women's Bill. It saw the Bill as "favoritism" and further "pampering" of the "spoiled" Muslims, and stepped up its activities. However, since well before Shah Bano, Muslim women have been acutely aware of their difficult position: they are frequently oppressed by their religious laws and customs, they belong to a beleaguered religious minority, and they have not gained from the many reformist debates among Muslim leadership continuing since the nineteenth century. Muslim women are now trapped between three major forces: reformist sympathizers who are predominantly Hindu (in a debate where religious affiliation is always relevant); defensive, protectionist, patriarchal Muslim leaders; and an ideological climate that is critical of all things Muslim.

The Hindu Right's hijacking of feminist language to support all women suffering under discriminatory personal laws underscores the irony of espousing simultaneously women's primary role in the home, and a UCC designed to eliminate women's religion-based subordination in the home. The Hindu Right's instrumentalizing of women of all communities is manifest in its support for a UCC within a framework of equality and justice for all, but only on clearly stated terms of woman's "natural" roles and obligations within the family. In its chapter on women, the BJP's 1998 Manifesto restates its commitment to a UCC. Such a UCC, however, includes among its components "an end to polygamy"—an unambiguous underscoring of the Hindu Right's anger at Muslim marriage practices. The virulent rhetoric of the Hindu Right has brought a chill to the equal rights debate. Women's groups reduced their support for the UCC when it became the Hindu Right's cause, although they still acknowledge its value. Recently, Muslim women's groups have begun to examine Muslim personal laws with an eye to reform. Political parties, such as the Communist Party of India, have started their own Muslim women's groups. The debate continues in seminars, the press, and on campuses. At the national level, the unfortunate alignment of the Hindu Right with women's rights issues has prompted progressive groups to move away from promoting the UCC toward a focus on reforming each religion from within. This is a cautious and much slower strategy, with not only an uncertain outcome but also the very real possibility of backlash against women from the threatened powerholders within the religious community.

Women in the Hindu Right

The presence of women in the most virulent and hate-filled Hindu right-wing groups calls into question the totalizing category of "women," even as women are targeted as a group for rape and mutilation in incidences of religious scapegoating. Recent examples include the anti-Sikh riots in 1984, the anti-Muslim agitation leading up to the destruction by the Hindu Right of the sixteenth-century mosque at Ayodhya in 1992, and the riots that followed.

There are over five hundred Hindu Right organizations in India today, many with paramilitary-style training for their male and female cadets. In response, some Muslim Right organizations have made their presence felt here and there, in Kerala, Hyderabad, Delhi. There are also a few right-wing Sikh groups in the Punjab. All these groups rely on rigid, clear notions of the "good" woman—all are willing to inflict strict punishment and humiliation on women who ostensibly dress improperly or behave in an unchaste fashion, including verbal harassment and abuse, floggings, and shaving of the woman's head.[43]

In writing of the riots in Bombay in December 1992 and January 1993, Sikata Banerjee observes that within Bombay's slums, where roughly 50 percent of Bombay's population lives and which are home to large sections of the Muslim minority as well as Hindu Right supporters, the Muslim areas were targeted with systematic and organized violence. In these riots, in which over one thousand persons were killed and many more injured, Hindu Right women mobilized in groups to show up at hotspots. They demonstrated their strength in numbers to prevent the arrest of Shiv Sena leaders, many of whom openly acknowledged their role in violence and incitement to riot. Hindu Right women attacked Muslim areas and participated in the violence, even assaulting Muslim women.

Hindu women with whom the right-wing ideology resonates can be seen as the key to the success of the Right's agenda. "The dominant familial ideology which underlies the women's rights agenda of the Hindu Right is effective precisely because it is not being imposed by fiat, but rather, because of the way in which it shapes the subjectivity of women within the movement, who in turn, are shaping the discourse within which these issues are being articulated."[44] Hindu Right organizations bring together women from the same background, class, and castes. Similarities of experience forge a sense of unity of identity alongside a unity of purpose, which encourages a heightened communal solidarity. The tree of beleaguered Mother India, they reason, must be watered with the blood of the Muslim tyrants and their children who continue to hold post-Independence India in thrall through "secular" liberal guilt and affirmative action policies. Feminist groups, by contrast, bring together women from diverse backgrounds to work on issue-based projects that benefit themselves as well as others.

Outstanding Issues and Questions

Relational Religions

In multireligious societies, how is a religion defined, by itself and by others, *in relation to* another religion or religions? I have shown that Hindus and Muslims in the highly politicized religious environment of contemporary India are able to reconstitute themselves as "true" Hindus or Muslims in significant part *in relation to* each other. The essential integrity of each religious group is relational rather than *sui generis*. The changing nature of this engagement gives reason to hope that the excesses of the religious Right can indeed be addressed.

If indeed all religious personal laws have discriminatory provisions that disproportionately disadvantage women, then that could be a starting point to talk about women as a social group. In such a discussion, certain aspects of a woman's religious identity may be temporarily bracketed to begin a conversation about the experiences of women. In this scenario, human rights can serve as a sharp reminder that women were an integral part of the original issue, and can provide the terms enabling all participants to define, grapple with, and find a use for principles of justice, fairness, equality, and opportunity.

Religions in Crisis Mode

One important lesson to be learned from India today is that people define themselves exclusively in terms of merely one component of their multiple identities only in times of crisis. Human rights advocates should not repeat the mistake of the Indian government, which views religious affiliation as the only, and trumping, identity of a person, thereby making "a clear equation between religious law and community identity."[45] Indeed, when we take into account the complexity of an individual self, religious identities show themselves to be as relational as other identities. For example, a woman's caste, along with her class, linguistic grouping, and marital status are seen by others to determine her ability to be a chaste, and therefore "true," woman.

The recent construction of "true" Hinduism and, in response, of "true" Islam, highlights the difficulties of deciding who the religious partner is in any engagement between human rights and the voices of religion. Muslim male leadership and Muslim female voices have found it hard to combat the weight of Hindu formulations of "Muslim," which are entrenched in ordinary social discourse. In writing of the myth of the self-evident and homogeneous community of Muslims, Amrita Chhachhi notes countering evidence of class, caste, and regional differences on a vast scale in practices such as marriage, veiling, and kinship. She quotes one of many writers on this subject who recognize Muslim community in primarily an emotional sense:

> The bond is quite tenuous, like all religious bonds, it acquires salience only when threatened; otherwise, it operates more at a sentimental rather than substantive level, and for real life issues it gets weak if not canceled, once it comes into contact with other more basic bonds of socio-economic cohesion.[46]

When Religion Itself Promotes Injustice

Where does the language of engagement lie when existing, on-the-ground religious notions promote intolerance and injustice? One way to accomplish a greater discussion of religion, gender, and human rights might be to insist that groups on the ground not use human rights as a yardstick (as if it were an outside, internally exclusive system), but as the immediate language of the argument. Rather than asking whether the religious practice or law in question, such as women's inheritance law, can measure up to human rights principles, why not start with the human rights understanding of fairness in property issues and ask what would change for religion if women received more equitable treatment in the division of property. Asking that question will set into motion directions of inquiry that might highlight the self-serving nature of the pious recourse to religion by the beneficiaries of the existing practice. This demystifying process, in turn, might unmask the politics of the religious defense and make the interaction between religion and human rights less implacably rigid. If this approach is followed to its logical destination, then perhaps considerations of gender will not throw religion into such a crisis that it cannot continue without major reconfiguration of doctrine. There is room for flexibility and maneuverability in the direction of greater justice. The details that govern our daily lives are rarely as cruelly rigid as a dominant (and domineering), no-way-out interpretation of religion may suggest.

What can human rights say to the millions who believe, however erroneously, that their current religious practices and laws are immutable and ahistorical, and therefore trump all argument? This is the reality that India is faced with today. Human rights must not turn a cautious or respectful approach into reverence to the point of paralysis. To say that religion is nothing more than faith and obedience to those who claim greater access to their god is simply wrong, on its own terms. The histories of all religions reveal them to be politics-driven, compromise-ridden, negotiated, flexible, temporary understandings of definitionally imperfect human beings. All religions contain widely differing schools of interpretation. It is the socially powerful group, with latent as well as displayed power, that wins the day and not the debate. And it is human rights language that can return monologue to conversation, and declaration to debate—because rights in religion will have to be debated, and announced.

India's Human Rights Obligations

In addition to India's constitutional and legal protections of religious rights and women's rights, the major international human rights instruments to which India is a party, but sadly violates, exemplify the general support of equality and nondiscrimination between the sexes.[47] For example, Article 27 of the International Covenant on Civil and Political Rights protects the rights of minorities to "enjoy their own culture, to profess and practice their own religion, or to use their own language." The Women's Convention contains several references, like Article 5, to the obligation of state parties to take appropriate measures, such as enacting legislation, to modify the social and cultural patterns that discriminate against women. Similarly, Article 2 of the Universal Declaration of Human Rights specifically protects rights without regard for religion or sex. In international human rights, there is clear recognition of the multiplicity of identity aspects of our lives in the denial of trumping privileges to religion when confronted by women's rights concerns.

Under the terms of these international treaties as well as domestic law, India can be held accountable for systematic failure to enforce the law, and systematic failure to guarantee equal protection under the law. The Indian government, both at the federal level and in various states, has remained inactive during times of religious ferment; it also has actively encouraged anti-minority violence. At the level of parliamentary action, governments such as Rajiv Gandhi's at the time of the Shah Bano crisis have pushed through gender-discriminatory legislation in order to appease the vocal male leadership of minorities who threatened the government at the ballot box. Even concern expressed in the platform of the 1994 Women's Conference in Beijing regarding the full and equal participation of women in all spheres of public and private life, including economic and political decision-making, has been countered by the Hindu Right's use of women's rights to score points against other communities, as well as to discipline its "own" women. The Indian government can be held accountable here as well, for failing to follow through on the promises it made in Beijing.

Speaking/Seeking a Common Language

We have seen that the multiple pressures of coexistence in a multireligious society like India's are complicated by gender in a variety of ways. The status of women, in India as elsewhere, very quickly becomes instrumentalized in the service of other agendas. The vocabularies of authenticity, liberation, protectionism, and self-assertion are interwoven at the levels of individual, community, and nation, catching the voiceless "woman" in their net of rhetorical posturings. The stresses of capitalist development, and the accompanying changes in social structures and women's roles, have generated an increased emphasis on traditional patriarchal structures and increasing attempts to control and contain women. Women's groups, whatever their position on religion, face the familiar human rights dilemma of asking the state (and the Third World state is heavily implicated in the daily lives of citizens at all levels—legal, economic, social, and political) to rectify the wrongs the state itself has perpetuated through neglect or action.

In such an India, women's rights advocates seek a common language across religions, recognizing both the differences in personal laws and the similarities in oppression. They seek to discuss with all women the discriminatory provisions regarding those areas of life that involve and affect women the most. Here, the language of human rights must not be trumped by religion. As I have suggested above, the two can indeed be interwoven and are not mutually exclusive.

The right to choose between personal laws and civil procedure already exists in India—for example, a person may elect to marry under one or the other. However, cultural norms and practices are so strong that the overwhelming majority of marriages are solemnized by religion. If reform is to come from within the religion, as many scholars and activists desire, it will be, perforce, reluctant, slow, and without respected input from the disadvantaged groups—here, women. Hence, change must occur at the same time from secular realms such as the law. The law is not particularly secular in India—it is a social and discursive process, addressing and reifying religion in significant and influential ways. The courts have never shrunk from delivering judgments on religious matters. Indeed, they have a long and established record of seeking legal solutions to religious disputes in an engaged and activist spirit. Within such a legal tradition, is a UCC to be set up as a secular code that ignores all religion, or takes religion into account only to end its discriminatory provisions? This is not a decision as yet but a process of engaged discussion, difficult as it is to achieve in an India where the religious lines have been drawn in the vocabularies of community solidarity and gender expendability.

The Hindu Right speaks many of the same words as women's rights advocates, but with opposite meaning and antagonistic intent. In the Hindu Right's understanding of secularism, and of a UCC, women are instrumentalized. The shameful appropriation of women's rights language to direct hate and violence against minority men—and in so doing, against all minorities—forces minority women to subsume their feminist awareness in solidarity with the rest of their beleaguered community. After all, women are viewed as representatives of their communities by others as well as by themselves. Further, the Hindu Right's targeting of Muslims hugely overrides their supposed concern for gender oppression among Muslims—the abuse and rape of Muslim women is an inherent part of anti-Muslim violence.[48]

In the midst of this is the "Hindu woman," seeking the terms of equality and strength and respect, and finding a seductive response only in the bad history and virulent hatreds of the Right. The failure of Indian society, government, and courts to respond to women's concerns on all fronts has left a gap which the Hindu Right, with its batons and mass demonstrations and riots, has attempted to fill and use to its advantage. The most successful challenge to the Hindu Right ultimately must come from human rights, in a sympathetic but tough engagement with all religions, all women, and all that is right in contemporary India.

Notes

1. See Abdullahi A. An-Na'im, "Religious Minorities Under Islamic Law and the Limits of Cultural Relativism," *Human Rights Quarterly*, vol. 9, no. 1 (1987), 1–18; An-Na'im, "The Rights of Women and International Law in the Muslim Context," *Whittier Law Review* vol. 9, no. 3 (1987): 491–516.
2. See Kevin Boyle and Julie Sheen, eds., *Freedom of Religion and Belief* (New York: Routledge, 1997).
3. Abdullahi A. An-Na'im, "Toward a Cross-Cultural Approach to Defining International Standards of Human Rights: The Meaning of Cruel, Inhuman or Degrading Treatment or Punishment," 20, in Abdullahi An-Na'im, ed., *Human Rights in Cross-Cultural Perspectives: A Quest for Consensus* (Philadelphia: University of Pennsylvania Press, 1992), 19–43.
4. Donna Sullivan, "Gender Equality and Religious Freedom: Toward a Framework for Conflict Resolution," *International Law and Politics* 24 (1992), 795–856: 795.
5. See Arati Rao, "Home-Word Bound: Women's Place in the Family of International Human Rights," *Global Governance* vol 2, no. 2 (May–August 1996): 241–60; Charlotte Bunch, "Women's Rights as Human Rights: Toward a Re-Vision of Human Rights," *Human Rights Quarterly* vol. 12, no. 4 (November 1990), 486–98; V. Spike Peterson, "Whose Rights? A Critique of the 'Givens' in Human Rights Discourse," *Alternatives* 15 (1990): 303–44; Rebecca J. Cook, ed., *Human Rights of Women: National and International Perspectives* (Philadelphia: University of Pennsylvania Press, 1994); Julie Peters and Andrea Wolper, eds., *Women's Rights Human Rights: International Feminist Perspectives* (New York: Routledge, 1995).
6. Floya Anthias and Nira Yuval-Davis, "Introduction, " in Yuval-Davis and Anthias, eds., *Woman-Nation-State* (New York: St. Martin's Press, 1989), 1.
7. See Riane Eisler, "Roles of Men and Women: Integrating the Public and the Private," in Peter Juviler and Bertram Gross, eds., *Human Rights for the Twenty-First Century* (Armonk, NY: M.E. Sharpe, 1993), 245–62.
8. Donna Sullivan, "Gender Equality," 856.
9. Kumkum Sangari and Sudesh Vaid, "Recasting Women: An Introduction," in Sangari and Vaid, eds., *Recasting Women: Essays in Colonial History* (New Delhi: Kali for Women, 1996), 1–25: 2.
10. See Amrita Chhachhi, "Forced Identities: The State, Communalism, Fundamentalism and Women in India," in Deniz Kandiyoti, ed., *Women, Islam and the State* (Philadelphia: Temple University Press, 1991), 144–75.
11. See Tapan Basu, et al., *Khaki Shorts and Saffron Flags: A Critique of the Hindu Right* (New Delhi: Orient Longman, 1993).
12. Richard W. Lariviere, "Justices and *Panditas:* Some Ironies in Contemporary Readings of the Hindu Legal Past," *The Journal of Asian Studies* vol. 48, no. 4 (November 1989), 757–69: 759.
13. See Partha Chatterjee, *The Nation and Its Fragments: Colonial and Postcolonial*

Histories (Princeton: Princeton University Press, 1993); Lata Mani, "Contentious Traditions: The Debate on *Sati* in Colonial India," in Sangari and Vaid, *Recasting Women,* 88–126.

14. Lariviere, "Justices and *Panditas,*" 757.

15. See Vasudha Dhagamwar, *Law Power and Justice: The Protection of Personal Rights in the Indian Penal Code* (New Delhi: Sage, 1992, 2nd edition). As early as 1833, Thomas Macaulay was saying in the English Parliament that while a single law for all Indians was desirable, it was also unattainable:

> We know that respect must be paid to feelings generated by differences of religion, of nation, of caste. Much, I am persuaded, may be done to assimilate the different systems of law without wounding those feelings. . . . Our principle is simply this: uniformity where you can have it; diversity where you must have it; but in all cases certainty. (39).

16. The Indian Constitution, Article 44.

17. Ratna Kapur and Brenda Cossman, *Subversive Sites: Feminist Engagements with Law in India* (New Delhi: Sage, 1996), 264.

18. See J.D.M. Derrett, *Religion, Law and the State in India* (New York: Free Press, 1968). Explaining his addition of the final chapter (on Muslim law), Derrett wrote:

> [A]lthough it is concerned with the perplexing topic of the future of the personal law of Muslims in India, its main object is to prefigure in some manner the Indian Civil Code which Article 44 of the Constitution of India promises and a few lively minds in India are already envisaging. . . . If such a Code comes to be passed the dimensions of contact between religion and the State in India will suddenly be greatly narrowed. (21).

In light of the events of the subsequent three decades, his words seem painfully prescient.

19. The Indian Constitution, Article 25.

20. Ibid., Articles 26–30.

21. Ibid., Article 51A(e).

22. Madhu Kishwar, "Denial of Fundamental Rights to Women," in Madhu Kishwar and Ruth Vanita, eds., *In Search of Answers: Indian Women's Voices from Manushi* (New Delhi: Horizon India, 1991), 191–203: 191.

23. Indira Jaising, "Women, Religion and Law," 59–69, in Kamla Bhasin, Ritu Menon, and Nighat Said Khan, eds., *Against All Odds* (New Delhi: Kali for Women, 1994), 62.

24. United States Department of State, *India Country Report on Human Rights Practices for 1997.* Released by the Bureau of Democracy, Human Rights, and Labor, January 30, 1997.

25. Boyle and Sheen, *Freedom of Religion,* 191.

26. Ironically, the word "secularism" entered the Constitution only in 1976 through the 42nd Amendment, passed during the two-year Emergency declared by Mrs. Gandhi in which civil liberties were effectively suspended.

27. Ratna Kapur and Brenda Cossman, "Communalising Gender/Engendering Community: Women, Legal Discourse and Saffron Agenda," *Economic and Political Weekly,* April 24, 1993, 35–44: 37.

28. Ibid., 37.

29. Ibid., 43, fn 20 (quoting L.K. Advani).

30. Kapur and Cossman, *Subversive Sites,* 239 (quoting L.K. Advani).

31. Sikata Banerjee, "Hindu Nationalism and the Construction of Woman: The Shiv

Sena Organizes Women in Bombay," in Tanika Sarkar and Urvashi Butalia, eds., *Women and the Hindu Right: A Collection of Essays* (New Delhi: Kali for Women, 1995), 216–32: 222.

32. Stanley Tambiah, *Sri Lanka: Ethnic Fratricide and the Dismantling of Democracy* (Chicago: University of Chicago Press, 1986).

33. Kapur and Cossman, "Communalising Gender," 37.

34. Ketu H. Katrak, "Indian Nationalism, Gandhian '*Satyagraha,*' and Representations of Female Sexuality," in Andrew Parker et al., eds., *Nationalisms and Sexualities* (New York: Routledge, 1992), 395–406: 396, 398.

35. Paola Bacchetta, " 'All Our Goddesses Are Armed,' " in Bhasin, *Against All Odds,* 134 (italics added).

36. Kapur and Cossman, "Communalising Gender," 39.

37. Ibid.

38. Kapur and Cossman, *Subversive Sites,* 263.

39. Kapur and Cossman, "Communalising Gender," 40.

40. Kapur and Cossman, *Subversive Sites,* 263.

41. Ibid., 254–55.

42. See Zakia Pathak and Rajeswari Sunder Rajan, "Shahbano," *Signs: Journal of Women in Culture and Society* vol. 14, no. 3 (Spring 1989): 558–82; Anika Rahman, "Religious Rights Versus Women's Rights in India: A Test Case for International Human Rights Law," *Columbia Journal of Transnational Law,* vol. 28, no. 2 (1990): 473–98.

43. Amrita Chhachhi, "Identity Politics, Secularism and Women: A South Asian Perspective," in Zoya Hasan, ed., *Forging Identities: Gender, Communities and the State* (New Delhi: Kali for Women, 1994), 74–95: 83–84.

44. Kapur and Cossman, *Subversive Sites,* 272.

45. Zoya Hasan, "Minority Identity, State Policy and the Political Process," in Hasan, *Forging Identities,* 68.

46. Rasheeduddin Khan, "Minority Segments in Indian Polity: Muslim Situation and the Plight of Urdu," *Economic and Political Weekly,* September 2, 1978, 1512, quoted in Chhachhi, *Forging Identities,* 145.

47. See UN Instruments: *International Covenant on Economic, Social and Cultural Rights*, entered into force 16th Dec. 1966; *International Covenant on Civil and Political Rights*, entered into force 23 Mar. 1976; *International Convention on the Elimination of All Forms of Racial Discrimination*, entered into force 4 Jan. 1969; *Convention on the Rights of the Child*, entered into force 2 Sept. 1990; *Convention on the Elimination of All Forms of Discrimination Against Women*, entered into force 3 Sept. 1981; and *Convention on the Political Rights of Women*, entered into force 7 July 1954, *193 UNTS135.*

48. See Amrita Basu, "When Local Riots Are Not Merely Local: Bringing the State Back In, Bijnor 1988–1992," in Partha Chatterjee, ed., *State and Politics in India* (Oxford: Oxford University Press, 1997), 390–435.

11

REPLY   JULIE STONE PETERS

Reconceptualizing the Relationships Between Religion, Women, Culture, and Human Rights

Arati Rao's evocation of the complex politics of gender and religion in India might serve as a paradigmatic case study for larger problems of the relation between religion and human rights, on the one hand, and women and human rights, on the other. The distinction here, or course, is an artificial one. Rao's analysis suggests how central religion is to the issue of women's human rights and how central an understanding of women's human rights is to an understanding of the relation between religion and human rights. Questions about whether "human rights" as a collection of instruments, institutions, and conceptions can inform a nuanced analysis of culture or implementation of desiderata are not before us here. In fact, the institutions that make up human rights have increasingly addressed themselves to questions of culture: to the production of law through culture and the places in which the boundaries between culture and law tend to dissolve; most classically, where religion constitutes itself as law.

Investigations into the relation between religion and women's human rights (the important work of Ratna Kapur and Brenda Cossman on India, for instance, or of Abdullahi An-Na'im on Islam)[1] have already played a central role in the broader reconceptualization of the relationship between religion and human rights. As this volume suggests, a central question for those investigating the place of religion in human rights has become not so much "how can human rights norms protect individuals from religious persecution?" (though this clearly remains critical) but both "how can human rights norms protect individuals from religion itself?" and "how can religion be an agent for the promulgation of human rights norms?" Those rethinking human rights have come to acknowledge that "religious law" may be, at one and the same time, a rhetorical device for enforcing a set of power relations (mandating, centrally, the subordination of women) and a way of describing the norms and commitments that bind a community through shared culture—classically the sphere to which women are relegated but, at the same time, the sphere in which their contributions may sometimes be recognized.

If such norms are often the basis for the legitimation of troubling cultural practices, they also offer a model for legal community built on values transcending relativist choice or the kind of mercantile exchange that is the foundation for the modern secular state ("you offer us security, we'll obey your laws"). What has now become the classic feminist account of religion as a vehicle for the subordination of women must acknowledge the equally powerful account of religion as a vehicle for the rearticulation of human rights (including women's rights) in the local context. The traditional view of the entrenchment of masculinist religion as an obstacle to women's rights must come to terms with the view of religion and "culture" as the potential bearers of women's rights. Religion is no longer merely the subject of rights or the enemy of rights, but may be an agent of rights.

One of Professor Rao's central points is that a conception of human rights working in conjunction with religious law need not treat religion's tenets as eternal and unchanging. Even the most cursory historical view must acknowledge religious law as a fluid series of decisions and relationships, which have developed and continue to develop within the power relations of a given legal community. The extended codification of Hindu law, for instance, took place in the context of the British colonial attempt to delegate administrative tasks (a cost-saving measure, as well as an implicit recognition of the impracticality of the wholesale imposition of British law) and, at the same time, to provide colonial administrators with a textual basis for overturning traditional interpretations of the Hindu code. The codification of Hindu law, as Rao points out, tended at once to freeze the law in its nineteenth-century form and, at the same time, to offer a text easily exploited by those in positions of power. It had its origin in the work of nineteenth-century administrator-ethnographers like Sir Henry Sumner Maine, whose sympathy for the culture whose law he was purporting to expound is suggested by his (typical) pronouncement that "irrational imitation has engrafted" into the Hindu code "an immense apparatus of cruel absurdities" that reflects "a civilization as feeble and perverted as that of the Hindoos."[2]

A glance at the past and contemporary history of India reveals, then, not only the extent to which purportedly eternal religious law is a historical product, but also the extent to which religions are relational. Just as a certain conception of Zionist Judaism has developed in reaction to the felt threat of Palestinian nationalism, even the more general conception of a national Hinduism in India has developed specifically in response to the felt threat of Muslim minorities. In Rao's powerful evocation, the modern legal identity of the Hindu woman (defined through measures that ostensibly protect her chastity and mandate her role) has been configured by a reactive Hindu image of the rapacious Muslim male, from whom the chastity of the Hindu woman is to be protected.

This is the oppositional side of Arati Rao's argument: traditional claims that pit religious norms against women's human rights need not be seen as unbending, but may be dismantled, reinterpreted from the point of view of women who are committed to the religious affirmation of rights. That oppositional side serves as the basis for the affirmative side of the argument, less explicit in Rao's essay but nonetheless central to the claim for the use of religion in human rights: through their access to educational and other cultural institutions, through their role as representatives and channels for culture, women already have power over a religious substructure capable of change, and may, in fact, learn to use that power to greater effect.

Professor Rao recognizes the danger in this argument. To see women as channels for culture is to risk reaffirming their marginalization. It is to risk reinforcing a public–private distinction in which the "private" is controlled by the (masculine) public. It is to risk reinforcing claims like those undergirding the Hindu political Right's version of women's human rights, whose central object is to reinforce the Indian woman's command of "the affection of the father, the love of the husband, and the respect of her son." It is to risk relegating women to the sphere of family: "No fundamental change in values is desirable. Women in India ever had a pride of place within the household," where, as Madhu Kishwar points out, "family structure ... ensures the subordination and exploitation of women in a way that puts them beyond the purview of most of the fundamental rights guaranteed by the Constitution."

If Arati Rao recognizes the danger in the argument about the power of women as agents of culture, she also recognizes implicitly that the claim for secularism as a ground for freedom from religion-based subordination of women may be illusory. Where secularism purports to neutrality, it serves most often to mask deeply held beliefs, some of which may in fact serve women, but some of which may underwrite discriminatory policies founded in traditional religious interpretation. In India, specific political point is given to general theoretical questions about the value of parallel religious legal systems through the proposed Uniform Civil Code (UCC), which would replace the various (mostly religion-based) personal laws established during the colonial period. As Rao points out, the subsumption of personal laws under the proposed UCC would, on the one hand, eliminate specific religion-based laws that discriminate against women but, on the other hand, it would eliminate adjudication between competing visions, leaving the areas previously covered by various personal laws dominated by Hindu majority religious views masquerading as secularism.

These theoretical obstacles, however, are less significant than the pragmatic constraints. The rise in fundamentalism globally—an assertion of cultural rights against threats from both majority and minority cultures—continues to call itself "tradition" and take as central to the program of "tradition" a reassertion of cultural controls over women. In the existing environment of resurgent fundamentalism, and with the rise in gender-specific abuses, how can we have faith in theoretical claims for the treatment of religion as fluid cultural capital translatable into a currency for gender equalization? The constraints in most places on, for instance, the creation of forceful women's coalitions transcending religious and community boundaries, coalitions in which, as Rao suggests, "parts of a woman's religious identity can be temporarily bracketed . . . to begin a conversation about the experiences of women," are overwhelming.

If the historical is not the inevitable, the aspirational is not the actual. Religious texts continue to be interpreted as providing unarguable authority for the dominion of fathers and husbands over daughters and wives, the exclusion of women from public life, the denial of women's property rights, the continuation of practices dangerous to women's health and lives, discrimination in healthcare, education, nutrition, and employment, in laws regarding adultery, divorce, and the custody of children (to mention just a few issues). All these are repeatedly justified by claims from religion, treated as immune from the kinds of change that takes place in other kinds of law. It is not merely that in India (as elsewhere), as Rao points out, "all religious personal laws have discriminatory provisions which disproportionately disadvantage women," but that there are social structures in place precisely to reinforce the legitimating link between religion and discrimination against women.

In this context, international conventions seem feeble interjections into local legal conversation, either obviated by reservations (for instance, granting trumping power to religious or customary law) or ignored. A case like *Ephrahim v. Pastory,* in which the High Court of Tanzania ruled that the Tanzanian Bill of Rights, the Women's Convention, the African Charter on Human and Peoples' Rights, and the International Covenant on Civil and Political Rights collectively preempted Haya customary law,[3] has been so widely noted in the literature precisely because it was so unusual. Political power is constituted to resist such rulings. The famous Shah Bano case discussed by Rao is only a more high-profile version of the subtle ways in which entrenched political power resists challenges to religious norms.

This said, however, discussions like those of Professor Rao open a pathway for rethinking the role of religion in women's lives and creating a conception of religion-based rights, however aspirational. Just as important, analyses like Rao's offer us critical insights into some of the artificial oppositions on which human rights discourse has depended: the opposition between the right to freedom of religion and the state's strictures on free exercise (secular or imposed by an established state religion); the opposition between a secular state and a religious one or a multireligious state and a monoreligious one; the opposition between the public and the private spheres; and the opposition between women's equal rights and a coercive masculinist religion. Perhaps most important, such analyses offer a window on the conjunction of the problem of women and religion as key to a series of larger issues that will continue to be central in reshaping human rights as an institution in the twenty-first century: the role of culture in mandating rights standards and trumping (or being trumped by) particular rights, the nature of jural communities in an increasingly global world order, the identity of those speaking for such communities, and the mechanisms that might give voice to those who do not yet have a common language.

Notes

1. Ratna Kapur and Brenda Cossman, *Subversive Sites: Feminist Engagements with Law in India* (New Delhi: Sage, 1996); Abdullahi Ahmed An-Na'im, "The Rights of Women and International Law in the Muslim Context," *Whittier Law Review* 9 (1987): 491.

2. Sir Henry Sumner Maine, *Ancient Law* 4, 10, 12, J.H. Morgan ed. (London: J.M. Dent, 1917) (originally 1861).

3. See Rebecca J. Cook, "State Accountability Under the Women's Convention," in Rebecca J. Cook, ed., *Human Rights of Women: National and International Perspectives* (Philadelphia: University of Pennsylvania Press, 1994), 250–51.

12

BLU GREENBERG

Feminism, Jewish Orthodoxy, and Human Rights: Strange Bedfellows?

Oftentimes, a new title or new context compels one to look at one's own work in an altogether new and different light. I must admit that until the invitation was extended to me to discuss my work on feminism and Jewish orthodoxy in the framework of this seminar series, and even more so until the post-lecture commentary by Alan Segal and others, I simply never thought of it as a human rights issue. This, though as the years have worn on, some bits and pieces, some specific issues, have evoked in me feelings of impatience, a sense of urgency, and even moments of despair—feelings familiar to human rights activists of every stripe—feelings that, along with those of hope and exhilaration at small strides, power every human rights struggle, each in its own way.

The question is, Why not? Why, during the course of two and a half decades of dealing with issues of feminism and orthodoxy, did the human rights connection never occur to me to be a logical one? After all, are these not issues that affect one's personal status? Do not matters of women's roles and status within their own communities strike at the core of a woman's being, her persona, her dignity, her personal happiness and welfare?

To discuss the issue of "Why not?" in the abstract would be meaningless. Therefore, I shall begin by defining the specific areas in which inherited tradition is seriously challenged by the feminist standard of women's equality.[1]

Discrepancies Between Feminist Expectations and Jewish Role-Definition

The first issue, and perhaps most urgent because it limits a woman's ability to get on with her life after a bad marriage, is Jewish divorce law. A Jewish marriage is legally terminated through the transfer of a *gett,* a writ of divorce. This transfer takes place in the presence of three witnesses who constitute the *beth din,* the religious court of law. Unlike civil divorce, the change of status from married to divorced is not that which is legislated by the court but rather is a transaction between the two parties to the marriage. If no *gett* is transferred, the Jewish marriage is still in effect even though the couple may have long been living apart or have been granted a civil divorce.

The core of the problem is that a husband has leverage over his wife insofar as he is the one empowered to give the *gett* to her, and not the other way around. True, though a wife cannot give the *gett* to her husband, tradition does recognize female-initiated divorce as a legitimate phenomenon. In fact, the Talmud gives numerous grounds for a wife to sue for divorce in the rabbinic courts of law. These range from a husband's inability to provide for his wife in the lifestyle to which she had been accustomed, to his refusal to accompany her move to the holy land, to an aversion to his occupation if it seems odious to her, such as leather tanning or dung gathering.

Moreover, throughout Jewish history, there was a continual expansion of the rights of the woman in divorce situations. In fact, there is good reason to believe that the original law source (Deut. 24.1), formulated in the times of patriarchal society, was intended to serve as a protection for women. A Jewish woman could not be handed off summarily by means of an oral divorce. Nor could a Jewish divorcee be permanently set aside as undesirable "spoiled goods," as was often the case for women of ancient societies who had lost their virginity. The very language of the *gett* ensures against the possibility of placing her on the shelf for life: it specifically states that the woman is now free to marry again.

Nevertheless, the actual dissolution of the marriage is dependent on the husband giving the *gett,* and if he refuses, for reasons of spite or blackmail, there is little that can be done to compel him, for the law also states that the husband must give the *gett* of his own free will. This is known as the principle of a man's absolute right.[2] A scoundrel, or even an otherwise perfectly decent man blinded by a hatred that is as intense as love once was, is sorely tempted to use whatever means are legally available to him to punish the object of his hatred. Some Jewish men, albeit relatively few, do exercise this right, rendering their wives *agunot,* women chained to recalcitrant, absentee, and often blackmailing husbands.

For all previous generations of Jewish history, the phenomenon of a woman divorcing a man was so rare that cases of a husband withholding the writ of divorce for reasons of spite hardly ever arose. And where they did, the rabbis created a legal fiction—"we force him until he says I want to"—to solve the problem. The principle of a man's right was maintained but the woman was enabled to be free. In these times of spiraling divorce, however, the story is altogether different. There has been a sharp rise in female-initiated divorce, and a consequent rise in the number of *agunot*. A divorce culture, the new self-dignity and self-perceptions of women, the psychic and financial independence they now experience, and the fact that Jews no longer live in a closed society have all played a role here.

To the uninitiated or, for that matter, to anyone outside of the Orthodox community, the problem of imbalance within the law would seem simple to resolve: rewrite the law. Or, where abuse exists, take away the husband's privilege of absolute right. But for anyone who is a member of a fundamentalist community, the point is to preserve the traditions and to remain faithful to them.[3]

Moreover, the source of the law is a factor. Jewish legal tradition ascribes greater weight and authority to laws that emanate from Scriptures (*d'oh'riyta*) than to laws developed in post-Biblical society (*d'rabbanan*). It is true that everything in Jewish law of the past three thousand years is either derived from Sinai or connected to Sinai, but the closer to the Commanding Voice of Sinai, the closer to Revelation, the more sacred and more resistant to later reinterpretation. While that legal-theological theory does not hold up under case-by-case scrutiny, it does dominate discussions about the law and can be used selectively to support the immutability of a particular law. Concerning divorce law and a man's absolute right, these come directly from the Torah, through a single brief pericope in Deuteronomy, 24:1: "If a man takes a wife . . . and she fails to please him because he finds something objectionable (*ervah*) in her, then he writes her a writ of divorce, places it in her hand, and sends her away from his house." Religious decisors throughout the generations have remained faithful to the Deuteronomic principle and the process for ending a marriage, even as they expanded protections for women in divorce law.

The second area of discrepancy between feminist expectations and Jewish role-definition/division is that of women and liturgical responsibilities. Women's presence in communal prayer was neither mandated by Jewish law nor formally recognized. Consequently, although women did attend the synagogue and did recite the prayers, they did not participate in public liturgical roles, such as being called up to the reading of the Torah or leading the congregation in prayer. And of course, women were not and are not considered part of the *minyan,* the classical term for a formally constituted prayer community consisting of ten men.

Here again, the sources of obligation in prayer have been interpreted differentially for men and women—man's prayer obligation (*d'oh'riyta*) is derived from the Torah, and women's prayer (*d'rabbanan*) is derived from the Talmud. In addition there is the broad Talmudic principle of exemption for women from responsibility for positive time-bound commandments—that is, those obligations that must be performed within a specific period of time, such as dwelling in the *sukkah* during the Festival of Booths, donning the phylacteries (by day and not by night), and so on. Although the exemption was not applied directly by the Rabbis of the Talmud to include daily, formal, fixed-time prayer, it was nevertheless bridged in consciousness to include it. A careful reading of the sources shows that women are formally obligated in daily prayer, but the broad exemption as well as peripheral status in communal prayer served to dull women's prayer reflex. The point is that women in traditional Judaism, by their own actions and by the sum of community expectations of them, play a second-class role in Jewish prayer, both as to their rights and responsibilities.

The third area in which feminism compels us to take a good look, resistant though we may be when it comes to challenging our sacred texts and hallowed liturgies, is that of language. Beginning with the Torah and continuing through generations of rabbinic creativity, the language is to a great extent non-inclusive. God is He; God is the God of our fathers. Community is often addressed as a community of men, as in "you and your wife (or wives)." A morning blessing recited daily by men is "Blessed are You Adonai, our God, ruler of the universe, who has not made me a woman." The parallel daily blessing recited by women is "Blessed are You . . . who has made me according to Your will." Whether the rationale offered is valid—that men have more commandments and obligations than women and therefore are thankful to God—the internalization of hierarchy goes on unabated, below the level of the conscious where all things are more powerful and spill over in one hundred ways into real life and gender valuations. Many Orthodox men (and Orthodox women as well) feel self-conscious about language issues, but are caught in the dilemma of tradition and change. One certainly cannot rewrite Scriptures. This is the eternal word of God. Neither does one easily tinker with prayers that have come to us intact through the centuries, nay, the millennia, sanctified by the lips of millions of Jews who went before us.

The fourth area is that of women in leadership roles. Tradition dictates, more by absence of discussion than by argument, the inadmissibility of women to leadership roles, rabbinic and lay alike. Not surprisingly, history has recorded very few models. And where there were models, such as the powerful judge Deborah, rabbinic commentary ascribed to her the more feminine role of mediator and pacifier rather than powerful political leader. Today, as the models of women in leadership roles abound, both in the liberal wings of Judaism and in the secular world all around us, the discussion of Orthodox women as rabbis is just getting under way. The earliest responses within mainstream orthodoxy have been to rule out the possibility.

A fifth area is that of legal testimony. The law is clear: With some very few exceptions, only men may serve as witnesses in the religious courts of law or in religious proceedings, such as the Jewish marriage ceremony, divorce proceedings, conversion, and other matters concerning personal status. The disqualification of woman as witness does not apply to torts or other matters, which are adjudicated in civil courts of law and where women function equally as defendants, plaintiffs, and witnesses. There are no judges in the Jewish legal system.

Sixth are all of those items negatively associated with a woman's sexuality. One example is the law of *kol isha* (literally, a woman's voice): the injunction against a man hearing a woman's voice in song. The Talmud describes certain types of behavior that could lead to unseemly behavior—and a woman's voice is among them. Though the injunction is directed toward a man to refrain from hearing a woman's song, to all intents and purposes this law becomes a curb on women's song rather than on men absenting themselves from places of Jewish celebration. What exactly is the connection to women's sexuality? A woman singing is distracting at best and seductive at worst.

The original Talmudic context of the law is that of a man's recitation of the Shema, the sacred creed that Jews recite daily, affirming God's oneness and teachings. The Shema is the one prayer in all of the extensive and rich Jewish liturgy that the rabbis determine requires absolute, total concentration. In that context, the law makes a great deal of sense, for extraneous song can be distracting and sexy. But the matter was broadened to include women's song in any kind of social setting, including the synagogue and a family Sabbath dinner.

Seventh, there is the matter of life-cycle and ritual celebration. Judaism abounds with rituals that celebrate peak moments in a person's life; it is rich with rites of passage that signify different stages of physical and emotional growth. For the better part of the last four thousand years, beginning with the covenant rite of circumcision, these rituals have been largely associated with men's lives. Women enter new stages silently. They were onlookers, and sometimes not even that, at birth rituals, the *bar mitzvah* rite marking puberty and entry into Jewish adulthood, the marriage ceremony, rituals associated with death such as the recitation of *kaddish,* the mourner's prayer—all of these were men's celebrations. In my mother's day, which was not that long ago as Jews count time, a mother did not even attend the circumcision ceremony entering her son into the covenant. It was thought that women were too frail. Moreover, in peak experiences that were unique to women, such as the act of giving birth, no ritual was created to celebrate the miracle of a woman's biology or to connect her emotions to the culture and sacred memory of the community. I have often wondered: Had Jewish men been the ones to give birth all these centuries, what magnificent sort of ritual would have been developed by now!

Finally, there is the matter of Talmud Torah. Women were not obligated to the study of Torah, though very high value was placed on such study. Men learned, institutions were created for them, and expectations were set for Everyman. Women, where they were taught at all, were taught at an inferior level. Much of the literature, such as Talmud and Codes, was closed to them, and no infrastructure was put into place for women's study for the better part of the last three thousand years. This explains why women did not have access to leadership roles. Jewish leaders were not political or military heroes, they were the learning heroes, the scholars. And once the access route—the scholarly enterprise—was closed to women, there was no possibility that they could succeed.

Human Rights: Why Not?

All of this would seem to warrant a positioning on the platter of human rights issues, for altogether it establishes women in a hierarchical relationship to men in the religious community. In so many areas of the tradition, the following axiom holds to be true: women are to men as men are to God.[4] And yet, for the past two decades of Jewish feminism, this hierarchy, its actual disabilities and its potential for abuse, has not earned even a whisper of the potent phrase, "human rights." Why not?

First and foremost are the real horrors in the human rights arena. It is an act of arrogance to attach the same label that one applies to the torture and imprisonment of thousands of Tibetan nuns and priests and the burning of their monasteries, to the issue of whether a woman may sing freely in the presence of men. Where the entire class of Orthodox woman may or may not sit in the synagogue, what they are entitled to do there, and how gendered language speaks to them all pale beside a single example of forced female circumcision, commercial sexual exploitation of children, or the impoverished and discontinuous life of a migrant worker family. Compared to the massive injustices on the human rights agenda, the feminist issues within orthodoxy seem like a great luxury, as indeed many judged the American feminist movement in its earliest years to be—nothing more than a petulant, middle-class woman's whim.

Second, orthodoxy is not a community with locked doors. Just as one may enter freely, as do the born again or returning Jews (*baalei teshuva*), so may one leave it. Inasmuch as many of the items on the Orthodox feminist's agenda are issues of access, most of which have been resolved in the liberal denominations, a woman who feels suffocated or abused within orthodoxy can find a very comfortable home within Conservative, Reform, or Reconstructionist Judaism. And if she chooses to flee to the traditional Conservative community, she will find a lifestyle not all that different from her previous one, except as regards women's issues. I was prepared to say that this is one way in which orthodoxy differs from other fundamentalist communities, but after reading the papers in this seminar, I think it holds true for many of us. We are not prisoners. We are free to leave, yet we choose to stay, preferring to be gadflies and critics in our spiritually rich communities rather than "full access women" outside of them. Human rights becomes a burning issue when you have no other options and no way out. Not so for women of most orthodoxies of modern times, but more of this later.

On a personal level, one feels the desire to protect one's own community from attack from without. This reminds me of an incident concerning my son David. David was born in 1963 and came of age in the seventies when feminism was very new to the Orthodox community. As a teenager and high school student, he carried on many a debate with me over our Sabbath table regarding my feminist views. At age twenty, David spent a year studying at a more traditionalist yeshiva in Israel. I came for a visit a few months later and during a friendly and confidential chat with his teacher (*rebbe*), I was amused to learn that whenever my views or other feminist views were discussed (my book and several articles had come out the year before), David jumped in to defend my position.

But it is more than the matter of rallying to the defense of family that makes me recoil from the idea of putting Orthodox Judaism up for scrutiny under the world's microscope. And that is the political reality. I, like many other Jews, feel that the human rights community and the political third world are an aligned group that has been too quick to censure Israel, too unevenhanded when it comes to criticism regarding the Middle East. Israel with all of its democratic institutions, openness, and procedures for self-correction is cited with human rights abuses far more often than is valid and far more often than other neighboring repressive communities. That is not to say that Israel has made no mistakes and committed no infractions of human rights. Rather, that in the context of a country often under siege with war waiting in the wings at its borders, Israel has done remarkably well in preserving the human rights of its citizens, Arab and Jew alike. One would not know this from reading "unbiased/uneven-handed" international human rights documents. I, for one, hesitate to add anything to the human rights watch that would be further used to delegitimate Jews, Judaism, or Israel as an upstanding nation. I say all this at the risk of sounding whiny to people whose judgment means a great deal to me, but I must speak out where I see blind-sightedness.

Aside from protecting community, which is no small matter, there are issues of self-preservation and of effectiveness within the Orthodox women's community. Until very recently, it was difficult enough to gain cohorts even with relatively mild internal criticism. The overwhelming majority of Orthodox women did not sign on to religious feminism. That is not to say that these women were unaware of the issues. Rather, they remained unsympathetic, suspicious, and antagonistic to identifiable Orthodox feminists as a group. Conditioning to hierarchical structures? Perhaps. Fear of changing the status quo or of speaking up? A suspension of independent thinking? A hesitation at challenging the rabbis? Perhaps all of the above. In most instances of human rights, the downtrodden or persecuted become emotionally joined to the issue, even if they fear to speak up or to be openly identified. But here, the greater number of Orthodox women simply deny that abuses exist. In that vacuum, making the human rights accusation would carry three strikes against the accuser—airing a community's private laundry in public, suggesting that Judaism is anything less than a religion par excellence of justice and ethics, and pointing a finger at the rabbis in whom is vested the power to reinterpret the law. It has been my experience that I can give a speech about orthodoxy and feminism and not once refer to contemporary rabbis, yet I will be attacked later for attacking the rabbis.

Lack of unanimity as to what is or is not a loss of rights is another deterrent. Even within the small Jewish feminist community, there is debate. Some believe that the ordination of women is a priority; others disagree about this being on the agenda altogether. Some feel that the women's prayer groups symbolize the cutting edge issue; yet there are many feminists who are not comfortable in women's prayer groups. The following anecdote sums up the situation well. At the recent Feminism and Orthodoxy conference, a private dinner was held for the speakers, committee members, and spouses. During dinner, one committee member stood to sing a song she had written, spoofing the right turn orthodoxy has taken in recent years. Among the dinner guests were two rabbis, both great sympathizers and supporters of Orthodox feminism. One of them closed his remarks earlier that day with a rousing "Next year, the title of the conference should be Feminism in Orthodoxy," for which he received a standing ovation from the two thousand participants. The other rabbi, also modern Orthodox, has been fearless in speaking his mind on many of these issues: He founded a program that trains women to be experts in the laws of divorce and empowers them to serve in quasi-judicial function in the religious courts, a place where no woman has functioned before. He is also one of the few Orthodox rabbis to come out in favor of the ordination of women. Yet, as the committee member began to sing, both rabbis discreetly left the room. Why? Because they observe the tradition of *kol isha*. To my mind, the muzzling of a woman in song comes close to a violation of her basic human rights. This is an issue that would be high on my list of things to set right, but there would be no agreement between us there.

Finally, there is the matter of amelioration. Not surprisingly, the impulse for bridging internal religious issues to the broader framework of human rights is weakened in inverse ratio to improvements made in the areas under question. This is as it should be. To its credit, there have been many changes in orthodoxy during the past two decades.

This matter of relative amelioration becomes even more complex when one considers the factor of intent. On the one hand, improvement could symbolize, as it does in some quarters, an attempt to throw a bone to the underdog in the hope that she and her defenders will go away. On the other hand, and I believe that this is more characteristic of orthodoxy than the former, halakhically legitimated improvements for women represent the desire by religious leaders to allow the maximum possible latitude under the dictates of canon law. It is less a matter of "us against them" than one of "we are all in this together, struggling to fulfill the word of God." It is one thing to plead human rights when your religious leaders say, "Too bad. Nothing doing." It is another when the response is, "I understand your feelings and feel bad about them, but these are the laws we inherited, these are the roles God assigned to men and women."

Therefore, let us now turn to the ameliorations. In every area, one can point to changes for women within orthodoxy, some more significant than others, but all worthy of recognition.

Changes for Women in Jewish Divorce Law

During the past few decades, as divorce has escalated and the *agunah* problem increased, there have been several attempts by community leadership to respond to the problem. In the 1970s, the civil court solution was introduced. In several precedent-setting cases, Jewish divorce was attached to civil divorce proceedings. If a recalcitrant husband refused to authorize the *gett,* the civil judge could fine or incarcerate him until he complied. This procedure was legally based on those aspects of a Jewish marriage that are contractual in nature. This solution was encouraged by many Orthodox rabbis, even the most right-wing. Why? Because it solved the problem without any change in *halakha*. However, it was opposed by liberals who feared a breach in the sacred principle of separation of church and state.

An interesting example of the internal division on this matter occurred in Australia, in the late 1980s. At the urging of the Orthodox rabbinate, the Australian federal government was prepared to make this a feature of civil law—that is, that cases of recalcitrance in Jewish divorce would be decided (penalized) in the civil courts. There was great debate, with the women of the Jewish social service organizations, who were mostly not Orthodox, calling for a halakhic solution and the rabbis calling for a civil solution. This is exactly the opposite of how one would expect the sides to line up. The government measure passed, because the Australian Jewish community is more traditional than those of most other Western countries.

Another solution, one that arose in the 1980s, was that of a prenuptial agreement. The engaged couple would agree that should they ever separate or seek a civil divorce and one or the other impeded the *gett,* both would submit to the authority of a rabbinic court and abide by its mandate. This might be to require the husband to give his wife a *gett.* Typically, the agreement stipulates that if the husband is recusant, he is liable to a financial penalty for each ensuing day. While it offers no guarantee—for a husband may still refuse or may flee the jurisdiction of the rabbinic court—it does add some pressure, and it does make a value statement about recalcitrance. But in truth, this procedure has not been widely used in the Orthodox community. A relatively small number of Orthodox rabbis who perform weddings require it; few others even make the suggestion, and some will not allow it.

Several activist organizations have been formed with a dual agenda of raising consciousness in the community and aiding individual *agunot* by mounting pressure on recalcitrant husbands. The effect of the activist organizations has been underrated. I believe that the formation of two special Jewish courts of law (*bet din*) to deal almost exclusively with the problem of *agunot* is a direct result of the work of these groups. What do these courts do that is different? One is altogether innovative, freeing women without requiring the presence of the husband, once abuse has been documented. This is based on an ancient principal in Jewish law of *havka'at kiddushin,* the retroactive setting aside of the marriage if certain circumstances warrant it. The other is a court that has as its unspoken mandate the finding of solutions in favor of the victimized woman. Though that would seem to be an obvious function of the *bet din,* the sad fact is that many of the courts in cases of *agunah* are biased in favor of the husband, at best working out a more "reasonable" settlement in cases of blackmail.

In Israel, where civil government can be joined to the matter, the procedures are slightly different. A recalcitrant husband can be fined, his wages garnisheed, his driver's license pulled. Also in Israel, the rabbinate has developed a training program for *toanot,* women advocates who become experts in Jewish law and represent women in the religious court proceedings. These women have had a strong effect on the proceedings and they convey support for women who are victimized by recalcitrant husbands. Still, though the religious and civil courts work together, there remain far too many cases of anchored wives. Unlike the diaspora communities, in Israel all cases of divorce, whether the couple is religious or not, are adjudicated in the religious courts.

In addition to organized structures, there are ad hoc groups that rise to protect an *agunah.* One such example is the group of several Canadian women who decided to take matters into their own hands. One young woman in their community was being blackmailed by her husband in return for the *gett.* Her parents were people of means and wanted to pay so as to release her. But she did not want to give the fellow a cent. One Sabbath morning, before the reading of the Torah, approximately twenty of her friends stood up and announced aloud in synagogue that none of them would go to the *mikvah,* the ritual bath, until their friend had her *gett* in hand.[5] Their Lysistrata-style announcement produced the quickest divorce ever in Jewish history! Levity aside, women in the Orthodox community are beginning to understand that they, too, have levers of power.

A different sort of activism, which is to me an embarrassment to Judaism, is used on occasion in certain fundamentalist communities. A husband who remains unyielding is physically assaulted until he "decides" that he wants to give his wife a *gett.* While more deserving of the term thuggery than activism, it nevertheless works against a husband's own brand of thuggery. In recent weeks, there has been much made of this in the secular press. A recalcitrant husband from Boro Park, a strong fundamentalist community, was beaten to the point where he agreed to give a *gett* "of his own free will." Thereafter, he brought a multi-million-dollar suit against several rabbis in the community who had sanctioned the strong-arm tactics. It will be interesting to see what the courts decide.

Meanwhile, the grave problem of the *agunah* remains. Currently, it is solved on an individual basis—one anchored woman by one anchored woman—as caring rabbis continue seeking ways to invalidate a marriage or free a woman with a *gett.* But what is now needed is a broad-scale solution, at the level of the law, so that the mere potential for inequity will be eliminated, and no victim of a recalcitrant husband will ever have to come before the rabbis, in humiliation, on her knee.

Changes for Women in Prayer

What do Orthodox women do, those who wish to remain faithful to the tradition yet who also want to experience fuller participation in communal liturgies? They organize women's prayer (*tefila*) groups. They do not call their assemblies a *minyan* because in halakhic opinion, women are not considered part of a *minyan* and may not constitute one. To win legitimacy, the women emphasize that they are not a *minyan*. Thus, they omit recitation of certain prayers that require a *minyan,* and they take care not to entitle themselves inappropriately.[6]

The women's *tefila* groups generally meet once a month, the rationale being that women want greater experience and participation but do not want to split off into separate his/her prayer communities. Thus, women's *tefila* remains a sub-community for women within their larger communities, not a break from them. The components of women's *tefila* are leading the services, offering a *d'var* Torah or sermon, reading from the Torah with proper cantillations, being called up for an *aliyah,* reciting special blessings of Thanksgiving or special saving, celebrating life-cycle ceremonies and special events in their lives. On the one hand, there is none of the creativity that exists in women's liturgy in the liberal denominations. On the other, it satisfies and gratifies traditional women to participate more directly in the familiar, the ancient, the hallowed. This, in itself, is abundantly innovative. And like any other prayer community, women's *tefila* offers occasional peak moments of spirituality.

It must be acknowledged that women's *tefila* groups have not attracted the majority of Orthodox women, even in communities that are hospitable and affirming of them. Nevertheless, they are a steady force and, in some communities, have grown in numbers and in size during the last decade. There has been rabbinic opposition from a significant part of the establishment, but there has also been a sufficient number of individual rabbis who have legitimated and supported these groups, including inviting them to hold their services in the synagogue itself.

Perhaps most interesting of all in the political struggle is the fact that none of the prayer groups folded in the face of opposition from establishment rabbis who attacked them as radical feminist enterprises and not liturgical gatherings in the name of God. After each attack, more prayer groups in more cities were opened. This would not have happened two decades ago, when Orthodox women were more docile. Armed with the knowledge that what they are doing is not in violation of *halakha,* and supported by individual rabbis, they stand their ground. Moreover, the heavy-handedness of the opposition made feminists out of some previously mild-mannered participants.

The Women at the Wall in Israel is a somewhat different and more complex story, but the basic issue is the same: the right of women to assemble and carry on a liturgy as a group, within the parameters of halakhic prayer. The women meet for services on the first day of the New Month. Here too, they were not intimidated, not even by threats of violence. An interim decision has been handed down in a case taken to the high court in Jerusalem, allowing the women to pray as a group, but to keep their voices at moderate levels so as not to disturb others at the Wall with this altogether new phenomenon. A final decision is pending.

This constitutes the very first time that women in religious community are resorting to the civil courts to intervene in a religious matter.[7] There has not been as much grass-roots support in Israel for the Women of the Wall. This is probably an indication that the factors cited above to account for resistance to the human rights association also operate here. On the other hand, politics and *halakha* have often been deeply intertwined in Israel, so the decision of the high court on this one will be most interesting to follow.

Another novel phenomenon in terms of women and liturgy is that of women convening themselves as a quorum to recite the grace after a meal. Tradition teaches that only men may be counted in the *zimmun,* the quorum convened for recitation of the grace.[8] However, there is also halakhic precedent for three or more women to constitute themselves as a *mezuman* when no men are present. For most of this century, and probably for the better part of Jewish history, women remained peripheral to the quorum.

Several years ago, I attended a beautiful pageant prepared by students in my daughter's yeshiva high school class. I remember quite vividly my daughter's particular project. Her task was to comb the biblical sources on water and then to highlight the relationship between water-as-a-source-of-life and Torah-as-a-source-of-life. In addition to her recitation, she created a large felt display of water and related symbols; in twelve-inch-high royal blue felt letters she "wrote" at the bottom of her banner the Hebrew words from Isaiah, "Yea, all who are thirsty go to the waters." Although she was then only fifteen, her project—oral and visual—was very sophisticated. And so were the presentations of many of her classmates.

At that time, the high school consisted of two hundred young women and a learned faculty that was primarily female. The day's program was concluded with a lovely feast, which had also been prepared by the girls. The meal began and ended with the appropriate blessings and grace. After being nurtured for two hours by the gifts of intellect and heart and hand of these young women, the principal called in from another part of the building three boys from the eighth grade (post *bar mitzvah*) to constitute the quorum for reciting the grace. The asymmetry was startling. Equally startling was the no one seemed to notice or mind whose maturity counted. When I delicately raised the issue afterward with several friends, I immediately saw the veil drop over their eyes. Recently, however, at first self-consciously and then quite as matter of fact, groups of women have begun to convene their own *zimmun* for recitation of the grace. The two primary Orthodox women's organizations have now made this their standard operating procedure. A dozen years ago, they would have scoffed at the idea.

Other liturgical acts new to women include the recitation by women of the *kiddush,* the sanctification over the wine. The Talmud does permit a woman to recite *kiddush,* but adds that a dire consequences will befall a man whose wife does so for him. Perhaps that stigma explains why historically women rarely recited the *kiddush.* In fact, for a woman to have to do so only seemed to heighten the fact that she had no man or boy in her life to fulfill this *mitzvah* for her. But today, in homes and in synagogues, at a family celebration, *bat mitzvah,* birth ceremony, or congregational *kiddush,* women have been heard to recite the *kiddush.* To be sure, it is still quite rare and in some quarters it still raises eyebrows, but it is not considered disgraceful behavior or an antinomian act. Rather, it is becoming more widely accepted.

Women are taking up other rituals associated with liturgy. For example, during the past few years on the feast of Tabernacles (Sukkot), an occasional woman or girl will carry the palm branch (*lulav*) and citron (*etrog*) to the synagogue to hold aloft at appropriate moments of prayer. This was certainly not part of a Jewish woman's repertoire in previous generations. Similarly, in a number of modern Orthodox synagogues, a women's *hakafah* has been organized for the holiday of Simkhat Torah. Women carry aloft the Torah scroll and dance around it. That these *hakafot* for women generally take place outside of the sanctuary or of the synagogue altogether, and that relatively few women join in, is all to be understood as a ritual-in-process.

In a most recent development, March of 1998, a prestigious, establishment modern Orthodox synagogue—one that does not host a women's prayer group—prepared to alter its standard operating procedure of the last forty-five years to allow the Torah scroll to be carried through the women's section on Sabbaths and holidays, just as it is carried through the men's section. The Torah processional ritual is lovely. Prior to and following the reading from the Torah, the scroll is carried aloft through the congregation to allow the worshipers to express their reverence and love for this sacred writing. But "the congregation" always meant the men's section. Under the new procedure, the Torah will be carried by a man through the men's section, then handed to a woman who will carry it throughout the women's section, then return it to a man to be placed on the reading table or returned to the ark. This seemingly small act is significant in that it represents a chink in the armor of keeping women disconnected from the sacred scrolls. The rabbi of the congregation, a learned man, knew that there would be some political cost, yet he determined that the law permitted women to touch or kiss the Torah and to honor it as men do, so he took a stand. He made the announcement several months before it will be instituted—upon completion of a new sanctuary—so as to allow the political dust to settle. It remains to be seen whether there will be a hospitable response by the majority of both men and women of the congregation. An indication of how change is resisted in the Orthodox community is the concern registered by a feminist in the congregation, "I wonder if there will be any women willing to carry the Torah."

Changes for Women in Language

As regards changing sacred tests and sacrosanct liturgies, it should come as no surprise to anyone that within orthodoxy, not a single word has been altered. This is in sharp contrast to the liberal denominations where inclusive, non-sexist prayer books are becoming the norm and not the radical exception. But traditionalists believe that one can no more tinker with sacrosanct prayers than rewrite Scriptures or censor the Talmud.

What is new and of interest in orthodoxy, however, is that the natives are beginning to get restless. For example, whereas a decade ago, one could hear only in the liberal denominations murmurings about the male preference blessing, mentioned above, today traditional women are calling that language into question. And not only women. Some men in the community, albeit a few, refrain from reciting that blessing as part of their morning prayers. They do this without fanfare, without publicly repudiating or changing its text. But they do it on the grounds that it is disrespectful of women.

At the Feminism and Orthodoxy conference, an entire plenary session was devoted to the subject of gender and sacred texts. This was something I did not imagine would happen for at least another decade. While no one publicly called for a rewriting of gender problematic texts or for striking hostile or belittling value statements from ancient sources, mere acknowledgment of the problem was a major breakthrough.

What is also new is that where there is a flowering of women's prayer, female persona and past models are often incorporated. For example, in women's prayer groups, the names of the matriarchs are added to certain sections of the liturgy where before only the patriarchs were mentioned. An indicator of the delicate balance between faithfulness and innovation is that the matriarchs' names are not added to all such sections.

The Eighteen Benedictions prayer is considered to be the central part of the morning, afternoon, and evening prayer services. It is recited silently by each individual worshiper. This prayer is of very ancient origin (at least two thousand years old), and is considered the essence of the conversation between human beings and God. It opens with the words, "Blessed are you Adonai, our God, and the God of our fathers, the God of Abraham, the God of Isaac, and the God of Jacob." In recent years, Conservative and Reform liturgists have added there the names, "Sarah, Rebecca, Rachel, and Leah," but Orthodox women would not consider changing the traditional text.

Language is a thorny issue. On the one hand, words are all the more powerful for their subtlety, all the more penetrating for their quiet constancy. Like water dripping on a rock, so does gendered language alter the psyche. God as male, community as the class of men, women as secondary citizens—all of this affects not only self-perception, but the formulation of law as well. On the other hand, the language of the texts has been hallowed by usage. Language links us vertically and horizontally, to our past, present, and future. I know that I can show up at any synagogue in the world, and the prayer service (with some very minor variations) will be identical to that of my own synagogue. Repair of language and creation of altered liturgies have effectively widened the rift between the denominations in that we can no longer pray together as one people. So the language issue is far more complex that it would seem at the surface, with issues of equality, self-dignity, and the integrity of community all coming into play. I do not know where the language questions will take us, but I take comfort in the fact that the issues will be dealt with not by isolated individuals but in the framework of a concerned community.

Meanwhile, it must also be said that the community has been greatly sensitized to language issues in general. Many Orthodox rabbis now take care in their sermons and teachings to use phrases such as "he or she," "men and women." This is in contrast to past universal use of male pronouns as the generic term for human beings and community. Not only does this change reflect increased sensitivity to issues of language and to the presence of women, but it also tempers somewhat the strongest arguments in favor of recasting language—that language and its images inform the psyche in a subtle, subconscious, and, therefore, all the more powerful way. If, in fact, those who are unalterably opposed to changing hallowed language are able to be mindful of women in other speech, then perhaps a compromise can be struck.

Changes for Women in Leadership

In the Jewish religious community, leadership is inextricably linked to learning. It seems not at all unreasonable, therefore, to conjecture that in the not-too-distant future, Orthodox women will also hold the title of rabbi. The meshing of two forces—the explosion of women's learning on the one hand, and the very powerful model of women rabbis in the liberal denominations on the other—is surely going to create that fact.

Although I have said that the majority response within the community has been to reject any such possibility, the very fact that the subject is now up for discussion is a sign that change is in the air. Equally important to the discussion among rabbinic leaders is the conversation among women scholars. As a group, they are not ready to say "yes" to the idea, but they are talking, analyzing, thinking. The fact that many are unsure about where they stand on the issue is a significant step forward from their flat rejection of it but a decade ago. And a few among them have come out in favor, saying "Why not us?"

In 1996, a young woman announced that she was going to be the first Orthodox woman rabbi. Unfortunately, she was only at the beginning of her rabbinic studies, she did not gather a group of cohorts about her, and the publicity generated by her announcement backfired to the extent that the individual rabbi who was prepared to ordain her several years down the road backed off from using the title rabbi. Yet I believe that she had much to do with widening the conversation.

In January 1998, something happened that will transform the situation again. Two modern synagogues in New York each engaged a woman to serve as a congregational intern. What this means is that two women are now serving in Orthodox synagogues in almost identical capacity to the male assistant rabbis in those congregations. It took me a while to realize how revolutionary this is. I had always believed that it would be highly unlikely for Orthodox women to serve in the capacity of pulpit rabbi, for the community would not be ready for that step. Thus, I reasoned, the first step should be the ordination of women—that is, women carrying the title of rabbi based on their mastery of texts, as it is for men. There would be plenty of time afterward to think about such emotionally charged issues as service in the pulpit. Besides, there are other jobs that a woman rabbi can hold, positions that are now closed only to Orthodox women. We can take it one step at a time, I argued, mindful of community sensibilities.

But the congregational interns have changed my mind. Though these two women and the rabbis who hired them have dissociated themselves from the idea of Orthodox women rabbis, resolutely disclaiming any and all connection to training as rabbis or serving as rabbis, they nevertheless represent a simultaneous thrust toward women in the Orthodox rabbinate. Serving in the public roles as they do, they make the possibility of a woman rabbi all the more accessible. And since much of the objection within the modern Orthodox community to women serving as rabbi is a psychological one, the presence of congregational interns helps to overcome a major hurdle.

Meanwhile, we can also take note of the fact that women have assumed lay leadership roles in Orthodox synagogues, up to and including the office of president. This is a broad leap from their status a generation ago when women were not even entitled to vote as members of an Orthodox synagogue.

Currently, women also serve as executive directors of Orthodox synagogues. They sit on rabbinic search committees, and some who do exercise the opportunity to query a rabbinic candidate on attitudes toward women's issues. Women serve as chairpersons and as guests of honor at the annual dinners held by religious institutions, a staple of Jewish communal life. The all-male dais can now be found only in the right-wing yeshiva world. And in Israel, women have been elected to town rabbinic councils following the landmark Leah Shakdiel case.

Changes for Women in Legal Testimony

Though there has not been much attention or pressure regarding the matter of women serving on the *bet din,* the religious court of law, I suspect that this matter will be raised at some point in the future, only because of the domino effect of one thing upon the other. Meanwhile, inasmuch as *halakha* on this subject is so explicit—only men may qualify as witnesses—the real issue here is less one of women's rights than of unity of the community. Initially, women in the Conservative rabbinate took the decision not to serve in the capacity of witness to marriage and divorce. They did this largely out of concern for unity issues. Recently, however, they reversed their original decision. Since legal documents like the *gett* and marriage contract (*ketubah*), when they are witnessed by women, are considered invalid according to Orthodox tradition, some argue that this step is even more divisive than the ordination of women.

Does all of this mean that within orthodoxy no woman can ever be legitimated to give testimony in the religious courts? Despite the unambiguity of *halakha,* the answer is not a categorical "yes" or "no." For one, it has been a practice of Israeli rabbinic courts for some time now to incorporate women's testimony, albeit through the back door. Technically, the court is disbanded and the "testimony" of a woman is taken. The court is then formally reconvened and those who deliberate on the issue may use the information supplied by the woman.

In Israel, where most issues of family status come under the jurisdiction of the religious courts, a special group of women trained in matters of Jewish family law (*toh'ah'noht*) are now part of the court system. Since 1990, any woman who is party to a divorce proceeding has the option of bringing along to the court such an auxiliary person—to give support and to speak on her behalf. Here again, the model of a woman serving in this capacity can overcome generations of conditioning about the religious courts as the exclusive purview/place of men.

Changes in Women's Sexuality as Taboo

I remain completely baffled as to why, in this time of feminism, with its proud values of self-expression and self-esteem, there has not been a large and vocal plea to reexamine the law regarding *kol isha*. On the contrary, women in their respective communities are part and party to careful observance of it, taking pains not to sing in the presence of men even at religious celebrations. This is axiomatic in the right-wing community, but it has also become increasingly true of the modern Orthodox as the influence of the former upon the latter has grown. It is worthwhile to digress a moment to trace this pattern, for it has far-reaching implications for feminism within the religious community. Also, it is a pattern that I believe characterizes other traditional religions.

In the modern Orthodox community of the forties and fifties, *kol isha* was not an issue. It was on the books, but without much discussion it had fallen into desuetude, like other customs and laws which the community let lapse over the generations. I recall that at Yeshiva University, which included the major seminary for training Orthodox rabbis, holiday pageants were held in the fifties in which young men and women from the respective branches of the institution acted and sang together. Today, my nephew, a product of Yeshiva University, will not go to a Broadway musical because of *kol isha*. His lovely young wife, who grew up in a modern Orthodox household similar to his, takes care in front of whom she sings, including the singing of Sabbath table songs at her own table when guests are present. While there are no accurate figures on this, I suspect they represent a good third of the modern Orthodox community today.

How did this happen? After World War II, there was a profound realization that modernity was not all that it was held out to be, at least not as far as Jews were concerned. Simultaneously, ethnic liberation and self-pride movements began to take root and a worldwide growth of fundamentalism strengthened Jewish fundamentalist groups as well. Out of this came much good: in general, a corrective to the excesses of modernity and its deracinated values; in particular, a great expansion of Jewish learning. But while all of this was happening, feminism was exerting its powerful influence, and fundamentalism and feminism locked horns. Within right-wing orthodoxy, there was broader separation of the sexes, arranged marriages, a more stringent dress code, and general sense of taboo about the female persona and sexuality. Although it is not quite accurate to say the revival of *kol isha* was a response to the new freedom of women to be seen and heard, the two phenomena are not totally unconnected.

Still, it is the lack of complaint that baffles me. For women who have a new sense of themselves just by virtue of living in contemporary society, including women in the right-wing community who are educated, savvy, raise girl children, have careers, and are modern in so many other ways, to acquiesce without any complaint to a stifling of the song in their hearts and a melody on their lips.

One additional comment about female sexuality, feminism, and human rights: The reader who knows something about Judaism may wonder why the large area of menstruation and its taboos has not been mentioned here. After all, the law calls for a complete physical separation of the menstruant women, not only during her menses but also during a seven-day period following her flow. This taboo would seem to represent a large stigma attached to a woman's body, and several contemporary scholars, Jewish and non-Jewish alike, have dealt with the Biblical and rabbinic tradition on this matter.

Yet, I believe that there is an even more significant stream in the sources—that of governing sexual relations between husband and wife. The law is not merely about woman's blood but about family purity, as in fact the laws of the menstruant women are referred to in English language sources. Though linked to a woman's bodily flow, the man must observe these laws of separation in conjunction with his wife. The range of interpretation of these laws is very wide, from separating out one who is impure and unclean to regenerating the relationship and renewing romance each month following the period of mutual physical separation. The matter is complex, far beyond the purview of this essay, and, in my opinion, not open to feminist or human rights scrutiny in the manner of other issues dealt with here.

Changes for Women in Life-Cycle Ceremonies

Here the significance lies in the anecdotal, the individual case, the single-not-yet-repeated case study. I have often referred to feminism in orthodoxy as a revolution of small signs, and nowhere is this more true than in the area of life-cycle ceremonies. A few of the many examples that have cropped up in recent years include the Rejoicing of the (birth of the) Daughter (*simhat bat*), using the mother's Hebrew name in her child's surname, the *bat mitzvah,* women's role in the wedding ritual, and women's participation in burial rites.

After almost four thousand years of communal celebration at the birth of a Jewish male child, birth ceremonies for baby girls are being woven into the fabric of Jewish life. This is a ritual in process, is by no means universally practiced, and has not yet been standardized or incorporated into the tradition or liturgy in a formal way. But where it is observed, it parallels the covenantal ceremony of *brit,* the circumcision rite for an eight-day-old Jewish boy, but without the medical rite. These ceremonies are largely the creation of individual families. The primary focus, as it is for a boy, is the entry of this infant girl into the covenant between Abraham and Sarah and God. Does that mean that for four thousand years of Jewish history, Jewish girls were not considered part of the covenantal family? Of course not. It does mean, however, that they were accessed to the covenant silently, without ritual or rite, with a whisper, as it were.

Giving a Jewish name is a matter of great significance. Traditionally, a Jewish name was composed of three parts: a given Hebrew name, son or daughter, of the father (his first name)—for example, David Cohen as Da'veed ben (son of) Avraham. Only in very special circumstances, such as when a special prayer for healing was made, was the mother's Hebrew name used as the child's surname. At the moment of giving the name and in all other formal usage, only the father's name was included. During this last decade, however, there have been glimmers of change. At an occasional baby naming, or birth ceremony, or even a *bar* or *bat mitzvah,* the child's name includes both the mother and father's names—for example, Da'veed ben Avraham Ve Sarah. Women called up to the Torah in women's prayer groups also use the Hebrew names of both parents.

The celebration of *bar mitzvah,* a boy becoming an adult Jew under the canopy of Torah, is a relatively late custom in Judaism, only several hundred years old. But the parallel celebration for girls, *bat mitzvah,* began only yesterday as Jews count time. It was an innovation of liberal Jews in the early part of this century. In fact, up until a score of years ago, *bat mitzvah* celebration evoked suspicion and derision within orthodoxy. Not so any longer. Today, no self-respecting Orthodox family would not mark in some special way the *bat mitzvah* of its daughters. *Bat mitzvah* celebrations within the Orthodox community run the gamut, from the girl's father reciting the blessing over the Torah in the synagogue on Sabbath morning, to the young woman herself reading the Torah at a women's prayer group service, and everything in between.

In the traditional Jewish wedding ceremony, the bride and female guests have few vocalized roles. The bride is covered with the veil by her husband (*bedeken*); she walks seven times around her husband under the wedding canopy; her husband recites the marriage declaration to her; she accepts the ring on her index finger; and she acquires the marriage contract (*ketubah*). Traditionally, she recites no words, nor do the women guests participate in any of the special honors associated with the wedding ceremony.

Today, some brides want to have their female friends share in the ritual, and some want to have a more expressive role themselves. Consequently, many new customs have grown during this last score of years. For example, during the *bedeken,* the father of the bride places his hands over her head and blesses her, and is followed by the father of the groom. In recent times, some mothers also join in blessing the bride. Women may hold up the poles of the portable marriage canopy (*huppah*), a female guest may read the *ketubah* during the ceremony,[9] or the bride may recite under the canopy some reciprocal words of love, usually taken from Song of Songs.[10] Where a bride wishes to give her husband a ring, she will do it in a manner that does not confuse it with a double ring ceremony.[11] Finally, at the conclusion of a traditional wedding, seven blessings are recited. As is the case for most public ritual, only men recite these blessings. A recent innovation has been to call up seven women, one at a time, to recite some words of blessing corresponding to the seven traditional wedding blessings that, moments earlier, had been recited by seven male guests. These and other rituals may seem inconsequential to the outsider. But within the Orthodox community, they convey a whole different sense of the presence of women in public ceremony, which explains why they are still very rare and considered somewhat controversial.

Because of its associated mystery and taboo, death has tended to sharpen the divide between the sexes. One example of this is women's participation in burial rites. In certain cemeteries run by the more right-wing burial societies, women must stand at a distance from the actual burial. In some extreme instances, this has included the female mourner as well. Even in the modern Orthodox community, the mourning rituals are different for women, most notably the recitation of the *kaddish,* the mourner's prayer. *Kaddish* is a most powerful healing ritual, for it helps a mourner knit together in the framework of a loving community. This prayer is recited daily at communal prayer services for a full year following the death of a parent or child, and for thirty days after the death of a spouse or sibling. As it is recited only in a *minyan,* for two thousand years, women did not recite this classical mourner's prayer. Oftentimes, a husband would take upon himself the obligation to recite *kaddish* for his wife's parents or sibling.

Recently, and in small numbers, Orthodox women have taken upon themselves the ritual of *kaddish* recitation, which means that they must attend synagogue services every day. Those who have, have described the spiritual experience, the psychological and emotional value, as well as the process of integration into the healing community. After the initial awkwardness and perhaps suspicion by the men, a woman is treated with graciousness and welcome. By the time the eleventh month rolls around, she has become such a regular feature of the group that the men are sorry to see her leave, which inevitably she does.

Another new phenomenon altogether is that of a woman teaching Torah at a *shiva minyan*. *Shiva* is the seven-day mourning period following burial. During these seven days, the mourners stay at home, sit on low wooden stools, and are visited by family and friends who come to comfort, distract, help, listen. A *minyan* is held at the home of the mourners so that the *kaddish* can be recited during the morning, afternoon, and evening prayers. In order to create a demarcation between the afternoon and evening prayers, which are usually held in tandem, five to ten minutes of study are inserted between the two. One of the male visitors will teach a few verses from the Talmud and then relate its context to the life of the deceased.

Now, how does it happen that after two thousand years, a new ritual is introduced and without fanfare? Let us look at this one, a history in the making. At a *kaddish minyan* not long ago, it was the granddaughter and granddaughter-in-law who taught the learning segment between the afternoon and evening prayers. Both granddaughters live simultaneously in the Orthodox community and in the modern world. Both are feminists. Because they loved their grandfather very much and were unusually close to him, they wanted to have some special part in this period of mourning.

Now the father/father-in-law of these two young women was not quite comfortable with their request, although his wife was altogether for it. In fact, had someone other than his children made the request, he would surely have said "No," not to be recalcitrant but simply because it had never been done before. But here it was his own children, and he heard their plea. Yes, they could teach the Talmud segment. However, reciting *kaddish* after a woman's learning was more than he could handle. His compromise was that after the two women finished teaching the Talmud, one male guest would read a single verse from the text and then the *kaddish* could be recited. Perhaps in a few years, a woman will teach the Talmud and those assembled will recite the *kaddish* immediately following her words.

Changes for Women in Learning

Search for the focus of feminist values in a particular Jewish denomination and you will find it in a different place in each one. In Jewish orthodoxy, it is in the study of sacred texts that feminism has most powerfully taken root. One example that points up the difference is the reclaiming of *Rosh Hodesh* as a woman's holiday. While a host of monthly rituals and worship have been introduced by religious feminists of other denominations, Orthodox women have tended to mark the New Month with special learning groups. In my own community, during the past few years, the local religious women's groups have scheduled *Rosh Hodesh* group study of texts (*sheurim*).

We are witnessing a virtual explosion of women's learning in the Orthodox community, modern and fundamentalist alike. Some would demur, saying that feminist values have had nothing to do with it, but I believe the timing is more than mere coincidence. The Orthodox community has always emphasized Talmud Torah, with particular attention to the study of Talmud. High value was placed on its learning, and great status was conferred upon the learned. Women, however, were simply not part of this exalted enterprise. My two sisters and I grew up in a home suffused with Jewish learning. My father was a Talmud scholar, who studied for one hour every single morning before he went off to work in the clothing industry. Primary emphasis was placed on our Jewish education. My parents uprooted themselves and moved across the continent in search of the best Jewish schooling that could be had for their daughters. But neither my sisters nor I were ever introduced to a page of the Talmud in all of our years of elementary, high school, and college education. By contrast, male cousins and friends had many pages of Talmud under their belts by the time they were thirteen.

Today, all of that has changed. Young women in yeshiva day schools are taught Talmud at an early age, at the very same ages as their brothers. Women fill the Honors Talmud class in Jewish high schools. Institutions of higher Jewish traditional learning, such as the renowned Drisha Institute in New York, have been created especially for women. In local communities, women study Torah, Talmud, and other serious texts. Of equal significance, they manage to carve out the time for regular learning. A once uncommon sight is now almost taken for granted: women walking through the streets on a Sabbath afternoon with a tractate of Talmud tucked under the arm as they wend their way to class.

As the pool of women who learn enlarges, so does the number of those who commit themselves seriously to long-term study of religious texts; so, too, does the number of women who become teachers in the community, including teachers of Talmud and *halakha*. Remarkably, there are now dozens of Orthodox women around the world who have spent the last decade concentrating on this field of study. And there are dozens more coming up through the pipeline.

Given all of these factors, does the human rights critique seem appropriate to apply to Orthodox Judaism where it falls short of the new standards for women? Is feminism a theology of women to be interpreted differently inside of each system it impacts upon, or is it a sweeping new operating standard for every configuration of contemporary society? If sacred ritual that was codified in times of social patriarchy fails the human rights test, what is to happen to it? Is there a pace at which a religion can be transformed that will meet the new definitions of human dignity, yet feel continuous with the past? Does gender difference within a traditional religion ipso facto mean discrimination, or can a religious tradition teach broader society that gender distinctiveness and equality can coexist?

These are not easy questions to contemplate, much less to answer. Indeed, I find myself left with more questions at the conclusion of this essay than I had when I began, placing me well within the Jewish analytic tradition. To begin, let us examine these issues in light of the objections raised earlier to applying the human rights yardstick to orthodoxy.

> (a) The real horrors of human rights are immense. Though emotions tell me to dissociate this cause from the arena of human rights, the intellect tells me another. Although one should have some modesty of language appropriate to the degree of suffering, I know that the relativist argument does not hold up. No cause would ever qualify, for there is always something more terrible to which to compare one's own need. Human rights is a broad canopy. One can learn from the most extreme violations to minor infractions, and vice versa. But more than that is the interconnectedness of all of life. The domino effect of one thing upon the other is always operating, and when one sector of society moves closer to perfection, every other sector potentially moves a notch closer as well.
>
> (b) Orthodoxy is not a system into which one is permanently locked. This "free-to-leave" response is no answer. If one believes that orthodoxy holds the most truths of inherited tradition, that it maintains that power of the commanding voice, that it is the richest way of Jewish life, and that Sabbath observance, education of the young, ritual, and prayer are kept with a greater degree of faithfulness than in any of the other modern denominations, then why should one have to take a walk on this issue?[12] Staying within and bringing the system to its own best values is the more rewarding challenge and responsibility. When someone says to me, "with your views on women's issues, why don't you join the Conservative or Reform movement," I find myself singing the praises of an orthodoxy in which I want the best of both worlds, tradition and feminism.
>
> (c) I am reluctant to add more cannon fodder for those who relish criticism of Jews, Judaism, and Israel. I have learned from contemporary Israel that, in the long run, the choice of honest self-criticism works best. This is the lesson of democracies, and is also the mark of persons of integrity. Embarrassment should not be an issue. The benefit is that when one criticizes

oneself, there is a good chance that one's self-defense will be believed. Yet one must state the obvious: criticism of the system must be balanced, relieved by pointing to the merits as well.

(d) Self-protection. To make a difference, one cannot run for cover. If it is time to make the human rights accusation, then one is obliged to do so. Besides, there is now a sufficient group of cohorts; there is support in many quarters all around. Those who object to feminism would surely feel betrayed and angered by a human rights critique, especially coming from an insider. On the other hand, such a critique might just as likely engage those who have remained passive in the past. It should also be said here that over the years, I have found the community that opposes the ideas of feminism to be civil, not personally abusive, nor myself in any danger, things which many heroic civil rights workers are not privileged to claim.

(e) Ameliorations. With apologies to the reader who may have thought this conversation leading elsewhere, the improvements of the past two decades give pause for thought on the human rights question. I believe the cup is half full on women's issues, and filling. The new fact of women's access to the full range of texts is a powerful symbol of a liberation in process. Women now have the wherewithal to accede to the highest positions of leadership and authority in the community. There is no going back, no matter how many new believers there are in the laws of *kol isha*. The new rituals, prayer groups, new roles—all of these are symbolic of women on their way to a fuller sense of equity and responsibility in the tradition.

I would be the first to admit that, taken item by item, few of the innovations mentioned above are earth shaking. But altogether, they add up to a matter of great significance: the redefinition of women's role in the liturgical, spiritual, and intellectual life of the community with its fundamental shift from private to public roles. All of the small steps reflect new spiritual expectations of and by Orthodox women. Each act proclaims the growing acceptance of women in public roles in Jewish life. The presumption today is that women will locate themselves in academy and synagogue, as well as in home and *mikvah*. Slowly but surely, a woman's presence in sacred settings is becoming normal, natural, familiar, everyday. The taboos against seeing her and hearing her in the performance of communal acts of holiness are being lifted.

It is true that this is all a far slower and more frustrating process, this cranking out of women's new roles and rights inch by inch. At one level, it would seem that whatever can speed up the process, such as human rights activism, should be introduced. Yet I believe that the incremental process has some advantages as well, particularly the sense of connectedness to the tradition. Change is perceived as being not in tension with what went before but rather as flowing forward smoothly through time, history, and community. This sense of connectedness is one of the great strengths of orthodoxy.

After all, modern Jews still do not know how to answer the vital question: To what extent and at what pace can you change from what was, yet continue to feel tied to Revelation? Introducing change can both enhance and diminish the ability to hear the Commanding Voice. What is the cut-off point that reverses direction downward? Orthodoxy offers a model of a community that, remarkably, has maintained both the authority and the sense of Revelation through all the intervening years since Sinai. Would the introduction of human rights into the question of what women may or may not do in marriage ritual change that balance? Conceivably so. In any event, community sensibilities are to be factored into the equation.

Second, the slower pace of orthodoxy offers another insight. All the answers about equality of roles are not yet in. Perhaps every differentiation between men and women should not automatically and categorically be equated with inequity. Who knows but that a blurring of all the lines, and at rapid pace, might not be a blueprint for great confusion ahead? There is already a significant body of post-feminist literature that suggests that definitions of male and female go beyond biology. Some of these findings suggest that there might be merit to gender-distinctive roles and that ritual and religious life may be among the appropriate places to allow for such differentiation. Why ritual? Because once you acknowledge that there is value to retaining gender definitions beyond biology, once you affirm that it is possible to hold in harmony equality and gender distinctiveness, then finely detailed ritual is a warm-spirited, non-self-centered way to differentiate. Ultimately, it is ritual that has the capacity to take differences beyond the immediacy of interpersonal relationships to a transcendent place.

Closing Caveats

But I must take yet one more turn. Having defended a religious community's right to proceed to at its own pace, with its internal considerations given primacy, I must add two caveats. First, there are instances when a community cannot be left to its own devices. When a community fails the test of internal repair, when the steps taken toward resolution are too slow, when the issue is not one of access but infringement on the basic rights of an individual to personal happiness, where the religion allows punitive measures to be brought by one individual against another, then all the force of the human rights movement—language and processes—must be brought to bear. This, no matter how primitive one's beloved religion will appear as the matter comes to broad public light. I speak of the tragic case of the *agunah* who cowers under the threat of blackmail or spite, whose life is on hold, whose potential for future marital happiness and whose right to bear children is curtailed, while the leadership debates whether this or that resolution is consonant with a man's absolute right.

Too much time has already passed and too much good will has been spent while the focus remains on individual cases rather than on a full-scale solution to the problem. Only the public embarrassment that comes of the human rights critique will enable rabbinic leadership to see how fully unethical and untenable the situation is. It is no accident that the loathsome case of the betrothal of a minor daughter by her father as a means of spiting his wife was solved by the rabbis two years after the problem was made known in the community and four days after it appeared on page eight of the *New York Times.* The most potent force in the human rights arsenal is the public press, and whatever the cost in image to an ethical community, all stops must be pulled out.

The second caveat is that although human rights tactics may not be used for internal problems, there is no reason why the language of human rights should not be used to wage the internal struggle. In fact, this is a perfectly Jewish thing to do, in the spirit not only of the prophets but of the basic Biblical credo of human life—that every human being is created in the image of God. When one side speaks of God-given roles, the other side should speak of the divinely mandated goal of human dignity. The language of human rights should be engaged in dialogue with the language of *halakha,* the development and interpretation of law and tradition. To separate these two, regrettably as is often the case among those most intensely committed to *halakha,* is to fail the real mission of Jewish law, the creation of a just and ethical society.

In that sense, perhaps, Orthodox Jews, myself included, should be willing to continue the conversation with others in the human rights community regarding the issue of feminism. We might have more to gain than we think.

Notes

1. But it is not a one-way street. Orthodox Judaism has as much to offer to feminism in the way of self-correction.

2. The principle of absolute right is discussed in the Talmud as differentiating between men and women. The Talmud is the quasi-canonical text, second to the Bible in Judaism, and the source of much of *halakha,* Jewish law and tradition. The Talmud comprises two parts: the Mishnah (six tractates of primarily legal content, civil and religious) and the Gemara (sixty-three voluminous tractates that contain an explication of the laws of the Mishnah, theology, liturgy, ethics, exegesis, lore, history, and more). It is the sum of the work of generations of rabbis who lived between the first century B.C.E. to the fifth century C.E. (some scholars say the seventh).

3. Unfortunately, the word fundamentalism has become synonymous with a repugnant political reality, but here I mean it to represent fidelity to canon law, to particular beliefs and a set of actions.

4. Judith Romney Wegner traces this theme throughout her book, *Chattel or Person? The Status of Women in the Mishnah* (London: Oxford University Press, 1988), 168.

5. According to *halakha*, husbands and wives may not resume sexual relations following menses until the wife immerses herself in the *mikvah*.

6. Interestingly, despite all of this care, women's *tefila* groups are often referred to as "women's *minyan*" by those who seek to discredit them.

7. Divorce and other family matters are not religious issues even though their jurisdiction comes within the religious courts.

8. Women are obligated to recite the grace but as individuals and not as members of a community.

9. Some rabbis will allow a woman to read only the English translation of the Aramaic *ketubah,* but there have been Orthodox weddings where a woman has read the *ketubah* in the original.

10. She does not repeat the groom's recitation of the marriage formula, "Behold, with this ring you are consecrated unto me according to the laws of Moses and Israel," for that would be considered a departure from the traditional marriage ritual.

11. Some Orthodox rabbis will not permit a bride to give a ring under the *huppah* altogether, but others who do so are careful to point out what is tradition and what is not.

12. An *agunah* who wants to remain faithful to her community of belief should not be forced out of it to find personal protection from abuse.

13

REPLY ALAN F. SEGAL

Jewish Orthodoxy, Modernity, and Women's Rights

The issues raised by Blu Greenberg are subtle ones. They do not involve the freeing of political captives or the violent oppression of a freedom-loving minority. One could easily argue that gender equality issues in Jewish *halakha* were not on the list of important human rights issues of the twentieth century. They do not rank as important as the Muslim–Hindu rioting, the solution to the Yugoslavian war, the oppression of the Kurds, the freedom of Africans in South Africa, the future of the former Soviet bloc, or the possibility of a democratic China.

Indeed, any oppression that an Orthodox woman might feel as a woman could easily be resolved by her leaving orthodoxy and entering a more egalitarian form of Judaism. She could continue to live as she liked and be as pious as she wished in Conservative or Reform Judaism. Reform Judaism for two decades and Conservative Judaism for almost one now have made the equality of women one of their main agenda items. Not only are women accepted as equals of men in all ritual occasions; they may study; may study the same texts as men, with men; stand on the dais and preach; even be ordained as rabbis. Both Conservative and Reform Judaism now have a significant and fast-growing minority of women rabbis who are experimenting with a very wide spectrum of ritual and moral stances about the gender equality of women. Only a small part of that spectrum would be practical for the Orthodox community.

Yet this is not an adequate response for those Orthodox women who want to remain in their community and to achieve within it some of the same kinds of rights that their Reform and Conservative sisters have achieved. They do not want to be Reform or Conservative Jews. They want to be equal and full members of the Orthodox Jewish community. Their identities are formed and fixed within that community. And, what is even more important, they have a vision of their own role in their community that they can communicate to their less cooperative brothers and sisters. In the end, by staying within that community they can change the male-only and male-superior culture that has characterized Orthodox Judaism for so long. So the appropriate question is not how much the Orthodox women will change the halakhic interpretation of gender roles, so much as how far they can raise the consciousness of Orthodox men and women who see the feminist requests as threatening or irreligious.

Blu Greenberg has summarized a series of issues that define the dispute of Orthodox feminists. Some of the issues are terminological and symbolic. Jews have traditionally referred to themselves as the sons or daughters of their fathers in Hebrew; it would be more equal and accurate to describe themselves as sons and daughters of both parents, especially when Jewish identity (Jew, non-Jew) is itself traced matrilineally, while only status within the community (Priest, Levite, Israel) follows the male line. Referring to the matriarchs too would make the prayers more gender equal. But changing the wording of prayer is not just changing a naming convention. Jews memorize their prayers, so any change is strange and unfamiliar, interrupting the rhythm. Furthermore, changing the order and wording of prayer was one of the hallmarks of Reform Judaism in the eighteenth and nineteenth centuries, making it an even more sensitive issue for the Orthodox community.

Beyond that, Blu raises issues of changing various ritual practices that exclude women or appear to mark women as inferior. Men are given special privileges in services by wearing distinctive ritual clothing. Men are given the right to lead prayers, to read from the scrolls of the law, and to preach from the pulpit. Some of these practices could be changed to accommodate more gender equality.

Finally, there are important ways in which long-lasting legal opinions have disadvantaged women. Women are not allowed to be witnesses; they are not counted for the *minyan*—the ten men needed for public prayer. On the whole, the laws concerning marriage and divorce were originally very fair to women but time has simply outrun the legal practice. Women may not divorce without the consent of their husbands, but husbands are free to divorce without their wives' consent. This has caused enormous hardships for some women, who must, in effect, bribe their husbands to grant them a legal divorce. The community is extremely sensitive to this issue today, seeking informal accommodations that protect women's rights. But the issue could be better resolved. Finally, women whose husbands are thought to be dead but not proven so, the *agunot,* are long-standing problems in Jewish law, and seekers of gender equality have raised the issue anew in a sharp way.

The issue of divorce within the Orthodox community is especially vexing. Whatever the legal precedents, in practice few rabbis have been willing to allow women to bring suit for divorce and so the plight of women seeking divorce from unwilling husbands has carried over for generations. More recently the number of women in this position has greatly increased. Not satisfied with the many different available avenues for easing these women's plight, Blu presses for structural change so as to eliminate the inequity permanently.

Blu raises important issues, not only for Orthodox women and not only for Jewish orthodoxy, but for the study of religious modernization generally. Orthodoxy in Judaism has always had resources that prevent it from becoming another form of "fundamentalism." I use quotations because fundamentalism is, properly speaking, a variety of Protestant denominationalism, but is applied by extension to other religious phenomena, often with the implication of terrorism or religious fanaticism. I would extend the definition beyond Protestantism but only with the proviso that it does not necessarily imply violence. Orthodoxy is not fundamentalist because it has always been able to discuss and debate, able to change, albeit slowly, in accordance with pressures from history.

The issue of gender equality, however, may prove to be the most difficult problem of all for orthodoxy, as it has been in numerous other places. Let us characterize the fundamentalist movements we have in mind here as religious movements that purposely eschew the results of Western science and culture as immoral. They are almost always trying in some central way to protect the supposed exalted and traditional role of women. This is a rallying cry for every major fundamentalist movement in the world right now. So we may say that issues of gender turn out to be fundamental for the dispute between mainline and liberal religious feelings on the one hand and "fundamentalist" views on the other.

In this regard, the dispute between feminist and non-feminist Jews is not so much a dispute over how much and what kind of equality women will achieve in twenty-first-century orthodoxy, so much as it is a life struggle within orthodoxy to decide whether it will remain a flexible and changeable force or will, along with religious conservatism elsewhere in the United States and the world, ossify further into a new kind of fundamentalism of the Jewish variety. The signs are not good: violent reactions to political events and extremist positions within the Jewish community are now emerging with halakhic justifications and a party of Orthodox Jews willing to justify the violence. The ability of Orthodox feminist women to make their positions known and understood, and to continue to influence the community and carry on dialogue within it, could make them a force for revitalization and against extremism.

14

ANN ELIZABETH MAYER

Islamic Law and Human Rights: Conundrums and Equivocations

Law is a central component of Islam, so it is not surprising that contemporary Muslims' attempts to come to terms with human rights should center on legal issues. The conversation on rights in Muslim milieus tends to focus on whether the civil and political rights afforded in international human rights law are compatible with Islamic law, with Muslims taking widely varying positions on this question. Although economic, social, and cultural rights are also bones of contention in contemporary Muslim societies, Islamic law is less likely to figure in debates in these areas.

A rough indicator of the areas where Islamic law competes with human rights law can be seen in the reservations that Muslim countries have entered to provisions in human rights conventions, many of which advise that the ratifying countries will uphold Islamic law at the expense of human rights where the two conflict. The pattern is instructive: not a single Muslim country has entered any Islamic reservations to the International Convention on Economic, Social, and Cultural Rights. Indeed, in ratifying this convention Egypt asserted that these rights presented no conflicts with the *shari'a*, Islamic law.[1] That is, the assumption seems to be that Islam and economic, social, and cultural rights are complementary. In contrast, many Muslim countries have entered reservations to provisions in human rights conventions guaranteeing, for instance, women's equality or freedom of religion on the grounds that these conflict with Islamic law. Moreover, in Muslim countries, laws that claim Islamic pedigrees often clash dramatically with civil and political rights under international law. Since this chapter is part of a volume that examines the competing claims of religion and human rights, civil and political rights are the logical centerpiece.

Most Muslim countries have largely discarded Islamic law and replaced it by laws along European lines. One might, therefore, ask why Islamic law should be referred to at all on a topic like human rights. However, dramatic recent cases illustrate how, even in Muslim countries where Islamic law plays only a marginal role, Islamic precepts come into play where civil and political rights are concerned. Moreover, Islamic law has grown in influence since the 1970s with the Islamic resurgence. This has led to selective reinstatements of Islamic law in several countries that had largely abandoned it in favor of laws of European derivation.[2] The Islamic rules embodied in the positive laws and court rulings of various Muslim countries can fly in the face of international human rights law.[3] Problematic features include severe deficiencies in criminal procedure, rules that discriminate against women and non-Muslims, harsh criminal penalties that entail great suffering, and a prohibition against conversion from Islam. What are often abstract theoretical disputes in other religious traditions about the compatibility of human rights and local religions can therefore be of great practical significance in Muslim countries.

But what is Islamic law? Many Muslims believe that their religious law crystallized centuries ago in the works of medieval jurists; others contend that Islamic principles must evolve as society evolves and should be rethought and reformed to suit current circumstances. In milieus where the ideas of medieval jurists remain influential, it is hard for human rights to make inroads. Medieval Islamic legal culture emphasized the duties of the believer toward the Deity rather than the rights of the individual vis-à-vis the ruler. According to the traditional perspective, rulers had obligations to implement *shari'a* law, and their subjects were to obey them unless ordered to do something sinful.

Legal and political institutions that could effectively curb despotism were not adopted in Muslim countries until Westernizing reforms in the nineteenth century. Before then, Islamic doctrine suggested that the only way to combat tyranny was through rebellion. In contrast, human rights theory presumes that governments are restrained by effective principles of constitutionalism and popular sovereignty. Since the nineteenth century there have been controversies in Muslim countries over the degree to which Western-style constitutionalism and democratic freedoms are compatible with Islamic law. Highly traditionalist Saudi Arabia remains one of the last hold-outs; absolute monarchy is still officially treated as the Islamic form of government par excellence. Article 6 of the Saudi Basic Law provides that citizens are to pay allegiance to the king in accordance with the Qur'an and *sunna,* in submission and obedience.[4] That is, the government still calls for citizens to render the kind of humble obedience to the sovereign that monarchs expected in Muslim societies centuries ago. By and large, contemporary Muslims have moved a considerable distance from the kind of Islamic

The Organization of the Islamic Conference

world view endorsed by the Saudis, tending to believe that their religion embrace some, if not all, human rights and modern democratic principle

Muslims' Human Rights: Between Islamic Law and International Law

Muslims are conducting their struggles to define where Islam stands on human rights after the establishment of international human rights law in numerous conventions and declarations produced under UN auspices since World War II.[5] All Muslim states, as UN members, are governed by international law. This is acknowledged in the Charter of the Organization of Islamic Conference (OIC), to which all Muslim countries belong, where members reaffirm "their commitment to the UN Charter and fundamental Human Rights, the purposes and principles of which provide the basis for fruitful cooperation amongst all people."[6] Any Islamic human rights project should thus take into account the existing international human rights regime.

Various Muslim countries have put forward Islamic human rights standards that are intended to replace the standards set in international law, and the OIC has encouraged Muslims to follow Islamic rights. In August 1990 a meeting of OIC foreign ministers endorsed the Cairo Declaration on Human Rights in Islam, one of the most widely touted of the new Islamic human rights schemes. Upon inspection, its protections turn out to be much feebler than those afforded by international law.[7] This OIC initiative suggests a weakening of Muslim countries' commitments to follow international law. Various rules in the Cairo Declaration are also impossible to reconcile with OIC members' obligations incurred via ratification of international human rights conventions.[8] How to resolve these conflicts was never explained by the OIC.

In terms of Islamic jurisprudence, what is the basis for the authority of Islamic laws promulgated by governments of modern nation-states? Documents like the Cairo Declaration are produced via secular political processes, as is public international law, in which nation-states act as the decision makers. However, nation-states possess no more authority to declare where Islamic law stands on human rights than NATO countries possess to pronounce on where Christian doctrine stands on human rights. The concurrence of Muslim states on supposedly Islamic human rights principles may give these principles a certain cachet in the eyes of their authors, but it signifies precisely nothing in terms of Islamic theology or law.

At the 1993 Vienna Human Rights Conference, Prince Saud al-Faisal made a statement extolling Islamic human rights that warrants dissection.[9] He asserted that the Cairo Declaration embodied "an expression of the will of over one billion people," a highly dubious claim since the OIC and its member nations, only a few of which were democratic, had made no effort to ascertain the views of Muslims on rights questions before issuing the declaration. Although he was a member of a ruling family that insists on all the prerogatives of absolute monarchy, the prince spoke as if Islam had its own efficacious scheme of rights. He maintained that Islamic law was "a comprehensive system for universal human rights."

In an example of the kind of equivocation so often encountered in this area, Prince Saud al-Faisal did not call for rejecting the universality of rights. Rather, he claimed to have accepted that the principles and objectives of human rights were universal, but maintained that it was necessary in their application to show consideration "for the diversity of societies, taking into account their various historical, cultural, and religious backgrounds and legal systems." That is, he seemed eager to downplay the conflicts with international human rights created by the Cairo Declaration and to persuade the international community that, in supporting this OIC initiative, Saudi Arabia was not breaking with the international consensus on human rights.

As noted, the sponsors of the Cairo Declaration claimed that it represented an Islamic consensus, when in reality no such consensus had been achieved, whether at the intergovernmental level or at the level of private institutions and groups. Sketching official stances on human rights is not too difficult, but it is virtually impossible to convey in a short paper the range of views on human rights that one could find among different categories of Muslims. In this connection, one needs to recall how decentralized Islam is. Islam lacks any single institution with power akin to that of the Vatican, which can pronounce on doctrine. With the rise in literacy, Muslims have increasingly shown a disposition to make up their own minds on contemporary controversies, disregarding the interpretations of learned legal scholars and instead reading the Qur'an or accounts of the Prophet Muhammad to extract their own lessons.

Reviewing Muslims' sharply conflicting conclusions regarding how their religion relates to human rights, one perceives that Islam per se cannot be the factor dictating the irreconcilable positions. Instead, these seem to be caused by a complex interplay of factors such as differing religious philosophies, political interests, local cultures and customs, social and economic backgrounds, levels of education, and the contrasting perspectives of urban versus rural dwellers and women versus men.

As disputes go on about where Islam stands on international human rights, the latter have won a considerable following among Muslims. As rights-consciousness has expanded and a number of energetic independent human rights NGOs have emerged, Muslims who support human rights have tended to treat the international standards as definitive. That is, alternative Islamic human rights principles have been put forward by the OIC and its member states while, at the grass-roots level, secular rights concepts have already established a sizable Muslim constituency.[10]

One could speculate that governmental schemes of Islamic human rights constitute a reaction to growing popular demands for the observance of international human rights. The Moroccan feminist and human rights advocate Fatima Mernissi suggests that regimes have tried to hide away international human rights law to avoid opening debates on the nature of power.[11] It seems that Muslim conservatives hope that by deploying the authority of religion they can maintain old hierarchies and forestall expansion of freedoms. To the extent that they are reactive in nature, the Islamic rights schemes proposed by governments are naturally more intelligible in terms of the politics of human rights than in terms of Islamic theology and law. That they are fraught with incoherence should come as no surprise.

Some representative provisions illustrate the character of the Cairo Declaration and typify many other recently concocted Islamic rights schemes. A striking feature is their evasiveness; their true purport will often only be apparent to persons who are familiar both with the original international rights formulations and with rules of Islamic law. Their wording frequently seems designed to camouflage divergences from international standards. In lieu of provision for equal rights for all persons regardless of sex or religion, Article 1 states that "all men are equal in terms of basic human dignity and basic obligations and responsibilities [not rights], without any discrimination on the grounds of race, color, language, sex, religious belief, political affiliation, social status or other considerations." Article 6 provides that "woman is equal to man in human dignity," omitting provisions for equality in rights and affirming the husband's responsibility for the support and welfare of the family. Article 6 thereby accommodates discriminatory Islamic laws on personal status that assign wives the status of dependents.

Article 5 provides that for the right to marry there should be "no restrictions stemming from race, color or nationality." By not prohibiting restrictions based on religion, Article 5 accommodates the bans on Muslim women marrying outside the faith and on Muslim men marrying women other than Muslims, Christians, or Jews. Article 2 prohibits the taking of life except for a *shari'a*-prescribed reason, and Article 19 states that there should be no crime or punishment except as provided for in the *shari'a*. Neither article explains what this entails. Persons knowledgeable about *shari'a* law will appreciate that these articles permit the death penalty to be imposed for crimes such as adultery or apostasy from Islam and accommodate corporal punishments like hand amputations and stoning to death that conflict with international standards prohibiting cruel, degrading, or inhuman punishments. Notable for their absence in the Cairo Declaration are provisions calling for the observance of democratic principles in political systems; protection for freedom of religion, freedom of association, and freedom of the press; and guarantees of equality in rights and equal protection of the law.

For the most part, Islamic human rights turn out to involve rights that are borrowed from international law and then qualified or distorted in some fashion. The misleading "equality" formulations already mentioned are perfect illustrations. These Islamic human rights initiatives represent hybrids of international rights principles and incongruous Islamic features. The borrowed rights are subject to supposedly "Islamic" limitations. For example, Article 24 says: "All the rights and freedoms stipulated in this Declaration are subject to the Islamic *shari'a*." Imposing such Islamic conditions is an exercise in vacuity so long as specific definitions of what these Islamic conditions entail are not forthcoming. The authors obviously have no wish to be explicit as to how they intend to circumscribe rights, preferring to equivocate and thereby accord governments the freedom to interpret Islamic limits as broadly as they please. Since modern civil and political rights are typically designed to protect the rights of the individual against the state, allowing the state complete discretion to define the scope of rights and freedoms renders them illusory.

Article 29.2 of the Universal Declaration of Human Rights (UDHR) stipulates that the exercise of rights and freedoms "shall be subject only to such limitations as are determined by law solely for the purpose of securing due recognition and respect for the rights and freedoms of others and of meeting the just requirements of morality, public order and the general welfare in a democratic society." International law does not allow rights to be compromised by the superimposition of vague conditions grounded in local laws and cultures. Regarding certain rights such as equality and freedom of religion, international law allows no qualifications, setting its own rules for when and how other rights can be qualified. Where Islam is so conceived as to limit rights, the result of using Islamic human rights schemes to supplant international law is, naturally, that Muslims and non-Muslims subject to the jurisdiction of Muslim states can wind up with rights provisions vastly inferior to those set in international law. No theoretical justification for assigning Muslims to an inferior standard of human rights has been offered by the OIC.

No persons or organizations with any competence or credibility in the area of human rights have endorsed the kinds of rights set forth in the Cairo

Declaration. They recognize the harmful impact of policies to eviscerate international human rights and to strengthen the hands of governments at the expense of the governed. Independent Muslim rights activists fighting to advance the cause of human rights have continued to work courageously for the advancement of human rights according to the international standards under highly adverse conditions. In other words, the "Islamic" rubric pasted on the rights afforded in schemes like the Cairo Declaration has not made its emasculated rights principles more palatable to Muslims who have embraced the ideals of human rights. Muslim women committed to feminist agendas have been particularly vigorous in demanding adherence to international norms that guarantee women full equality, and in rejecting the notion that they are governed by a different and more restrictive Islamic standard.

Muslims' Conflicting Views on Women's Rights

Many traditional-minded jurists and fundamentalist groups are convinced that Islam supports the established patriarchal order. They assume that men alone are equipped for roles in politics and society and that women are meant to serve men as house-bound dependents whose lives center on family tasks. (Of course, this model of the male–female relationship does entail duties for men, who are meant to look after the women in their charge.) Depending on one's interpretation, imposing such Islamic conditions on women's rights means that women might be deprived of education, mobility, job opportunities, guardianship of children, voting rights, equal shares of inheritance, and the like, and that they might also be subjected to sex segregation, child marriage and forced marriage, genital mutilation, veiling requirements, sharing their husband with co-wives, beatings and arrests for disobeying their husbands, arbitrary divorce, restrictions on giving testimony, and other degrading treatment. A woman whose rights are circumscribed by doctrines exposing her to these ills is not remotely close to enjoying the equality accorded her by international human rights law.

Some of the most scathing critiques of traditional interpretations of Islam that clash with human rights come from feminists, who speak out despite the grave risks that they may incur in calling for reforms to accommodate equality for women. Islamic feminists challenge the whole notion of a necessary conflict between Islam and women's international human rights. They differentiate between the discriminatory rules found in the works of Islam's medieval jurists and the ideologies of contemporary fundamentalists from the ideas set forth in the text of the Qur'an and the example of the Prophet. A typical feminist view is that the Islamic sources have been distorted by biased male interpreters eager to rationalize their privileges and power and that the original sources, when properly understood, support the equality of the sexes.[12] Islamic feminism is turning out to be a potent force for Islamic renewal and one of the most dynamic influences contributing to the integration of human rights within a reformed Islam.

The reactions to contemporary Islamic feminism vary. Depending on their outlook, some Muslims welcome proof that Islam can be reconceived as a progressive force that supports women's advancement and participation in society. In some milieus Muslim women who question what Islamic jurists or fundamentalist leaders decree about women's status may be denounced as heretics. The rise of a militant Islamic fundamentalism that effectively mobilizes support for its populist programs has correlated with escalating denunciations of Muslim women who demand freedom and equality in rights; they are castigated as traitors to their own cultures and agents of Western imperialism. To counter attacks on feminism as "un-Islamic," women's NGOs have circulated feminist analyses and adopted programs of outreach to encourage Muslims to learn about the emancipatory aspects of the Islamic heritage.[13] Impeding the ability of women to carry out the mission of Islamic reform has been their long exclusion from high positions in Islamic institutions. There is no woman sheikh of al-Azhar, no woman *mufti* (an official qualified to issue rulings on Islamic law), no woman ayatollah (the highest rank in the Shi'i clerical hierarchy). Women thus lack the institutional credentials and prestigious titles that can lend authority to men's pronouncements on behalf of Islam.

Women's Rights Versus Religious Freedoms

When women challenge the restrictions on their freedoms that conservatives claim Islam requires, Westerners may view these as assaults on religious freedom. Such challenges typically arise when men and women have sharply conflicting views on women's rights, as happens when men cling to religious tradition to justify denying women rights and the women try to overthrow traditional doctrines in the interest of enhancing their rights. Westerners may link Muslims' disputes about whether women must defer to traditional strictures to current controversies over how to balance the principle of religious freedom against the principle of women's equality. Whether such balancing is permissible is not expressly addressed in texts of international human rights instruments, but analysis reveals that elevating conformity with religious dogmas above fundamental principles like the right to equality leads to conflicts with the essence of international human rights.

To illuminate how this issue is being addressed, one might review two problematic recent pieces on Islam and women's rights. Westerners often act unsettled and even aggrieved when confronted by Muslim women who, in disregard of time-honored religious strictures, demand the equality in rights that international law affords them. A good example is a review by Matthew A. Levitt of a volume on women's human rights in the Muslim world, *Faith and Freedom,* in which Muslim women's aspirations to enjoy international human rights are excoriated.[14] Levitt seems grievously offended by the female authors' appropriations of ideas that he associates with secular human rights, objecting that "there must be a willingness to accept and respect religion and to find space for women's human rights within religious parameters."[15] Levitt does not insist that Muslim men's rights be similarly restricted by religious parameters, which apparently leaves that half of the Muslim population free to benefit from human rights, secular though they may be. While insisting that women may enjoy rights only insofar as their religious traditions permit, Levitt incongruously asserts that the need to protect women's human rights is a given. In this he perversely denies an obvious fact: rights that are subordinated to religious criteria cannot be accurately termed human rights.[16] In this self-contradiction, Levitt resembles the Iranian officials discussed below, who are anxious to maintain the pretense that they support human rights for women while at the same time they endorse incompatible religious doctrines.

These days it is a rare man who, in fighting against women's international human rights, will confess to being determined to exclude women from enjoying these rights. This leads to the incongruous use of the term "human rights" for policies aiming to uphold discriminatory rules affecting women. The practical results of using religious criteria to circumscribe Muslim women's rights will be "rights" far different from the human rights guaranteed by international law. The rights enjoyed by women in countries like Iran and the Sudan, where "religious parameters" determine the scope of women's rights, are distinctly inferior to the standards of rights enjoyed by women in Scandinavia, where international human rights conventions are rigorously adhered to. The situation of women in countries like Afghanistan and Saudi Arabia, where the governments follow particularly reactionary interpretations of Islamic requirements affecting women, affords an even starker contrast with the rights picture in Scandinavia. Thus "human rights" for women, as propounded by Levitt and others who insist that women's rights must be set within religious parameters, amount to a subset of inferior rights specially tailored for women and designed to keep them in their place. Women are thereby implicitly excluded from the category of humans entitled to benefit from the protections of human rights.

A related attitude is evinced in an article attacking the bolder premises of Islamic feminism by Anouar Majid, an academic who has recently written on the politics of feminism. Majid shares Levitt's view that Muslim women are precluded from seeking emancipation via secular rights, but he also faults Muslim women who find a warrant for claiming too many rights within an Islamic framework.[17] Although censuring feminists who explore innovative approaches to harmonize Islam and full human rights for women, Majid does not want to say outright that he envisages treating women according to standards that relegate them to an inferior, subordinate status. Majid tries to have it both ways: paying lip service to the need for women's liberation and professing sympathy for feminist goals, while stipulating that women's liberation should respect Islamic boundaries on individual freedom, which he insists are set by divine decree. Majid criticizes Fatima Mernissi for not deferring to the mandates of Scripture. Since Mernissi reads Scripture as emancipatory, Majid must mean that her interpretations of Islamic law are not legitimate. Majid seems to assume that Muslim women should abide by his views of scriptural constraints on their freedoms. Whereas Levitt emphasizes that Muslim women are precluded from enjoying secular human rights, Majid seeks to delegitimize the projects of Muslim women who seek equal rights within an Islamic framework. The two concur in one area: by implication they both treat men's religious convictions regarding what restraints should be placed on women's freedoms as definitive and binding on women.

To illustrate what the clashes in this area entail, let us consider two very simple scenarios, which could and should be expanded if this essay were longer. Assume that in each case we have a Muslim man who is sincerely convinced that Islamic law entitles him to subjugate and control a woman and who complains that affording her human rights interferes with his religious freedom. When he is confronted by a Muslim woman who sincerely believes that her religion affords her equality in rights, is protecting religious freedom the issue? Or, are the woman's human rights the real issue? Unless we assume that the only religious freedom that is at stake is the man's, phrasing the question in terms of religious freedom gets us nowhere. The parties' religious convictions are diametrically opposed, and calling for them to have the freedom to act according to their respective religious beliefs only leads to an impasse. Neither his nor her religious position can be vindicated without one thwarting the other. Although conservatives often speak in such conflicts as if it is self-evident that the man's religious freedom should prevail, this does not logically flow from any principle of international human rights. Instead, it seems to reflect a bias in favor of the status quo.

A second scenario might involve a conflict between this same man and a Muslim woman who believes strongly that she should be protected by international human rights, but does not believe that Islamic law is relevant or has become alienated from it. Is protecting religious freedom the issue? Or, are the woman's human rights the real issue? We have a clash between one party whose position is grounded in religion and the other whose position is grounded in human rights law. Should we say that any time a religious belief leads to clashes with human rights law, the latter must give way? That religious beliefs should always override human rights claims? The proposition that women should forfeit human rights where these conflict with religious traditions would, if accepted and translated into a generalizable principle, indicate that religious principles should always trump conflicting human rights claims. But, again, such a view diverges from international human rights law, which never assigns primacy to religious precepts over principles like the right to equality.

Significantly, where religious beliefs mandating racial discrimination conflict with the human rights of a racial group (as they did, say, in the case of the beliefs of the Afrikaaners' Dutch Reformed Church or the U.S. Southern Baptists), few would insist that the right to equality should be compromised. The notion that religious beliefs mandating discriminatory treatment should be held sacrosanct where women's human rights are at stake but must cede to human rights claims where racial discrimination is involved has no warrant whatsoever in international human rights law, where discrimination on the basis of sex and race are equally prohibited. ICCPR Article 26 affirms that all persons are equal before the law and calls for law to "guarantee to all persons equal and effective protection against discrimination on any ground such as race, color, sex, language, religion, political or other opinion, national or social origin, property, birth or other status." Allowing one person's liberties to be circumscribed simply because they offend the religious beliefs of another who is convinced that there is a divine mandate for inequality would entail rejecting one of the fundamental underpinnings of human rights law—that equality in liberty is a basic right of all persons.

The urgency of upholding the woman's right to decide what freedoms she wants to claim in the hypotheticals above becomes apparent when balancing the respective harms that would result from insisting that the woman defer to the man's claim of religious freedom against the harms that flow from upholding the woman's rights at the expense of the man's religious beliefs. This reveals a clear disparity in the degrees of loss involved. Deferring to the man's religious freedoms will expose the woman to oppression and loss of vital freedoms. In contrast, upholding the woman's rights will not unduly interfere with the man's leading a full life as a Muslim and fulfilling his religious obligations. It will mean that he cannot exert his dominion over a woman whose freedom he is entitled to fetter, according to his religious views, over her objections. In sum, weighing the respective harms produces additional reasons for concluding that the woman's human rights are more deserving of protection, because their loss would be of far greater consequence.

Constraints on Reformist and Innovative Islamic Thought

Of course, human rights issues would not occasion such sharp clashes if some entrenched interpretations of Islamic law did not lag so far behind human rights law. That Islamic thought has not yet made a more positive contribution to human rights does not imply that human rights cannot be successfully developed within an Islamic framework. The rich source material and the complex legacy of Islamic civilization offer many avenues for meshing human rights law with Islamic values. However, progressive trends in Islamic thought are being impeded by forces of reaction, which threaten progressive and creative thinkers in Muslim societies.

Reactionary clerics and fundamentalist leaders have anathematized Muslims who dare to challenge traditional dogmas or to argue that Islam should accommodate rights and freedoms. For example, some of Iran's most liberal-minded senior clerics have been placed under house arrest or jailed to stop them from speaking out against the idea that Islam mandates repression and intolerance. One of the most influential Iranian advocates of a rational and humanistic Islam that can accommodate human rights, Professor Abdol Karim Sorush, has been harassed, physically attacked, and threatened. Nonetheless, during a recent lecture in Washington, D.C., at considerable risk, he dared to state publicly that Islam was subordinated to criteria of justice, not the other way around—a direct challenge to a fundamental tenet of Iran's official Islamic ideology.[18] He has since been dismissed from his academic posts and prevented from traveling abroad. Under fundamentalist rule in the Sudan, Mahmud Muhammad Taha, a Gandhi-like proponent of Islamic reform and human rights, was denounced by reactionary Islamic groups as an apostate and hanged in 1985. The tightening noose of repression under Umar al-Bashir's dictatorship has forced Taha's disciple, Abdullahi An-Na'im, into exile in the United States, where he continues his writing, which shows that Islam can be interpreted in constructive ways that provide cultural legitimacy for human rights.[19]

Similarly, the bold ideas for modernist interpretations of the Qur'an put forward by the Syrian intellectual Muhammad Shahrur can only circulate clandestinely in many Muslim countries because their governments have banned Shahrur's book under pressures from conservatives and fundamentalists, who charge Shahrur with undermining sacred truths. In response to a suit brought by irate fundamentalists, Egyptian courts ruled in proceedings during 1995–96 that Professor Nasr Hamid Abu Zaid was an apostate and that he had to be divorced from his Muslim wife. This was punishment for his proposing innovative ways of viewing the Qur'an. This disturbing case showed how, even under a basically secular military regime, proponents of Islamic renewal could be terrorized. Faced with the threat of assassination for his supposed apostasy, Abu Zaid may never be able to return safely to Egypt from his current exile in the Netherlands. As the Center for Human Rights Legal Aid in Egypt has noted, this ruling "has created an atmosphere of blindness, tension, and intolerance which stunts the growth of thought in scientific research."[20]

Brave feminists like Fatima Mernissi who have stood up to assert that Islam supports women's freedoms have been slandered, threatened, and assaulted. In 1989 Toujan Faisal, the Jordanian parliamentarian and outspoken proponent of feminist readings of the Islamic sources, was labeled an apostate by Islamic fundamentalists, who tried unsuccessfully to have her marriage invalidated and asserted that killing her was licit. Taslima Nasreen, the iconoclastic feminist writer from Bangladesh, has had to abandon her home country and flee to the West in the face of death threats. Many more examples could be cited of how innovative Islamic thinkers are menaced and throttled or are forced offshore, where they are cut off from their natural constituencies, attenuating the impact of their ideas in their own societies.

Not surprisingly, in conditions so unpropitious for innovation, Islamic thought tends to ratify existing hierarchies and legitimize restrictions on freedoms. The relative paucity of contributions to human rights that are grounded in Islamic principles ties in with the repressive political climate in which Islamic thought is being elaborated. Like the innovative Muslim intellectuals whose freedom is inhibited by autocratic and intolerant regimes, Islam itself has become a prisoner of politics. As a precious legitimating device, Islam has often been appropriated and monopolized by undemocratic regimes, which are terrified lest Islam should ever become conceived of as a tool of liberation.

Iran's Struggles to Define a Human Rights Policy

The record of the Islamic Republic of Iran illustrates the complexity of the relationship between Islam and human rights. Iran has struggled inconclusively to define a tenable "Islamic" position vis-à-vis human rights. As an example of Iran's ambivalence, one could cite the fact that the Islamic Republic has not chosen to terminate its status as party to the ICCPR, even though it has regularly violated ICCPR principles and has endorsed Islamic rights at odds with those principles. In the early 1980s, the Iranian representative bluntly told the UN that, because of its Islamic values, the Islamic Republic would have no qualms about violating human rights. According to the paraphrased record of his speech, he announced that:

> conventions, declarations and resolutions or decisions of international organizations, which were contrary to Islam, had no validity in the Islamic Republic of Iran.... The Universal Declaration of Human Rights, which represented secular understanding of the Judaeo-Christian tradition, could not be implemented by Muslims and did not accord with the system of values recognized by the Islamic Republic of Iran; his country would therefore not hesitate to violate its provisions, since it had to choose between violating the divine law of the country and violating secular conventions.[21]

Far from settling matters, this statement turned out to represent only one of many contradictory positions on rights to be articulated by the postrevolutionary regime. Although any critical review of Iran's human rights practice would reveal that Iran has repeatedly used "Islam" as a pretext for denying rights and freedoms, spokespersons for the Islamic Republic have for the most part tried to obscure as far as possible the degree to which Iran's purportedly "Islamic" approach to rights involves curtailing internationally protected rights. In so doing, Iran's clerical leaders have revealed that they actually believe that international human rights remain binding and that they lack real confidence in their Islamic rationalizations for violating rights.

The 1979 Iranian constitution provides Islamic grounds for restricting human rights protections. Islamic qualifications are repeatedly stressed in the constitution, but not in a coherent way. Although the constitution is replete with borrowed Western ideas and principles, Article 4 stipulates that all laws, including the constitution itself, must be based on Islamic criteria. This principle is echoed in the Preamble, which states that the constitution is based on Islamic principles. Article 20 provides that all citizens enjoy human rights according to Islamic standards. One would surmise from this that the constitutional rights principles should have an Islamic character. However, Article 20 also stipulates that human rights are to be subordinated to Islamic criteria. This indicates that constitutional human rights principles are not deemed to be Islamic but that the criteria that override and qualify them are Islamic. Article 21 declares that women's rights are guaranteed in accordance with Islamic criteria. It is significant that Islamic qualifications are specifically imposed on the rights of women, not on the rights of men. This signals the establishment of a hierarchy in which Islamic criteria are used to ensure that men rank above women and to provide pretexts for depriving women of human rights. Here one sees a direct correlation between the use in the constitution of Islamic criteria to restrict human rights and the regime's actual policies, which discriminate on the basis of sex in ways that violate principles of international law.

An intention to employ Islamic law at the expense of rights can be detected in some constitutional provisions that do not specifically invoke Islamic law. Article 19 provides: "The people of Iran, regardless of their ethnic, family and tribal origins, shall enjoy equal rights. Color, race, language and the like shall not be a cause for privilege." This formulation avoids altogether the question of whether equality can be denied on the basis of sex or religion, even though in any rights scheme based on Islamic law one would expect that the issues of equality of women and non-Muslims would be the among the most sensitive. The actual treatment of women and religious minorities in the wake of the 1979 revolution suggests that the omission of these two categories was designed to open space for the application of retrograde versions of *shari'a* law. One contrasts the equivocation in Iran's equality provisions with the clear statement in the UDHR, which in Article 1 provides that "[a]ll humans are born free and equal in dignity and rights," and in Article 2 provides that "Everyone is entitled to all the rights and freedoms set forth in this Declaration, without distinction of any kind, such as race, color, sex, language, religion, political or other opinion, national or social origin, property, birth or other status." Nothing in these vital provisions suggests that discrimination based on sex or religion becomes acceptable when religious doctrines are behind the curtailment of rights and freedoms. Paradoxically, Iran's constitution, in which Islamic criteria are used to subordinate women, includes in Article 20 an unqualified guarantee of equal protection of the secular law [*qanun*], for all citizens, both men and women—without mention of any Islamic qualifications. The inclusion of a secular equal protection clause is emblematic of how ideas taken from Western constitutions and international human rights law are pressed into a matrix of Islamic principles. The constitution also guarantees the equality of men and women before the secular law [*qanun*] in Article 3.14. However, in the light of other provisions like Articles 4 and 20, it is "Islamic criteria" that ultimately govern in rights questions. That these secular guarantees are included only to be nullified by religious qualifications is one of the many conundrums in Iran's official stances on human rights.

Article 10 calls for the family to be safeguarded according to Islamic rights and morality. What this entails was revealed immediately after th revolution, when the government harshly suppressed women's protests against its mandatory veiling requirements. Important reforms advancing women's status in the liberal Iranian Family Protection Act were abrogated and women were pressured to abandon their jobs and return to the home to devote themselves to maternal and housewifely duties. There were many setbacks for the progress toward equality that Iranian women had made in the 1960s and 1970s. Although women were not altogether precluded from working or undertaking advanced studies, they were removed from desirable professional and governmental positions and their educational opportunities were sharply curtailed. Notably, women could no longer serve as lawyers or judges. Iranian women have fought determinedly to roll back these discriminatory policies; they have had some successes regaining ground lost after the clerical takeover, but are still a long way from having dismantled all obstacles to women's advancement. Meanwhile, the threats of criminal prosecutions and punishments for minor infractions of the strict Islamic dress rules have been augmented by a 1996 law adding jail terms and fines to existing flogging penalties.

The Islamic Republic has accumulated an exceptional record of religious intolerance, persecuting persons it deems to have abandoned Islam or, in the case of Baha'is, persons whose ancestors may have converted from Islam. These may be compelled to choose between death and returning to Islam. Harsh crackdowns on the Baha'i minority since the clerical takeover have earned the Islamic Republic repeated condemnations.[22] In connection with this pattern of persecution, it is hardly coincidental that Baha'is insist on the full equality of men and women.

Iran's religious persecutions clash with the principle of freedom of religion, which in international law is a freedom not subject to any constraints. In yet another sign of equivocation, attacks on people for their religious beliefs have generally been accompanied by official attempts to hide any religious motives lying behind them. Iran's repeated insistence that it is executing people for spying, treason, or drug trafficking, when their actual crimes are abandoning Islam or religious dissent, reveal the government's lack of confidence that criminalizing religious belief can be justified in today's world. Ayatollah Khomeini's notorious *fatwa* condemning Salman Rushdie is the exception in this regard. The opprobrium that this provoked may well have strengthened the determination on the part of Iranian officialdom to hide the religious motivations behind its brutal treatment of converts from Islam, non-Muslims, and dissenting Islamic thinkers.

The Politics of Repression

There are reasons for saying that Iran's dismal post-revolutionary human rights record should be seen as a reflection of political choices rather than as a consequence of a commitment to implement Islamic law. Some of Iran's most egregious rights violations—like complete disregard for due process, harsh repression of the political opposition, routine recourse to torture, suppression of restive ethnic minorities, and sending assassination squads abroad to murder dissidents—have nothing to do with following Islamic requirements. Instead, they reflect contempt for the rule of law and the determination of ruling clerics to terrorize and decimate the ranks of their critics.

The repeated arrests and protracted detention of the prominent editor and journalist Faraj Sarkuhi during 1996–97 exemplify how dissidents may be treated. It is probably no coincidence that Sarkuhi had been one of the 134 writers who had signed a petition in October 1994 calling for more freedom of expression, since few things seem to irritate the regime more than having Iranian citizens criticize its suppression of dissent. After Ayatollah Yazdi stated in June 1997 that Sarkuhi was charged with attempting to leave Iran illegally and spying for a foreign country, a capital offense, in September 1997 Sarkuhi was sentenced in a secret trial to a year in prison for the less serious offense of spreading propaganda against the Islamic Republic of Iran. One might assess the outcome of this process as yet another example of Iran's ambivalence and equivocation. Powerful hard-liners would probably have liked to see Sarkuhi executed on specious charges of "spying" as a deterrent to further expression of dissent. More moderate members of the regime most likely calculated that executing yet another critical intellectual would set back their campaign to establish friendlier relations with the West, and that the international outcry already occasioned by Sarkuhi's imprisonment would only mushroom unless he were let off with a mild penalty. Probably all factions within the regime concurred that the way Iran conducted political trials made them unsuitable for public viewing. The unsavory aspects of such trials were exposed when the regime imprudently televised the prosecution of Tehran's mayor in 1998.

Despite exposure to intermittently harsh repression, Iran's dissidents have remained steadfast in their demands for democratic freedoms and human rights. For example, in 1995, at great risk to themselves, eighty-six Iranian activists published and signed a statement of protest against clerical misrule. They condemned the regime for preventing the Iranian people from governing themselves and participating in determining their destiny. They also proclaimed their indignation over being denied the benefit of rights set forth in Iran's constitution. In this protest, they touched on the root of the problem: the government's actual policy of ignoring any rights principles, regardless of whether they were secular or nominally "Islamic."

The politically contingent nature of Iran's official "Islam" was highlighted in January 1988, when Ayatollah Khomeini made his famous pronouncement that the Islamic state was entrusted with absolute power that freed it to do as it chose, even if this meant violating fundamental pillars of the Islamic religion like the pilgrimage.[23] His pronouncement indicated that the same regime that vaunted its Islamic ideology and that aggressively prosecuted its citizens for infractions of Islamic law felt free to run roughshod over Islamic law whenever this served its political objectives. Khomeini's idea that the interests of the nation-state should override fundamental Islamic tenets has never been repudiated. Thus, Iran's official "Islam" turns out to be highly malleable, and the cynicism of the leadership has been increasingly echoed by cynicism among the populace.

Recent developments suggest that the political exploitation of religion has ultimately been counterproductive for the regime. The level of alienation was revealed in the 1997 presidential elections, when Mohammad Khatami, a candidate who was only supposed to represent one of the token opponents for the candidate blessed by the ruling elite, Majles Speaker Nateq-Nuri, won in a landslide. Mohammad Khatami was known to be a relatively liberal cleric who had called for greater tolerance and more freedoms. He was elected president with 70 percent of the vote after a campaign in which he committed himself to ensuring enhanced civil rights and respecting diversity of opinion. Nateq-Nuri, a religious hard-liner known for his harsh policy on enforcing the official version of Islamic morality, went down to a humiliating defeat despite the enormous advantages that he had enjoyed in terms of access to the media, financing, and public forums.

The regime has continued to flail about in its attempts to respond to negative UN reports and foreign criticisms, attacking the motives of its accusers and dismissing as lies any charges that it violates human rights. Iran was obviously disturbed by criticisms of the UN Human Rights Commission in March 1995, and its assessments that Iran's Islamic laws violated human rights. Ayatollah Yazdi tried to depict the report as an attack on Islam:

> The new issue is this: who says that human rights devised by the West should be applied to the whole world? Who has said such a thing? Some nations have their own cultures, some nations have their own religions, you cannot describe as human rights violations the issues which concern their religion and culture. You cannot impose the human rights as you have translated and defined them.... Islamic human rights differ from the Declaration of Human Rights. Islam has its own rules and regulations.... Human Rights must be Islamic human rights.[24]

Yazdi apparently felt compelled to argue that Islam required Iran's human rights violations, thereby absolving the regime of blame. Here, however, the defense was offered not to the international community but to Iranians in an effort to discredit external critics by portraying them as insensitive to Islamic beliefs and culture. In another statement broadcast the same year, Yazdi shifted his position, speaking as if Iran's policies did adhere to international law and insisting that "realistic investigations" by international human rights organizations would show that protecting human rights "in its true sense, is one of the goals of the holy, divine, and popular system of Iran."[25] This was yet another sign of the ongoing ambivalence about whether it was prudent to concede that Iran's official Islam entailed violating human rights.

Curiously, Iran has shown no qualms about attacking other Islamic states, including Saudi Arabia, for violating human rights, even where the violations are tied to policies of implementing Islamic law. Apparently, only Iran's official Islam gives it a special warrant for deviating from international law. Indeed, Iran seems to enjoy attacking other Islamic regimes for their rights violations, as if doing so would make Iran's official Islam look relatively progressive by comparison. The actions of the fiercely and unapologetically reactionary Taliban after taking Kabul in 1996 gave Iran's leaders a golden opportunity to pose as enlightened defenders of women's international human rights. After all, when compared with their cloistered and downtrodden Afghan sisters, Iranian women were faring relatively well and were blessed with considerable freedom.

Ayatollah Jannati denounced the Taliban and their "fossilized" policies of stopping girls from attending school and banning women from working outside the home in the name of Islam. What could be worse, he asked, than the violence, narrow-mindedness, and limits on women's rights which defamed Islam?[26] Iran hosted an international conference in October 1996 on the Afghan crisis. In a statement, the conferees decried "evident violations of human rights, especially women's rights," and urged an end to the violations according to the UN Charter.[27] That a regime with such a troubled record on women's rights would seek to position itself as a champion of international human rights illustrates the impact that such ideals can have even on their foes. Iran's wish to act the part of the defender of enlightened Islam and women's rights and to deprecate measures that associated Islam with curbs on women's freedoms was revealing. Iran's efforts to place maximum distance between its policies affecting women and those pursued by the Taliban indicated that at least some in the clerical elite had come to appreciate that, for a regime that relied on Islam as a legitimating device, it was becoming increasingly awkward to have this pillar of its authority associated with sex discrimination and reactionary policies on women.

Conclusion

While repressive regimes and Islamic conservatives industriously press the notion that there are religious barriers to Muslims' enjoying the human rights set in international law, in general Muslims seem to be moving toward the position that Islam and human rights do not have to be competing systems. So great is the legitimacy that international human rights have won that many Muslims who actually oppose human rights have felt compelled to reformulate their discourse and pretend that their Islamic rights agendas are compatible with respect for international human rights. The result has been a mess of conundrums and equivocations. But, as the impetus for fusing elements of the Islamic heritage with international human rights law spreads, a more straightforward and more coherent Islamic discourse on human rights may be emerging.

Notes

1. Reservations to human rights conventions can be found under the respective convention headings at http://www.un.org/Depts/Treaty/final/ts2/newfiles.
2. See the debates about Islamic fundamentalism and human rights recorded in Lawyers Committee for Human Rights, *Islam and Justice: Debating the Future of Human Rights in the Middle East and North Africa* (January 1997). For assessments of the impact of fundamentalism, see Ann Elizabeth Mayer, "The Fundamentalist Impact on Law, Politics, and Constitutions in Iran, Pakistan, and the Sudan," in *Fundamentalisms and the State: Remaking Polities, Economies, and Militance,* Martin Marty and R. Scott Appleby, eds. (Chicago: University of Chicago Press, 1993), 110–51. For comparisons of how Islamic and various other fundamentalisms affect women's human rights, see Courtney W. Howland, "The Challenge of Religious Fundamentalism to the Liberty and Equality Rights of Women," *Columbia Journal of Transnational Law* 35 (1997), 272–377.
3. For discussions of the relationship of Islamic positions on human rights and the rights provisions in international law, see generally Ann Elizabeth Mayer, *Islam and Human Rights: Tradition and Politics,* 2d ed. (3d ed. to appear in 1998) (Boulder, CO: Westview Press, 1995).
4. For an assessment of this law, see Middle East Watch, *Empty Reform: Saudi Arabia's New Basic Laws* (May 1992).
5. Mayer, *Islam and Human Rights,* 10–11, 19–20, 38–39, 55.
6. Hasan Moinuddin, *The Charter of the Islamic Conference* (Oxford: Oxford University Press, 1987), 186.
7. Ann Elizabeth Mayer, "Universal Versus Islamic Human Rights: A Clash of Cultures or a Clash with a Construct," *Michigan Journal of International Law* 15 (1994), 327–50.
8. Ibid., 348–50.
9. "Islam Guarantees Human Rights, Says Saud," *Riyadh Daily,* June 17, 1993, available in LEXIS, Nexis Library, Saudi File.
10. For some indications of attitudes on rights, see Kevin Dwyer, *Arab Voices: The Human Rights Debate in the Middle East* (Berkeley: University of California Press,

1991); Susan Waltz, *Human Rights and Reform: Changing the Face of North African Politics* (Berkeley: University of California Press, 1994). See also Lawyers Committee, *Islam and Justice.*

11. Fatima Mernissi, *Islam and Democracy: Fear of the Modern World* (Reading, MA: Addison-Wesley, 1992), 60–64.

12. See the discussions and sources in Fatima Mernissi, *The Veil and the Male Elite: A Feminist Interpretation of Women's Rights in Islam* (Reading, MA: Addison-Wesley, 1991); Mahnaz Afkhami, ed., *Faith and Freedom: Women's Human Rights in the Muslim World* (London: I.B. Tauris, 1995). For a provocative essay challenging the effectiveness of the Islamic feminist strategy, see Reza Afshari, "Egalitarian Islam and Misogynist Islamic Tradition: A Critique of the Feminist Interpretation of Islamic History and Heritage," *Critique: Journal of Critical Studies of Iran and the Middle East* (Spring 1994), 13–34.

13. Programs disseminating instruction on women's rights and Islam have been pursued by groups like Women Living Under Muslim Laws (WLUML) and the Sisterhood Is Global Institute (SIGI). A SIGI manual providing guidelines for organizing human rights workshops is Mahnaz Afkhami and Haleh Vaziri, *Claiming Our Rights: A Manual for Women's Human Rights Education in Muslim Societies* (1996).

14. The book is *Faith and Freedom,* cited above, and the review was published as Matthew A. Levitt, "Faith and Freedom: Women's Human Rights in the Muslim World," *Journal of International Affairs* 50 (Summer 1996), 305–10. I have discussed how Orientalist and cultural relativist proclivities disincline Westerners to take Muslim women's human rights claims seriously in "Universal Versus Islamic Human Rights," 393–402.

15. Levitt, "Faith and Freedom," 309. A more nuanced but related assessment can be found in the work of Theodor Meron, *Human Rights Law-Making in the United Nations: A Critique of Instruments and Process* (Oxford: Clarendon Press, 1986), 62–66, 153–60.

16. His comment professing a belief in human rights for women—as if this were consistent with his demands that women defer to "religious parameters"—is found in Levitt, "Faith and Freedom," 309. Courtney Howland persuasively explains why under international human rights law it is impermissible to use religious criteria to circumscribe women's human rights. See Howland, "The Challenge of Religious Fundamentalism," 327–32, 340–46.

17. See the article by Anouar Majid, "The Politics of Feminism in Islam," forthcoming in *SIGNS,* an important feminist journal that has quixotically elected to publish this piece. Some commentaries will be appended, including one that I have written.

18. This bold statement was made during a speech at American University on March 26, 1997.

19. See Abdullahi An-Na'im, *Toward an Islamic Reformation: Civil Liberties, Human Rights, and International Law* (Syracuse: Syracuse University Press, 1990).

20. These comments can be found at http://www.chrla.org/reports/zayd/abu3.htm. Many insights into the Abu Zaid case can be gleaned from materials indexed at http://www.chrla.org/chrla/zaydindex.htm.

21. Quoted in Mayer, "Universal Versus Islamic Human Rights," 316.

22. This is discussed in Mayer, "The Fundamentalist Impact," 193.

23. See, for example, Final Report on the Situation of Human Rights in the Islamic Republic of Iran by the Special Representative of the Commission on Human Rights, Mr. Reynaldo Galindo Pohl, pursuant to Resolution 1992/67, March 4, 1992, UN Doc. E/CN.4/1993/41, January 28, 1993, 54–55, and the sections on Iran in the annual reports of Amnesty International and Middle East Watch, later Human Rights Watch/Middle East.

24. "Head of Judiciary Comments on Bank Fraud Case," Human Rights in Iran, Reuters Textline, BBC Monitoring Service, March 13, 1995, available in LEXIS, Nexis Library.

25. See "Egyptian President in Jordan," BBC SWB EE/D2495/ME, December 28, 1995, available in LEXIS, Nexis Library.

26. "Iranian Cleric Blasts Taleban for Defaming Islam," Reuters North American Wire, October 4, 1996, available in LEXIS, Nexis Library.

27. "Iran Conference Urges Halt to Afghan War," Reuters World Service, October 30, 1996, available in LEXIS, Nexis Library.

About the Editors and Contributors

Kenneth Anderson, Associate Professor of Law at the Washington College of Law, American University, has taught the laws of war and international human rights at Columbia and Harvard law schools, and was the John Harvey Gregory Lecturer on World Organization at Harvard Law School between 1993 and 1995. Previously he was director of the Human Rights Watch Arms Division and general counsel to the Open Society Institute–Soros Foundations.

Margaret E. Crahan, Dorothy Epstein Professor of Latin American History at Hunter College, City University of New York, is the author of more than sixty articles and books, including *Africa and the Caribbean: Legacies of a Link* and *Human Rights and Basic Needs in the Americas.* She has done extensive field work in Argentina, Brazil, Chile, Colombia, Costa Rica, Cuba, El Salvador, Guatemala, Honduras, Mexico, Nicaragua, Panama, Paraguay, Peru, Spain, Switzerland, and Uruguay and is an authority on Catholicism in Latin America.

Patricia A. Daly, O.P., Executive Director of the Tri-State Coalition for Responsible Investment, is a member of the Governing Board of the Interfaith Center on Corporate Responsibility whose members use their investment power to raise social and moral issues before transnational corporations and to finance economic development projects at home and abroad. She has a special interest in human rights, ecology, and food safety.

Blu Greenberg writes and lectures on issues of contemporary Jewish interest. She is the author of several books, among them, *On Women and Judaism: A View from Tradition* and *How to Run a Traditional Jewish Household.* In 1997 and 1998 she chaired the historic International Conference on Feminism and Orthodoxy.

Carrie Gustafson, Associate-in-Law and MIA/JSD candidate, Columbia Law School, is a practicing lawyer and recipient of a Mellon dissertation fellowship to study transitional justice issues at Columbia University, is a member of the Minnesota Bar and the Columbia University Seminar on

Human Rights. She has undertaken extensive pro bono work in the areas of criminal and civil law, and was an advisor to the U.S. Delegation to the UN Commission on Human Rights in 1995.

Louis Henkin, University Professor Emeritus, Board Chair of the Center for the Study of Human Rights, and Special Service Professor at Columbia University, served as law clerk to Judge Learned Hand and Justice Felix Frankfurter, and as a lawyer in the U.S. State Department. He is the author of many publications, including *The Age of Rights, The Rights of Man Today, Democracy and Foreign Affairs,* and *Constitutionalism.* Among his public and professional activities, he was President of the American Society of International Law from 1992 to 1994, and has received numerous awards, among them the annual human rights award from the Lawyers Committee on Human Rights.

James F. Joyce, S.J., Director of Social Ministries, New York Province, Society of Jesus, has extensive humanitarian experience overseas and an ongoing interest in issues of human rights, particularly labor rights.

Peter Juviler, Professor of Political Science at Barnard College, is Co-Director of the Center for the Study of Human Rights, Columbia University. Along with numerous articles and chapters, his recent books include *Freedom's Ordeal: The Struggle for Human Rights and Democracy in Post-Soviet States,* and *Human Rights for the 21st Century* (co-edited with Bertram Gross).

Ann Elizabeth Mayer, Associate Professor of Legal Studies at the Wharton School of the University of Pennsylvania, holds a Ph.D. from the University of Michigan and a J.D. from the University of Pennsylvania, as well as a certificate in Islamic and Comparative Law from the University of London. She has written extensively on issues of Islamic Law, human rights, and the status of women, including *Islam and Human Rights: Tradition and Politics.* She has done human rights work with several Western and Middle Eastern organizations.

Julie Stone Peters, Associate Professor of English and Comparative Literature at Columbia University, teaches courses on law and literature, drama, and cultural theory. She is co-editor of *Women's Rights, Human Rights: International Feminist Perspectives,* and has written on the history of intellectual property, technology and culture, customary law, and human rights. She received a B.A. from Yale, a Ph.D. from Princeton University, and a J.D. from Columbia University.

Arati Rao, Associate Director of the Southern Asian Institute at Columbia University, teaches about women and human rights at the School of International and Public Affairs, and has published on a wide range of international rights–related issues, including women and the family, the politics of women and culture, human rights instruments, and the South Asian diaspora. She is a Research Associate at the Centre for Feminist Legal Research in New Dehli.

Larry Rasmussen, Reinhold Niebuhr Professor of Social Ethics at Union Theological Seminary, is the author of numerous articles and books, most recently *Earth Community, Earth Ethics* (winner of the 1997 Grawemeyer Award in Religion of $150,000), and *Moral Fragments and Moral Community.* He currently serves as co-moderator of Unit III (Justice, Peace, Creation) of the World Council of Churches.

Alan F. Segal, Professor of Religion at Barnard College, is the recipient of the Guggenheim and other fellowships for distinguished research. He was the first Jewish member of the *Studiorum Novi Testamenti Societas* (Cambridge) to address the society, and the first American elected President of the Canadian Society of Biblical Studies. His books include *Rebecca's Children: Judaism and Christianity in the Roman World* and *Paul the Convert: The Apostolate and Apostasy of Saul of Tarsis*—selection of the Book of the Month Club and the History Book Club.

Donald W. Shriver Jr., President Emeritus and William E. Dodge Professor of Applied Christianity at Union Theological Seminary (1975–96), is an ordained Presbyterian minister, a member of the Council on Foreign Relations, and past president of the Society of Christian Ethics. He has held adjunct professorships at the Jewish Theological Seminary and the Schools of Business, Law, and Journalism at Columbia University. His most recent books include *An Ethic for Enemies: Forgiveness in Politics* and *Beyond Success: Corporations and Their Critics.*

Max L. Stackhouse, Stephen Colwell Professor of Christian Ethics at Princeton Theological Seminary and Director of the Project on Public Theology at Princeton University, is the author and editor of twelve books, including *Creeds, Society, and Human Rights, Christian Social Ethics in a Global Era,* and *Public Theology and Political Economy.* He is an ordained minister of the United Church of Christ, and President of the Berkshire Institute for Theology and the Arts. His teaching has taken him around the world to India, former East Germany, Canada, the Philippines, and China.

Index

Academic public, 20
American Civil Liberties Union, 17, 29*n.17*
Amnesty International, 19
Anthropocentricism, 4–5, 37–38, 44
Asian Values, 17–18, 29*n.20*

Banzer Plan, 83, 87*n.1*
Bar mitzvah, 149, 165
Base Christian Communities (CEBs), 60, 68, 70–71, 79*n.6,* 82
Bharatiya Janata Party (BJP) (India), 118–19, 120–21, 124, 127, 129
Bill of Rights (1791) (America), 38
Bill of Rights (1689) (England), 38
Biotic/human environmental rights
  anthropocentricism and, 4–5, 37–38, 44
  argument for, 40–44
    modernism and, 40, 44–45, 46, 49
    nature morality and, 40–42, 51*n.18*
    nature value and, 41–44
    non-religious, 41–42
    religious, 41
  Brundtland Report, 39, 51*n.10*
  Community of Life concept, 39, 43, 46, 47–49, 53
  convergence of, 44–48
  distinction between, 36
  Enlightenment and, 36–37, 42, 44, 46
  framework for, 38, 40, 42, 44, 46–48
  global ethic for, 39, 53–55
  life system deterioration, 38–39, 44–45
  morality and, 4–5, 37–38
    of nature, 40–42, 51*n.18*
  natural law, 37–38

Biotic/human environmental rights *(continued)*
  non-governmental organizations and, 39
  religious involvement in, 39–40, 41, 45, 48–50
    first world responsibility, 54–55
    international economic investments, 54
    sacred images, 55–56
  rights defined, 36–38
  social justice and, 39–40, 47–48, 50
  Universal Declaration on Human Rights, 36, 38, 48
Birth ceremony, Jewish Orthodoxy, 150, 164–65
  baby naming, 165
BJP. *See* Bharatiya Janata Party
Brundtland Report, 39, 51*n.10*
Buddhism, 4
  Indian Hindu Right and, 122
Burial rites, Jewish Orthodoxy, 149, 166–67

Cairo Declaration on Human Rights in Islam, 179–80, 181–83
Cambodia, 96, 97
Caste system (India), 119, 121, 125, 128
Catholic Church. *See* Latin America, social change in
CEBs. *See* Base Christian Communities
Charter of the Organization of Islamic Conference (OIC), 179, 180, 182
Church of England, 3
Circumcision, 149–50, 165

203

Civil rights, 14
Colonialism (India), 121, 138*n.15,* 141
Community of Life, 39, 43, 46, 47–49, 53
Constitution (1950) (India), 122–23
Criminal justice systems
 causal theories, 99–100
 communities and, 94–95
 forgiveness and, 100–101
 international courts and, 107–15
  class interests, 112–15
  religious roots, 109–12, 115
  International Criminal Court (ICC), 6, 88, 90–91, 92–99
 local judiciaries, 96–97, 102–3
 punishment and, 89, 90–94
  cultural norms, 93–94
  means vs. end, 97–98
  social justice, 93
  social norms, 95–96
 satyagraha and
  defined, 89
  feminine values of, 89–90
  humanizing strategies of, 6, 89, 92, 96, 97–98
  punishment and, 93
  religion and, 89
  social norms and, 95–96
  truth and, 99
  victims and, 100–102
 truth in, 98–99
 ubuntu, 102, 106*n.67*
 United Nations Security Council, 90
 victims and, 101–2
 violence/power legitimization
  deterrence theory, 91
  reprobative theory, 92
  retributive theory, 91–92
 violence/power of, 88–89, 90
Cultural norms
 criminal justice and, 93–94
 Indian Hindu Right, 119–20, 130, 136, 140–41, 142

Declaration of Independence (1776), 12–14, 27*n.6*
Declaration of the Rights of Man and the Citizen (1789) (France), 38

Descartes
 biotic rights, 37
 public theology, 24
Deterrence theory, 91
Divorce, India, 130
Divorce, Jewish Orthodoxy, 145–47, 175–76
 agunot and, 146–47, 154, 155
 changes in, 153–55, 163
  agunot, 154, 155
  gett transfer, 153–54, 155
  havka'at kiddushin law, 154
  Israel, 155
  prenuptial agreement, 154
 gett transfer, 146, 153–54, 155, 162
 man's absolute right in, 146–47, 172*n.2*

Earth Summit (Rio) (1992), 39, 54
Ecological Society of America, 39
Economic public, 20
Enlightenment
 biotic rights and, 36–37, 42, 44, 46
 public theology and, 13, 19, 20–21, 22, 23–24, 25, 31
Entitlements, 12–13, 31
Environment. *See* Biotic/human environmental rights
Ephrahim v. Pastory, 143
Eugenics, 21

Family Protection Act (Iran), 192
Fundamentalism
 Indian Hindu Right, 124–26, 143
 Jewish Orthodoxy, 176
 Latin America, 57, 66, 77*n.1,* 83

Gandhi, Mahatma, 89, 90, 91, 92–93, 95, 96, 97–98, 100
Germany, 3
Global ethics
 biotic rights and, 39, 53–55
 economic investments, 54
 Latin America, 5–6, 85–86
 See also Morality; Universalism, public theology and

Hinduism. *See* Indian Hindu Right, women and
Hindutva ideology, 118–19, 120–21, 122, 125–26
Hindu Women's Code Bill, 121
Hobbesian perspective, public theology and, 18–19, 23
Holidays, Jewish Orthodoxy and, 158–59, 168
Human rights, public theology validation of
  Declaration of Independence, 12–14, 27n.6
  Enlightenment perspective, 13, 19, 20–21, 22, 23–24, 25, 31
  Hobbesian perspective, 18–19, 23
  human rights bases, 24–27, 30n.34
  human rights progress, 12
  human rights threat, 12–15
    civil rights, 14
    entitlements, 12–13, 31
    historical perspective, 13–15, 31
    universal moral laws and, 13–14, 27n.5
  modernism and, 20–21, 25–26
    eugenics, 21
    racial hygiene, 21
  modernism challenges
    hypermodernism, 22–24
    liberationist collectivism, 22
    libertarian individualism, 22
    postmodernism, 22–24
    traditionalism, 22–24
  Nietzschean perspective, 14, 18–19, 23
  public theology defined, 19–20, 32
    academic public, 20
    economic public, 20
    legal public, 20
    political public, 20
    religious public, 20
  public theology limitations, 31–35
    religion and, 31–32, 33
    universalism and, 31, 32–35
  theological indispensability, 15–17, 33–35
    government and, 16–17
    metaphysical morality, 16–17, 28n.14

Human rights, public theology validation of *(continued)*
  religion/theology distinction, 15, 33
  universal moral laws and, 16–17
  Universal Declaration of Human Rights, 12, 21, 34
  universalism and, 4, 17–19, 25–27, 31, 32–35
    Amnesty International, 19
    Asian Values, 17–18, 29n.20
    limitations of, 31, 32–35
    moral laws, 13–14, 16–17, 27n.5
Human Rights Watch, 6
Hypermodernism, 22–24

ICC. *See* International Criminal Court
IMF. *See* International Monetary Fund
Indian Hindu Right, women and, 7–8
  Bharatiya Janata Party (BJP), 118–19, 120–21, 124, 127, 129
  British colonialism, 121, 138n.15, 141
  Buddhism and, 122
  caste system, 119, 121, 125, 128
  cultural norms, 119–20, 130, 136, 140–41, 142
  fundamentalism and, 124–26, 143
  gender manipulation
    male leadership, 128–29
    Muslims and, 126–27
    token liberation, 127–28
    traditional role emphasis, 127–29
  Hindutva ideology, 118–19, 120–21, 122, 125–26
  Jains and, 122
  multireligious societies and, 117, 119–20, 144
    relational religions, 132–33, 141–42
    religion as identity, 133
  Muslims and, 118, 121, 124–25, 126–27, 130–31, 132–33, 133, 136
    gender manipulation, 126–27
    Muslim Women's Bill, 130
  personal laws, 121
  Rashtriya Swayamsevak Sangh (RSS), 124
  reformist legislation
    common language for, 135–37, 144

Indian Hindu Right, women and *(continued)*
  Constitution (1950), 122–23
  divorce, 130
  government obligation toward, 134–35
  Hindu Women's Code Bill, 121
  Muslim Women's Bill, 130
  National Human Rights Commission (NHRC), 123
  religious rights, 123–24
  Shah Bano case, 130, 143–44
  Uniform Civil Code (UCC), 119, 122, 129–31, 142–43
  women's rights, 121–23
  in secular India, 124–26, 142–43, 144
  Sikhs and, 122, 131
  social justice and, 133–34
  Universal Declaration of Human Rights, 135
  women's participation in, 131–32
Inter-American Development Bank, 5, 74, 83
International Criminal Court (ICC), 6, 88, 90–91, 92–99
International Monetary Fund (IMF), 5, 74, 83, 85
Iran, Islamic law and, 189–92
  Family Protection Act, 192
  religious freedom, 8–9, 192, 194
  repression politics, 192–95
  women's rights, 190–92, 195
Islamic law
  European derivation of, 177–78
  historical perspective, 178–79
  human rights and
    Cairo Declaration on Human Rights in Islam, 179–80, 181–83
    Charter of the Organization of Islamic Conference (OIC), 179, 180, 182
    convention reservations, 177, 196n.1
    international law, 8, 179–83, 196
    language ambiguities, 181–82
    reform constraints, 188–89
    Universal Declaration of Human Rights, 182
  Iran and, 189–92

Islamic law *(continued)*
  Family Protection Act, 192
  religious freedom, 8–9, 192, 194
  repression politics, 192–95
  women's rights, 190–92, 195
  women's rights, 183–84, 189, 197n.13
  in Iran, 190–92, 195
  vs. religious freedom, 184–88
Israel, 151–52, 155, 157

Jains, 122
Jewish Orthodoxy, women and
  divorce law, 145–47, 175–76
    agunot and, 146–47
    gett transfer, 146, 162
    man's absolute right in, 146–47, 172n.2
  divorce law changes, 153–55, 163
    agunot and, 154, 155
    gett transfer, 153–54, 155
    havka'at kiddushin law, 154
    Israel and, 155
    prenuptial agreement, 154
  fundamentalism and, 176
  human rights and, 7, 145, 150–53, 169–72, 174–76
  Israel and, 151–52, 155, 157
  language, 148
    changes in, 159–60
  leadership role, 148–49
    changes in, 161–62
  legal testimony, 149, 175
    changes in, 162–63
  life-cycle ceremonies, 149–50
    bar mitzvah, 149
    birth ceremony, 150
    burial rites, 149
    circumcision, 149–50
  life-cycle ceremony changes, 164–67
    baby naming, 165
    bar mitzvah, 165
    bat mitzvah, 165
    birth ceremony, 164–65
    burial rites, 166–67
    circumcision, 165
    wedding ceremony, 165–66
  liturgical role, 147–48, 175
  liturgical role changes, 156–59

Jewish Orthodoxy, women and
  (continued)
    after-meal grace, 157–58, 173*n.8*
    holiday celebrations, 158–59, 168
    in Israel, 157
    minyan and, 156, 173*n.6*
    prayer groups (*tefila*), 156, 173*n.6*
    Torah processional ritual, 158–59
    wine sanctification (*kiddush*), 158
  sexuality, 149
    kol isha law, 149
  sexuality changes, 163–64
    kol isha law, 163–164
    menstruation, 164
  Talmud and, 148, 149, 158, 167, 168
  Talmud learning, 150
    changes in, 167–68
  Torah and, 147–48, 150, 156, 158–59, 165, 167, 168

Kant, Immanuel
  biotic rights, 36–37, 42
  public theology, 24, 31
Kol isha law, 163–164

Language
  Indian Hindu Right and, 135–37, 144
  Islamic law and, 181–82
  Jewish Orthodoxy and, 148
    changes in, 159–60
Latin America, social change in
  Banzer Plan, 83, 87*n.1*
  Brazil, 62, 63
  Catholic Church, 63–65, 77*n.1*
    agenda of, 58–60
    Base Christian Communities (CEBs), 60, 68, 70–71, 79*n.6*, 82
    CELAM II (1968), 59, 65, 67, 68, 69, 75
    CELAM III (1979), 61, 67–69, 70, 75
    CELAM IV (1992), 60, 67, 70, 72, 73, 75
    change impediments, 61–62, 66–69, 72–73
    change realities, 72–73
    change strategies, 69–71
    conscientization and, 61–62

Latin America, social change in
  (continued)
    goal commitment, 58, 60
    ideology of, 57–58, 65, 66, 72–73, 82, 84–85
    impact of, 74–77
    internal consensus, 58, 60, 72–73
    leadership, 61–63, 72, 81–82
    liberation theology and, 60, 61, 65, 68, 70–71, 76, 80*n.20*
    Marxism and, 59–60, 65, 67–68, 71, 73, 75, 78*n.5*, 80*n.20*
    politics and, 57–58, 60, 63–69, 72–73, 75, 76
    resources of, 58, 61–62, 63, 72, 73, 75
    social class and, 60, 64–65, 68, 72–74, 75, 76–77
    social justice and, 5–6, 58–60
    Vatican II (1962–1965), 59, 65, 68, 69, 70, 76, 81, 82
  Chile, 62, 63, 76
  fundamentalism and, 57, 66, 77*n.1*, 83
  global ethics, 5–6, 85–86
  neoliberalism, 73–74, 83, 84, 85
  organizational conditions for, 58, 60–63
  poverty and, 73–74
  Protestantism and, 57, 66, 74, 77*n.1*, 83
  spiritism and, 57, 77*n.1*
  unionization, 85–86
Leadership
  Catholic Church and, 61–63, 72, 81–82
  Indian Hindu Right and, 128–29
  Jewish Orthodoxy and, 148–49
    changes in, 161–62
Legal public, 20
Legal testimony, Jewish Orthodoxy and, 149, 175
  changes in, 162–63
Levitt, Matthew A., 185–86
Liberationist collectivism, 22
Liberation theology, 60, 61, 65, 68, 70–71, 76, 80*n.20*
Libertarian individualism, 22

Life-cycle ceremonies, Jewish
    Orthodoxy
  bar mitzvah, 149, 165
  birth ceremony, 150, 164–65
  burial rites, 149, 166–67
  changes in, 164–67
    baby naming, 165
    bar mitzvah, 165
    bat mitzvah, 165
    birth ceremony, 164–65
    burial rites, 166–67
    circumcision, 165
    wedding ceremony, 165–66
  circumcision, 149–50, 165
Liturgical role, Jewish Orthodox
    women, 147–48, 175
  changes in, 156–59
    after-meal grace, 157–58, 173*n.8*
    holiday celebrations, 158–59, 168
    Israel and, 157
    kiddush (wine sanctification), 158
    minyan and, 156, 173*n.6*
    prayer groups (*tefila*), 156, 173*n.6*
    Torah processional ritual, 158–59
Locke, John, 24, 31

Majid, Anouar, 185–86
Marriage, Jewish Orthodoxy, 165–66
  prenuptial agreement, 154
  See also Divorce, Jewish Orthodoxy
Marxism, Latin America, 59–60, 65, 67–68, 71, 73, 75, 78*n.5*, 80*n.20*
Menstruation, Jewish Orthodoxy and, 164
Metaphysical morality, 16–17, 28*n.14*
Modernism, biotic rights and, 40, 44–45, 46, 49
Modernism, public theology and, 20–21, 25–26
  challenges to
    hypermodernism, 22–24
    liberationist collectivism, 22
    libertarian individualism, 22
    postmodernism, 22–24
    traditionalism, 22–24
  eugenics, 21
  racial hygiene, 21

Morality
  biotic rights and, 4–5, 37–38
  nature morality, 40–42, 51*n.18*
  public theology and metaphysical
    morality, 16–17, 28*n.14*
  universal moral laws, 13–14, 16–17, 27*n.5*
  See also Global ethics
Muslims, Indian Hindu Right and, 118, 121, 124–25, 130–31, 132–33, 133, 136
  gender manipulation, 126–27
  Muslim Women's Bill, 130
  See also Islamic law

National Human Rights Commission
    (NHRC) (India), 123
Natural law, 37–38
Nietzschean perspective, public
    theology and, 14, 18–19, 23
Nuremberg Doctors Trial, 21

Parliament of World Religions, 39
Political public, 20
Postmodernism, 22–24
Poverty, Latin America, 73–74
Protestantism, 57, 66, 74, 77*n.1*, 83
Punishment. *See* Criminal justice
    systems

Racial hygiene, 21
Rashtriya Swayamsevak Sangh (RSS), 124
Religion
  ambiguities of, 3–4, 9
  criminal justice systems, 6–7
  human rights advocacy, 5–6, 9
  human rights validation, 4–5, 9
  politics and, 7–9
  state-church separation, 3
  state religious suppression, 3
  state-supported religion, 3
  Universal Declaration of Human
    Rights, 3
  biotic rights and, 39–40, 41, 45, 48–50
  first world responsibility, 54–55

Religion *(continued)*
  international economic
    investments, 54
  sacred images, 55–56
  public theology and
    religion limitations, 31–32, 33
    religion/theology distinction, 15, 33
    religious public, 20
  See also specific religions
Religious public, 20
Reprobative theory, 92
Retributive theory, 91–92
Rolston, Holmes, 40–41, 42, 43
RSS. *See* Rashtriya Swayamsevak
    Sangh
Russia, 3, 17
Rwanda, 96–97, 99

Satyagraha
  defined, 89
  feminine values of, 89–90
  humanizing strategies of, 6, 89, 92, 96, 97–98
  punishment and, 93
  religion and, 89
  social norms and, 95–96
  truth and, 99
  victims and, 101–2
Sexuality, Jewish Orthodoxy and
  changes in, 163–64
  kol isha law, 149, 163–64
  menstruation, 164
Shah Bano case, 130, 143–44
Sikhs, 122, 131
Social class
  criminal justice and, 112–15
  Latin America, 60, 64–65, 68, 72–74, 75, 76–77
Social justice
  biotic rights and, 39–40, 47–48, 50
  criminal justice systems, 93
  Indian Hindu Right and, 133–34
Social justice
  Latin America, 5–6, 58–60

Social norms, criminal justice and, 95–96
Spiritism, 57, 77*n.1*

Talmud, 148, 149, 158, 167, 168
  learning and, 150
  changes in, 167–68
Taylor, Paul, 41–42
Torah, 147–48, 150, 156, 158–59, 165, 167, 168
Traditionalism, public theology and, 22–24

Ubuntu (South Africa), 102, 106*n.66*
Uniform Civil Code (UCC) (India), 119, 122, 129–31, 142–43
Unionization (Latin America), 85–86
United Nations Security Council, 90
Universal Declaration of Human Rights
  biotic rights and, 36, 38, 48
  Indian Hindu Right and, 135
  Islamic law and, 182
  public theology and, 12, 21, 34
  religious ambiguities and, 3
Universalism, public theology and, 4, 17–19, 25–27, 31, 32–35
  American Civil Liberties Union, 17, 29*n.17*
  Amnesty International, 19
  Asian Values, 17–18, 29*n.20*
  limitations of, 31, 32–35
  moral laws, 13–14, 16–17, 27*n.5*

Value of nature, 41–44

War Crimes Tribunal, 6
Women. *See* Indian Hindu Right, women and; Islamic law; Jewish Orthodoxy, women and
World Bank, 5, 74, 83, 85
World Council of Churches, 39
World Future Society, 3
World Trade Organization, 85